# DEVELOPING GRADING AND REPORTING SYSTEMS FOR STUDENT LEARNING

# EXPERTS IN ASSESSMENT

## SERIES EDITORS
### THOMAS R. GUSKEY AND ROBERT J. MARZANO

JUDITH ARTER, JAY MCTIGHE
SCORING RUBRICS IN THE CLASSROOM: USING PERFORMANCE CRITERIA FOR ASSESSING AND IMPROVING STUDENT PERFORMANCE

JANE M. BAILEY, THOMAS R. GUSKEY
IMPLEMENTING STUDENT-LED CONFERENCES

THOMAS R. GUSKEY, JANE M. BAILEY
DEVELOPING GRADING AND REPORTING SYSTEMS FOR STUDENT LEARNING

EDWARD KIFER
LARGE-SCALE ASSESSMENT: DIMENSIONS, DILEMMAS, AND POLICY

ROBERT J. MARZANO
DESIGNING A NEW TAXONOMY OF EDUCATIONAL OBJECTIVES

JAMES H. MCMILLAN
ESSENTIAL ASSESSMENT CONCEPTS FOR TEACHERS AND ADMINISTRATORS

JEFFREY K. SMITH, LISA F. SMITH, RICHARD DE LISI
NATURAL CLASSROOM ASSESSMENT: DESIGNING SEAMLESS INSTRUCTION AND ASSESSMENT

DOUGLAS B. REEVES
HOLISTIC ACCOUNTABILITY: SERVING STUDENTS, SCHOOLS, AND COMMUNITY

ISBN 0-7619-7756-2 (7-BOOK PAPER EDITION)
ISBN 0-7619-7757-0 (7-BOOK LIBRARY EDITION)

# Developing Grading and Reporting Systems for Student Learning

Thomas R. Guskey
Jane M. Bailey

## Experts in Assessment

### Series Editors
Thomas R. Guskey and Robert J. Marzano

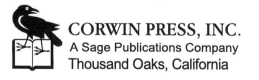
CORWIN PRESS, INC.
A Sage Publications Company
Thousand Oaks, California

*For information:*

Corwin Press, Inc.
A Sage Publications Company
2455 Teller Road
Thousand Oaks, California 91320
E-mail: order@corwinpress.com

Sage Publications Ltd.
6 Bonhill Street
London EC2A 4PU
United Kingdom

Sage Publications India Pvt. Ltd.
M-32 Market
Greater Kailash I
New Delhi 110 048 India

Printed in the United States of America

**Library of Congress Cataloging-in-Publication Data**

Guskey, Thomas R.
     Developing grading and reporting systems for student learning / by Thomas R. Guskey and Jane M. Bailey.
     p. cm. — (Experts in assessment kit)
     Includes bibliographical references and index.
     ISBN 0-8039-6853-1 (cloth: alk. paper)
     ISBN 0-8039-6854-X (pbk.: alk. paper)
     1. Grading and marking (Students)—United States. 2. School reports—United States. I. Bailey, Jane M. II. Title. III. Series.
     LB3060.37 .G87 2000
     371.27'2—dc21                                              00-011400

This book is printed on acid-free paper.

01   02   03   04   05   06   10   9   8   7   6   5   4   3   2   1

Acquiring Editor:  Rachel Livsey
Corwin Editorial Assistant:  Phyllis Cappello
Production Editor:  Nevair Kabakian
Editorial Assistant:  Cindy Bear
Typesetter/Designer:  Rebecca Evans
Cover Designer:  Tracy E. Miller

# Contents

**Series Editors' Introduction**     ix

**About the Authors**     x

**Introduction**     1

Our Guiding Premises     2

Our Purpose     3

Our Organizational Scheme     3

Other Resources     5

Our Hope     6

**1. Defining the Impetus for Change**     9

Developments That Compel Change in Grading and Reporting     10

Standards for Teacher Competence     11

The Task at Hand     13

A Personal Reflection     14

Teachers' Perceptions of Grading and Reporting     15

Sources of Teachers' Grading and Reporting Practices     16

Students' Perceptions of Grading and Reporting     17

The Points-Driven Academic Economy of Classrooms     19

Parents' Perceptions of Grading and Reporting     20

Parents' Perceptions of Teachers     22

Summary     23

**2. Exploring the History of Grading and Reporting**     24

Early Developments     25

Problems With Subjectivity in Grading     26

Modern Grading and Reporting Systems     27

The Effects of Grading on Students     28

Summary     29

**3. Laying a Foundation for Change**     30

Grading and Reporting Are Not Essential to Instruction     30

Grading and Reporting Require Subjective Judgments     32

Bias Must Be Avoided in Grading and Reporting    33

Grades Have Some Value as Rewards, But No Value
     as Punishments    34

Grading and Reporting Should Be Done in Reference
     to Learning Criteria    36

Alternative Strategies for Selecting Valedictorians    39

Clarifying Learning Criteria    40

Summary    43

**4. Building a Grading and Reporting System**    **44**

Problems in Grading and Reporting Reform    44

The Basis of Good Reporting Is Good Evidence    45

The Purposes of Grading and Reporting    50

The Importance of a Reporting System    52

Statements of Purpose    55

Sources of Grading and Reporting Evidence    56

Relating Evidence to Purpose    61

Summary    63

**5. Grading and Reporting Methods I: Letter Grades,
Percentage Grades, and Other Categorical Grading**    **64**

Letter Grades    65

Plus and Minus Letter Grades    70

Other Categorical Grades    74

Percentage Grades    77

Summary    82

**6. Grading and Reporting Methods II: Standards-
Based, Pass/Fail, Mastery Grading, and Narratives**    **83**

Standards-Based Grading    84

Pass/Fail Grading    93

Mastery Grading    96

Narratives    103

Summary    108

**7. Grading and Reporting for Students With
Special Needs**    **109**

Students With Disabilities    109

Students Who Are English Language Learners (ELLs)    122

Students Considered Gifted or Talented 125

Summary 127

8. **Special Problems in Grading and Reporting** **128**

Technology and Grading 128

Weighted Grades 134

Grade Inflation 135

Questionable Grading Practices 139

Summary 145

9. **Model Reporting Forms** **147**

Developing a Model Reporting Form 147

Using Checklists and Rubrics to Evaluate Students'
    Performance 155

Communicating Information on Self-Assessment and
    Goal Setting 159

Special Comment Sections and Parent Reports to School 161

Reports of Special Services 165

Reports on Physical Growth 165

Secondary Level Reporting Forms 166

Combining Methods of Reporting 168

Format, Organization, and Graphic Layout 168

Encouraging Input in the Design Process 169

Consistency in Reporting Forms 170

Frequency of Reports 171

Summary 172

10. **Guidelines for Developing Effective Reporting Systems** **173**

The Importance of Purpose 173

The Challenge of Communication 175

Tools for a Comprehensive Reporting System 175

Guidelines for Better Practice 191

Conclusion 193

**Resource A** **195**

**References** **198**

**Name Index** **213**

**Subject Index** **217**

# Series Editors' Introduction

Standards, assessment, accountability, and grading—these are the issues that dominated discussions of education in the 1990s. Today, they are at the center of every modern education reform effort. As educators turn to the task of implementing these reforms, they face a complex array of questions and concerns that little in their background or previous experience has prepared them to address. This series is designed to help in that challenging task.

In selecting the authors, we went to individuals recognized as true experts in the field. The ideas of these scholar-practitioners have already helped shape current discussions of standards, assessment, accountability, and grading. But equally important, their work reflects a deep understanding of the complexities involved in implementation. As they developed their books for this series, we asked them to extend their thinking, to push the edge, and to present new perspectives on what should be done and how to do it. That is precisely what they did. The books they crafted provide not only cutting-edge perspectives but also practical guidelines for successful implementation.

We have several goals for this series. First, that it be used by teachers, school leaders, policy makers, government officials, and all those concerned with these crucial aspects of education reform. Second, that it helps broaden understanding of the complex issues involved in standards, assessment, accountability, and grading. Third, that it leads to more thoughtful policies and programs. Fourth, and most important, that it helps accomplish the basic goal for which all reform initiatives are intended—namely, to enable all students to learn excellently and to gain the many positive benefits of that success.

— *Thomas R. Guskey*
*Robert J. Marzano*
*Series Editors*

# About the Authors

**Thomas R. Guskey** is Professor of Educational Policy Studies and Evaluation at the University of Kentucky. A graduate of the University of Chicago, he has taught at all levels, served as an administrator in Chicago Public Schools, and is author/editor of 11 books including *Implementing Mastery Learning, Improving Student Learning in College Classrooms, Communicating Student Learning,* and *Evaluating Professional Development.* He has won many awards for his work, including the National Staff Development Council's prestigious Article of the Year and Book of the Year awards. He is a frequent presenter at national conferences, was recently featured in a special segment on National Public Radio, and has worked with educators throughout the United States and Canada, as well as in Europe, Asia, and the Middle East.

**Jane M. Bailey** is Curriculum and Staff Development Coordinator for the Public Schools of Petoskey in northern lower Michigan. In addition to providing district leadership in the areas of curriculum and staff development, she serves as special education and federal programs director. She has more than 20 years of experience in education in a variety of roles including high school English teacher, special education consultant, high school principal, and staff development coordinator for an intermediate school district (regional service agency). She is coauthor of a chapter titled "Reporting Achievement at the Secondary Level: What and How" in the 1996 *Yearbook* for the Association for Supervision and Curriculum Development (ASCD). She is on the executive board of the Michigan affiliate of the National Staff Development Council and consults with school districts in the areas of assessment, grading, and school improvement.

# Introduction

Few topics in education generate more controversy than grading and reporting student learning. Teachers, parents, students, administrators, and community members all generally agree that we need better grading and reporting systems. The problem is that none of these groups seems to agree on what form those new systems should take. Even within each group there is little consensus as to what type of grading and reporting is best. Most teachers, for example, try hard to develop grading policies and reporting methods that are accurate and fair. Nevertheless, the policies and methods they use tend to vary widely from one teacher to another, even among those who teach at the same grade level within the same school (Brookhart, 1993, 1994; Cizek, Fitzgerald, & Rachor, 1996; McMillan, Workman, & Myran, 1999).

This lack of consensus about grading and reporting makes change exceptionally difficult. Efforts to introduce even moderate revisions in current systems typically are met with loud protests from one group or another, despite attempts to involve these various stakeholders in the change process. As a result, most educational leaders shun modifications in their reporting policies and practices simply to avoid these troublesome disputes (Allison & Friedman, 1995; Pardini, 1997).

So why enter this murky, disagreement-fraught quagmire, especially knowing the troubles it can bring? Why take on such a challenging topic when there seems to be so little agreement about what ought to be done or what changes are best?

We believe there are two important reasons for taking a serious look at the issues related to grading and reporting student learning and to do so right away. First of all, our work over the past several years has convinced us that a lot of current practice in grading and reporting is shamefully inadequate. We persist in the use of particular practices not because we've thought about them in any depth but, rather, because they are part of a tradition that has remained unquestioned for years.

Second, our recent work has shown that with relatively modest change, we can do a much better job of grading and reporting student learning. Today we know more than ever before about grading and reporting practices. We have better information about what works and is helpful to students. We are also much more knowledgeable about what doesn't work and is potentially harmful to students. This extensive knowledge base offers explicit direction for our change efforts and provides clear guidance for making improvements.

It also convinces us that there is no better time to implement these changes than the present. Change in our current grading and reporting policies and practices is not only needed—it is imperative.

## Our Guiding Premises

To fully understand the perspectives presented in this book, it is important for readers to know our operational premises. From the very beginning our work in developing this book has been guided by the following four basic premises:

1. The primary goal of grading and reporting is *communication*. Regardless of the format, its purpose is to provide high-quality information to interested persons in a form they can understand clearly and use effectively.

2. Grading and reporting are integral parts of the instructional process, much like assessment. When done well, they provide vital information to students, parents, and other interested persons that can be used to enhance both teaching and learning. Grading and reporting certify the attainment of learning goals, identify where additional work is needed, and provide a basis for improvement efforts.

3. Good reporting is based on good evidence. The usefulness of the information offered in any reporting device depends on the quality of the evidence on which that information is based. Even the most sophisticated, technologically advanced reporting system cannot compensate for poor, inadequate, or unreliable evidence on student learning.

4. Improvements in grading and reporting are best accomplished through the development of a comprehensive *reporting system*. As the goals of schooling become more complex, the need for better quality and more detailed communication about student learning becomes increasingly important. No single reporting device, such as a report card, can adequately serve these diverse communication needs. Instead, it requires a multifaceted reporting system that communicates multiple types of information to multiple audiences in multiple formats.

These premises directed our exploration of the topics of grading and reporting and shaped our vision of what we hoped this book would be. In addition, they served as the foundation upon which we framed the critical issues to be addressed in the book. We encourage readers to keep these premises in mind as they consider the topics presented and the recommendations offered.

---

**Guiding Premises in Developing Grading and Reporting Systems**

1. The primary goal of grading and reporting is communication.

2. Grading and reporting are integral parts of the instructional process.

3. Good reporting is based on good evidence.

4. Changes in grading and reporting are best accomplished through the development of a comprehensive reporting system.

---

## Our Purpose

Our purpose in developing this book was to provide all those involved in grading and reporting student learning with a coherent and thoughtful framework from which to view the complex issues related to this process. Since our principal focus was grading and reporting as it takes place on a regular basis in classrooms and in schools, we considered teachers our primary audience. Teachers are, after all, chiefly responsible for collecting evidence on student achievement and performance, evaluating that evidence, and communicating the results of their evaluations to others. Nevertheless, parents, administrators, community members, and students themselves all have important roles in the process and are important audiences for this work as well.

We believed that providing such a framework would help this diverse group of stakeholders develop a deeper and more reflective understanding of the various aspects of grading and reporting. We also believed it would provide a mechanism for making sense of the vast knowledge base accumulated over the past century on grading and reporting. We recognized, of course, that given the complexity of the issues involved in grading and reporting, it would be impossible to recommend a single set of "best" policies and practices. The tremendous diversity of contexts in which grading and reporting occur would make any attempt to do so completely foolish. Still, we were convinced that a coherent and thoughtful framework for viewing these complex issues could lead to better, more efficient, and much more effective grading and reporting policies and practices that would benefit all.

## Our Organizational Scheme

With our guiding premises as a foundation and our purpose clearly established, we framed a set of critical questions about grading and reporting student learning. These questions related to the issues that we found to be the most perplexing and troublesome to educators, parents, students, and policymakers. In the first section of the book, we clarify these questions and define the major issues that must be confronted in efforts to improve grading and reporting policies and practices.

With these critical questions clarified, we next searched the extensive literature on grading and reporting to find well-designed research studies that had addressed these questions and offered at least tentative answers. We also interviewed various groups of teachers, parents, and students to gain a better understanding of their perspectives and concerns with regard to grading and reporting. The second section of the book presents the results of our explorations and interviews and briefly explains the implications for practice that they offer.

Finally, we sought out educators who have been working on grading and reporting questions and have developed what they consider useful and practical answers. Our hope was to gain a better understanding of these issues and problems and to gather a variety of sensible and pragmatic solutions. In the final section of the book, we describe these solutions and offer specific guidelines for improving grading and reporting policies and practice.

One of the most basic questions we needed to address was *"Why should we change our current grading and reporting methods?"* Chapter 1 explores this question and explains why change is essential. Through examples from recent developments in education, our own experiences as classroom teachers, and information gathered from interviews with teachers, students, and parents, we illustrate the many problems inherent in current grading and reporting practices and the potentially detrimental effects of these practices.

*"What have we learned about grading and reporting over the years?"* is the question addressed in Chapter 2. Here we point out that, although many of our current reporting dilemmas are not new, lessons from the past and more recent research evidence are frequently ignored in efforts to develop better reporting policies and practices.

Chapter 3 focuses on *"How can we use our knowledge base to improve grading and reporting practice?"* Based on the major findings of past and current research studies, we offer several broad guidelines for improving practice. In particular, we describe those aspects of grading and reporting for which we have strong evidence to guide our reform initiatives. The ideas presented here provide a foundation for making reporting a more meaningful experience for teachers, parents, and students.

The central question of Chapter 4 is *"Why are report cards not enough?"* Here we delve into the problems that schools and school districts have faced in their attempts to implement report card reform. After showing that most of these problems arise from attempts to do too much with a single reporting device, we illustrate how the solution lies in developing a comprehensive, multifaceted reporting system.

Chapter 5 is the first of two chapters that explores the question *"What grading methods work best?"* Our focus in this chapter is on letter grades, percentage grades, and other categorical grading methods. Then in Chapter 6 we turn to several of the most common alternative grading methods, including standards-based grading, pass/fail grading, mastery grading, and narratives. For each method we describe its relative strengths and shortcomings. We also point out common fallacies related to each of these methods and illustrate how such fallacies can lead to misinterpretation and miscommunication.

*"How do we grade and report on the achievement and performance of students with special needs?"* is the focus of Chapter 7. Here we consider the special adaptations in grading and reporting that educators have made to better communicate information about the achievement and performance of students with disabilities, students who are English Language Learners (ELL), and students considered gifted or talented.

In Chapter 8 we turn to *"What special problems need to be addressed in grading and reporting?"* The major issues explored in this chapter include the use of technology and computerized grading programs, as well as the matter of grade inflation. We also raise questions about several commonly employed grading practices that can have damaging effects on students' learning, self-confidence, and motivation to learn.

*"Are there exemplary models of reporting that educators find to be working well?"* is the question that guided the development of Chapter 9. Here we describe a variety of elementary and secondary reporting forms and techniques that teachers say are helping them meet the challenge of effective communication. These include novel approaches to report cards and other reporting forms.

Finally, in Chapter 10 we turn to *"What guidelines can be offered for better grading and reporting systems?"* We describe the variety of reporting tools that might be included in a comprehensive reporting system. Then, arguing that honesty and fairness should direct all efforts in this area, we outline a set of guiding principles for educators to follow to ensure that their reporting systems focus on the qualities of effective communication and serve as enhancements to student learning.

Obviously, the issues addressed in these chapters are highly diverse. Our intent in addressing this broad array of issues, however, was not to offer a comprehensive treatise on the topic of grading and reporting student learning. Rather, we simply hoped to provide a thoughtful analysis of the most basic issues that would be useful to those engaged in the challenging task of developing better grading and reporting policies and practices.

## Other Resources

Within the past decade, several excellent books have been published on the topic of grading and reporting. Although each of these books takes a slightly different approach to the topic, all contribute significantly to our understanding of the problems and issues involved in this complicated area. Those that are best known and have most influenced our work include the following:

Azwell, T., & Schmar, E. (Eds.). (1995). *Report card on report cards: Alternatives to consider.* Portsmouth, NH: Heineman.

Guskey, T. R. (Ed.). (1996a). *Communicating student learning: 1996 yearbook of the Association for Supervision and Curriculum Development.* Alexandria, VA: Association for Supervision and Curriculum Development.

Haladyna, T. M. (1999). *A complete guide to student grading.* Boston: Allyn & Bacon.

Hargis, C. H. (1990). *Grades and grading practices.* Springfield, IL: Charles C Thomas.

O'Connor, K. (1999). *How to grade for learning.* Arlington Heights, IL: Skylight.

Turmbull, E., & Farr, B. (Eds.). (2000). *Grading and reporting student progress in an age of standards.* Norwood, MA: Christopher-Gordon.

Several other books and publications on grading also have gained a lot of attention in recent years, mainly because of their harsh criticism of specific grading practices. Some of these works blatantly attack nearly all forms of grading and are specifically designed to evoke a strong emotional response (e.g., Kohn, 1993, 1994). Although certain points made in these works have validity, careful reading reveals they are based on an extremely narrow view of existing research evidence (see Cameron & Pierce, 1996). Their authors emphasize the findings from a few investigations that correspond with the points they want to make, while ignoring numerous other studies that present strong but contradictory evidence. Furthermore, they appear to be either unaware of political realities in schools, or purposefully choose to ignore these realities (see Wiggins, 1996, 1997). Although we carefully considered the perspectives and ideas presented in these books and publications, we didn't find them particularly useful in helping us formulate workable guidelines for better practice.

Our goal in developing this book was not to replicate the excellent work already done. Rather, our goal was to extend the ideas presented in earlier works, add further clarification to those ideas, develop additional ideas based on current evidence, and within the context of current political realities, offer guidance for the practical implementation of these ideas in modern classrooms.

## Our Hope

It should be obvious from this brief description that it is not our intent to offer definitive solutions to all of the vexing problems that educators confront as they consider the various forms of grading and reporting student learning.

The issues involved in grading and reporting are too diverse and far too complex to be addressed with simple ideas or strategies. Instead, we designed this book to help readers think about grading and reporting in the most basic and fundamental terms. Rather than offering readers "the answer," we chose to show that improvements in reporting systems are possible and that specific and practical ideas are available to guide us in making those improvements.

Our grandest hope is that this book won't be just another volume that sits on a bookshelf in educators' offices or in professional libraries. Above all, we hope it will be used and reused, more as a workbook than as a textbook. We hope it will be incorporated in undergraduate education courses to help those preparing to become teachers develop a deeper understanding of grading and reporting issues, and that it will be the focus of study groups and faculty retreats where the ideas we present are discussed and debated. We would like to see well-worn, coffee-stained copies of this book in teachers' lounges, where it serves as a basis for brief conversations and extended planning sessions.

We hope readers will take an active, thoughtful, reflective, and perhaps even skeptical approach to the ideas we present. As a result, we hope it simulates further inquiry and action. Most important, we hope this book prompts the development of more thoughtful and more critically informed reporting systems that will be considered by all as models of effective communication.

# CHAPTER 1

# Defining the
# Impetus for Change

Change is never easy. It's especially difficult in education because so much current practice is based on tradition rather than compelling evidence of effectiveness. We continue to use certain practices not because we've thought about them deliberately or evaluated them thoroughly but, rather, because it is easier to continue doing what we have always done. In no area of education is this truer than the area of grading and reporting student learning.

In essence, grading is an exercise in professional judgment. It involves the collection and evaluation of evidence on students' achievement or performance over a specified period of time, such as 6 weeks, 9 weeks, or an academic semester. Through this process, various types of descriptive information and measures of students' performance are converted into grades or marks that summarize students' accomplishments, usually in reference to specific criteria or standards. Although some authors distinguish between "grades" and "marks" (see, for example, O'Connor, 1999), we consider these terms synonymous. Both imply a set of symbols, words, or numbers used to designate different levels of achievement or performance. These might be letter grades such as *A, B, C, D,* and *F*; symbols such as ✔+, ✔, ✔–; descriptive words such as *Exemplary, Satisfactory,* and *Needs Improvement*; or numerals such *4, 3, 2,* and *1.* Reporting, on the other hand, is the process by which these judgments are communicated to parents, students, or others.

Grading and reporting have been an integral part of education for the better part of the past century. But while most aspects of education have seen radical change during that time, in many ways grading and reporting have remained much the same. In recent years, however, new developments in education have made it imperative that we give serious attention to the issues of grading and reporting student learning and also consider thoughtful, carefully designed, and well-reasoned change.

## Developments That Compel Change
## in Grading and Reporting

Five different but interrelated developments in education have brought increased attention to grading and reporting. First is the growing emphasis on educational standards and performance-based forms of assessment. Educators today are no longer satisfied with instruction that focuses on only basic skills. Instead, they want students to engage in "authentic" problem solving tasks that require them to think, plan, analyze, integrate, and construct. In developing learning standards that emphasize these skills and assessments that measure how well students can perform them, educators discovered that their traditional marking systems were inadequate and obsolete. This, in turn, prompted calls for the development of better and more appropriate reporting systems.

A second development is the growing criticism of education and a skeptical public that doubts the quality of what is going on in schools and the capabilities of educators. The negative tone of various reports and polls has diminished the public's trust in educators to make decisions that are always in the best interests of students (see Carnevale & Desrochers, 1999). As a result, parents and community members are demanding more information than ever before about schools, instructional programs, and student learning progress.

The third development that spurred this effort is advances in technology. These advances present educators with many new challenges but also offer many new opportunities. Today, we are able to record and disseminate vast amounts of information with infinite detail. These advances also make it possible for us to do things that were unimaginable in the past. For example, the same technology that allows supermarkets to itemize every purchase on an individualized charge slip and permits businesses to provide individualized billings for items bought at locations throughout the world can be used to produce individualized report cards that show what students are working on and what progress they have made on a daily basis.

Fourth is growing recognition that grading and reporting are one of educators' most important responsibilities. Teachers today engage in some form of reporting every hour they are in the classroom. These reporting activities range from informally checking and correcting students' learning errors to scoring and recording the results from quizzes, examinations, and performance assessments. Reporting student progress can take the form of checklists, written comments, narrative reports, numerical scores, letter grades, or a formal or informal student conference. Yet despite the importance of these activities, few teachers have any formal training on grading or reporting. Most have scant knowledge of the various reporting methods, the advantages and disadvantages of each, or the effects of different grading policies (Stiggins, 1993, 1999). As a result, even educators dissatisfied with their present practices lack direction in their efforts to make changes.

Fifth, and perhaps most important, is increased awareness of the large gap between our knowledge base on grading and reporting, and what is common practice. Despite the fact that grading and reporting have been the subject of innumerable studies, current policies and practices tend to be based more on opinion than on thoughtful analysis of this growing evidence. As we described earlier, far too often we persist in the use of particular practices simply because "We've always done it that way" or because "That's what was done to us." While researchers have confirmed that some of the grading and reporting practices used by our former teachers were sound, others clearly were not. To make progress as a profession and to benefit our students, we must ensure this extensive knowledge base on grading and reporting makes its way into practice.

---

**Developments That Make Change in Grading and Reporting Systems Imperative**

1. The growing emphasis on standards and performance assessments makes current reporting practices inadequate.

2. Parents and community members are demanding more and better information about student learning progress.

3. Advances in technology allow for more efficient reporting of detailed information on student learning.

4. Grading and reporting are recognized as one of educators' most important responsibilities.

5. There is growing awareness of the gap between our knowledge base and common practice in grading and reporting.

---

## Standards for Teacher Competence

A related development that brought increased urgency to efforts to change grading and reporting practices was the publication of *Standards for Teacher Competence in Educational Assessment of Students* in 1990. These Standards were developed jointly by the American Federation of Teachers, the National Council on Measurement in Education, and the National Education Association. Two of the Standards relate directly to the issues of grading and reporting student learning.

Standard 5 states, "Teachers should be skilled in developing valid pupil grading procedures which use pupil assessments." The array of skills associated with this Standard include not only knowing how to combine various

sources of information in order to generate grades but also being able to articulate how those grades reflect students' performance and the teacher's value
of that performance. Standard 5 recognizes the subjective and judgmental
nature of grading and points to the need for teachers to acknowledge such
tendencies. Not only must good teachers know the assumptions underlying
varying grading procedures, they also must know how to accurately put valid
grading and reporting systems into place. Furthermore, Standard 5 makes
clear that teachers must constantly evaluate and modify their grading procedures in order to make them more valid (Whittington, 1999).

Grades have long been recognized in the measurement community as
prime examples of unreliable measurement. What one teacher considers in
determining students' grades may differ greatly from the criteria used by another teacher (Cizek et al., 1996; McMillan et al., 1999). Even in school districts
where established grading policies present guidelines for teachers to follow in
assigning grades, there remains significant variation in the grading practices
that teachers employ. While teachers certainly have the right to set their own
criteria and to determine grades based on their ideas of what a grade represents, they also need to recognize how they differ from others and to articulate
why.

Then, according to Standard 6, "Teachers should be skilled at communicating assessment results to students, parents, other lay audiences, and other
educators." Standard 6 calls for not only knowledge of assessment results and
what they mean but the ability to translate results in such a way that others
can make sense of them. This kind of communication requires not only an
understanding of the concepts of validity and reliability but the ability to
translate these concepts in a fashion that a student, a parent, or another adult
can comprehend (Whittington, 1999).

The validity of grades for communicating information on students'
achievement and performance depends in part on the quality of the assessment information on which grades are based and in part on the procedures
used to derive the grade from that information. Once highly valid results have
been obtained from individual classroom assessments, teachers need to know
how to derive grades from that information (Brookhart, 1999). They need to
recognize the importance of looking for consistency in that evidence and to
understand inconsistency as a signal to look deeper and to search for reasons
why. Such recognition and searching not only improve the validity of grades as
accurate representations of achievement, they also promote better student
learning.

Clearly if classroom assessment information is of poor quality or incomplete, the teacher will not be able to effectively communicate information
about student achievement and performance. That is why teachers need to
know (a) how to assign grades or other reporting marks in ways that maximize

validity and reliability and (b) how to communicate classroom assessment information in ways other than grades. They also must be prepared to advocate change in these methods whenever such change would result in clearer communication of classroom assessment results (Brookhart, 1999).

Sadly, research on teachers and teacher education suggests that preservice training for teachers in assessment and grading is sorely inadequate (Gulliksen & Hopkins, 1987; Stiggins, 1991, 1999). Some suggest this failure is due to the lack of alignment between assessment preparation and what teachers are required to do in the classroom (Ferrara, 1995; Gulliksen, 1993; Stiggins, 1993, 1999). Whatever the reasons, the Standards make clear the need for increased attention and practical solutions to the problems associated with grading and reporting student learning.

## The Task at Hand

With the five developments and the Standards in mind, we set out to gather and organize the information presented in this book. Much of our time in preparation was spent talking with teachers, students, and parents about their perceptions of grading and reporting. Through a series of informal interviews and discussion sessions, we asked individuals from each of these groups what they thought of the grading policies and practices they had experienced and how those policies and practices might be improved. We also spent significant time exploring the research literature on grading and reporting, drawing from that literature the most salient points to use in framing our ideas for improvement. Finally, we gathered information on grading policies and collected a wide variety of reporting forms from schools and school districts throughout the United States and Canada. While we cannot claim that these policies and forms constitute a truly representative sample, we believe they offer a basic idea of the diverse array of reporting practices currently in use.

As we described in the Introduction, our work was guided by a profound sense of the need for better reporting systems. Our personal experiences as educators made us well aware of inadequacies in many current reporting policies and practices. We had seen firsthand the frustration, confusion, and misinterpretation they frequently brought. We also were convinced that muddled thinking in the past had led to these muddled practices in the present. But most important, we shared the belief that better thinking, a better knowledge base, and a better understanding of the critical issues involved could bring significant improvements. That is precisely what we hoped this book would provide.

## A Personal Reflection

Like most teachers, we gave little thought to grading and reporting prior to beginning our first teaching assignments. One of us began our career in education as a middle school teacher while the other started at the high school level. In both cases, every 9 weeks we were required to reduce all the impressions and information we had gathered on the learning of each of our students to a single symbol. We recorded this symbol on a report card that was carried home by students, signed by one of their parents, and then returned to the school until the end of the next 9-week cycle. When the school year drew to a close, we tallied, summarized, and then recorded yet another symbol that represented our judgment of students' cumulative accomplishments. This symbol became part of students' "permanent record" and determined in large part what type of academic program they would enter the following school year.

In my case, I initially approached the process of grading and reporting rather casually, with little doubt I could be fair and objective. After all, during my 17 years as a student from kindergarten through college, I had experienced a variety of grading practices and policies and had a good idea of what worked. The first time I sat down to complete report cards, however, I quickly discovered the process was far more complicated than I ever anticipated.

I began at the top of my class list with Natalie, who clearly deserved a high mark. She consistently attained the highest score on examinations, and all of her work was well organized and exceptionally neat. But I also knew that none of what we worked on in class required serious effort from Natalie, and I had not done a very good job of challenging her capabilities. Still, I recorded the mark and moved on.

Next came Michael. Although he hadn't done well on examinations, Michael worked very hard, and his class assignments showed exceptional creativity. I certainly did not want to give him a mark that would discourage the extra effort he was exhibiting. Since I would need to consider his case more carefully, I set his report card aside with the intention of coming back to it later.

Then there was Nicole. At the beginning of the marking period she really struggled but in recent weeks had shown remarkable progress. Somehow, the mark I gave her needed to reflect her most recent work and show how far she had come. I set her report card aside too.

With each student the process of grading and reporting became more frustrating and confusing to me. The cases I needed to consider more carefully greatly outnumbered those I could mark with ease. What I imagined to be a simple and straightforward process turned out to be extremely complex. It seemed impossible to capture all that I wanted to communicate about each student in a single symbol. Furthermore, I began to see the whole process as counter to my role as a teacher. How could I be an advocate for my students and also serve as their evaluator and judge?

## Teachers' Perceptions of Grading and Reporting

Since those early years, the issues of grading and reporting have continued to fascinate and perplex us. Even today, in conversations with teachers we frequently ask "What grading and reporting practices do you use?" Elementary teachers typically describe standards-based reporting systems that include checklists of competencies and narrative reports. Some relate their recent efforts to develop progress-oriented reporting forms that attempt to illustrate students' achievement and performance on a developmental continuum. They are quick to add, however, that they have experienced difficulties in helping parents make sense of these forms. Nearly all also express personal dilemmas with the grading process. While they recognize the need to offer parents information about the achievement and performance of their children, the vast majority of elementary teachers indicate that the evaluative aspects of grading run counter to their perceived roles as teachers. They want to be an advocate for their students, but the process of grading requires them to be a judge.

The responses of secondary teachers tend to be different. Most begin by opening a grade book or computer file that contains page after page of meticulously kept spreadsheets. Each page lists the names of the students in each of their classes, followed by a series of columns filled with an intricate array of numbers and symbols. They go on to explain the process they use in determining students' grades, which typically involves complex mathematical formulae that include percentages, weighted averages, and various point-tallying options. With the aid of statistical software, they then calculate a number to the one hundred-thousandth decimal point that is finally converted to a letter grade.

When we follow this initial question with "Why do you grade?" the answers always come more slowly. Elementary teachers usually say, "Well, we have to, don't we?" Others respond, "Parents and administrators demand it!" Secondary teachers also mention parental demands and often point to college and university admission requirements. In the final analysis, nearly all teachers admit they really don't like grading and reporting. They describe the process as troublesome, time-consuming, and counter to what they consider to be their major responsibilities as teachers, which involve engaging students in a variety of high-quality learning experiences. What they want is a more effective reporting system that would enhance these instructional responsibilities rather than detract from them.

## Sources of Teachers' Grading and Reporting Practices

As our discussions continue, it becomes evident that most teachers haven't thought deeply about the issues involved in grading and reporting. When we ask, for example, "How did you decide on the grading and reporting practices you use?" most teachers describe some combination of four different sources of influence. First and foremost, they refer to the policies and practices they experienced as students. In other words, they do what was done to them. Prior to entering teaching, most teachers complete 5 or 6 years of elementary education, 3 years in middle school, 4 years in high school, and another 4 or 5 years at the college or university level. During those 16 or 17 years they were probably taught by 60 to 80 different teachers, all of whom were responsible for evaluating and grading their achievement and performance. From this wide array of grading policies and practices, they select for their classes those that they believe work best and are most appropriate.

A second important influence on teachers' grading and reporting practices is their personal philosophies of teaching and learning (Barnes, Bull, Perry, & Campbell, 1998; Frisbie & Waltman, 1992). Some teachers believe their major purpose in teaching is to identify the various talent levels of students, ranging from those who display exceptional ability and skill, to those who may need specialized assistance. Other teachers object to these sorting and selecting functions and insist, instead, that their major purpose is to develop talent and foster personal growth in all students. These different philosophies typically translate into very different grading policies and practices. The first group of teachers is likely to emphasize the evaluative nature of grading and the use of grades to recognize excellence in the performance of a few students. The second group of teachers, on the other hand, will stress the communicative and formative functions of reporting and how it can be used to facilitate the learning process.

The third source of information from which teachers draw is district-, building-, department-, or grade-level grading policies. A recent nationwide survey found that about two thirds of all schools have established policies on grading (Polloway et al., 1994). Unfortunately, the majority of teachers describe these policies as ambiguous and unclear and indicate they had little or no role in developing them. Nevertheless, teachers at all levels generally feel compelled to follow these policies and make adaptations only when they are convinced that such changes are both legally and educationally defensible.

The final factor that influences teachers' grading and reporting practices is what they learned in their undergraduate teacher preparation programs. Although this information is generally restricted to what was presented in a single unit of a required educational psychology course (Stiggins, 1993), it provides prospective teachers with the opportunity to explore a number of grading issues. At the very least, this unit usually helps them understand the difference between norm-referenced and criterion-referenced grading standards.

Because the influence of these four sources on teachers is uneven and inconsistent, the personal grading and reporting practices teachers develop tend to vary widely, even among teachers in the same school or in the same academic department. This puts students in the difficult position of having to learn a new set of grading policies and rules in every class. While some students become highly skilled at deciphering these differences, understanding the consequences, and manipulating each system to their advantage, others remain painfully unaware and confused, often suffering tragic results.

---

### Sources of Teachers' Grading Practices

1. The policies and practices they experienced as students

2. Their personal philosophies of teaching and learning

3. District-, building-, department-, or grade-level policies on grading and reporting

4. What they learned about grading and reporting in their undergraduate teacher preparation programs

---

# Students' Perceptions of Grading and Reporting

Students' perceptions on grading and reporting tend to be quite different from those of teachers. Most students' experiences with assessment and evaluation date back to their earliest childhood years. The things they do as toddlers are observed and appraised by their parents and other adults who communicate the results of these appraisals through direct and immediate feedback. This feedback is usually verbal and occasionally is accompanied by corrective action. Behaviors considered appropriate are encouraged with praise and recognition, while those judged to be inappropriate or potentially harmful are discouraged through reprimand or punishment. Expressions such as "Good job, Christopher!" and "That's right, Jennifer!" communicate acceptance and approval, whereas "No, no, Elizabeth!" or "Don't do that, Joseph!" let children know their behaviors are not permissible and need to be altered. Thoughtful adults, whether parents and/or teachers, try to ensure that the feedback they offer is clear, consistent, and an aid to children's learning.

When children get older and enter school, their learning experiences become more formalized and structured. But more important, a person outside the family organizes these learning experiences: a teacher. Similar to parents, teachers in the early elementary grades use direct verbal feedback to communicate appraisal results to children. They regularly observe children's behavior in class and then offer immediate feedback to guide and direct children's learning. Teachers praise children for appropriate actions and help them correct behaviors that are inappropriate or unacceptable.

In addition to the direct feedback they offer students, teachers must communicate the results of their appraisals to parents. Parents want to know how their child is doing in school and care deeply about the teachers' judgments. Teachers, in turn, want to inform parents about their child's learning progress and are eager to engage parents as partners in the learning process.

Sharing the results from *all* of their observations, however, is both impractical and inefficient for teachers. Therefore, teachers must distill the information they have gathered into a single symbol or collection of symbols designed to provide an overall summary of each student's performance. These symbols are typically recorded as marks or grades on a report card or reporting form. To teachers, marks and grades represent a simple and concise way to encapsulate and present the results of their appraisals to parents. Students generally view the grade as the teacher's summary judgment of their work and their accomplishments over a specific portion of the school year.

Around the middle school years and sometimes earlier, however, student's perceptions of grades begin to change. Although the reasons for this change are uncertain, it seems likely due to teachers' shifting emphasis from the formative aspects of grades to their summative functions. As a result, students no longer see grades as a source of feedback to guide improvements in their learning. Instead, they regard grades as the major commodity teachers and schools have to offer in exchange for their performance. This change brings a slow but steady shift in students' focus away from learning and toward what they must do to obtain the grade commodity.

For those who are successful in acquiring it, the grade commodity takes on great value. These students work hard to procure it and take pride in what they possess. Those who are less successful protect their self-images from guilt by attaching less importance to the grade commodity. Some may even consider it insignificant or irrelevant. This change in students' perceptions is reflected in the questions that they ask teachers on entering a class. Instead of inquiring about "What are we going to study?" or "What will I be learning?" students are more likely to ask "What must I do to get a good grade?"

The principal currency students must use to obtain the grade commodity, of course, is points. Over the course of a marking period, almost everything students do in class has a point value attached to it. Quizzes, tests, assessments, projects, laboratory experiments, and homework assignments all represent opportunities for students to earn points (Feldman, Kropf, & Alibrand, 1996). The number of points the teacher assigns to a particular activity determines its value. That is why, for example, the first questions students ask when the teacher announces an upcoming project or event are "Does it count?" and "How many points is it worth?" Teachers' answers to these questions give students a clear idea of how much importance they should attach to that particular event.

## The Points-Driven Academic Economy of Classrooms

From that time on, the currency of points dominates the academic economy of classrooms. Students begin to view academic wealth as determined by the number of points they can accumulate. Teachers set the currency exchange rate when they establish their grading standards and simplify the required bookkeeping with modern computerized grading programs. Savvy students keep track of current exchange rates, calculating far in advance the exact number of points they need to attain the grade they want, and adjust their efforts accordingly. They know they must plan cautiously since they can lose points or be fined for certain transgressions, such as not completing a homework assignment or turning in a project late. They also make note of contingencies that allow them to earn extra points or bonuses, such as doing special projects or volunteering for work outside of class.

Students also learn that the grade commodity can be gained through actions outside their actual academic performance. Their behaviors in class, the effort they appear to be making, their politeness in interacting with the teacher, the neatness of their work, and even their appearance can influence the grade they attain. Students sometimes label this the "Eddie Haskell Effect" in reference to the manipulative antics of a character portrayed in the 1960s' television show *Leave It to Beaver* (reruns of which now air in syndication). While points are clearly important, students also recognize that these other factors can be crucial in the grade commodity market.

Students who accumulate large amounts of points and are able to attain high grades qualify for distinctive labels such as "gifted" or "talented." Often, their wealth in the grade commodity allows them to qualify for special "honors" or "accelerated" classes. Students who acquire few points and are grade-commodity poor typically are referred for further evaluation. This, in turn, often leads to them being assigned special titles such as "slow learner" or "learning disabled." Although some may dispute this practice, it is well established that high grades are considered a prerequisite to "academically talented" programs, while failing grades are the first diagnostic step in the identification of students who are learning disabled (Hargis, 1990).

Sadly, this emphasis on earning points in order to procure the grade commodity diminishes the value of learning. Students are drawn into a points-driven, academic economy system that detracts from education's true purpose. What was originally designed to be a means of summarizing appraisals of student learning becomes the end in itself. Rigid adherence to points-driven systems may appear to bring objectivity and precision to the grading process. But as we will see in later chapters, this objectivity and precision are far more imaginary than real. In the long run, such systems detract from the central purposes of teaching and learning.

We hasten to add that the emphasis on points is not an immutable characteristic of grades or grading and reporting systems, as some might suggest. Rather, it stems from the procedures used in determining grades and the way those grades are then used or misused. Thoughtfully designed grading and reporting systems that emphasize the formative and communicative aspects of grades can maintain students' focus on important learning goals. Such systems can actually serve to enhance instructional processes. Especially when combined with other more descriptive information within a comprehensive reporting system, grades can communicate information that is accurate, meaningful, and constructive (Guskey, 1993).

## Parents' Perceptions of Grading and Reporting

Parents have unique perceptions of grading and reporting as well. We learned from our informal interviews and discussion sessions with parents that while few are enamored with the new forms of reporting that educators have developed, many do favor change in current reporting policies and practices. At the same time, however, most parents' ideas about grading and reporting tend to be limited by the narrow array of practices they experienced as students. For this reason it is imperative that parents not only be involved in planning reforms in grading and reporting policies but that change efforts also be accompanied by well-designed, high-quality parent education programs. Such programs should help parents understand the rationale behind changes in grading policies and practices, as well as the advantages of the alternative forms of reporting that might be included in a new reporting system. They should also illustrate to parents how this information can best be put to use.

Nearly all of the parents with whom we spoke indicate that they would like to receive more and better information about their child's learning progress in school. They stress first that they would like to receive that information more regularly. For example, if given the choice most parents indicate they would like to have report cards sent home every 6 weeks rather than every 9 weeks. This runs counter to the desires of most teachers, of course, who consistently report that completing report cards every 9 weeks is challenging enough. When we pressed this issue in our interviews with parents, however, we discovered that parents don't necessarily want report cards more often. Instead, they simply want information about their child's learning progress on a more regular basis. Because most parents see report cards as the principal source of such information, and sometimes the only source, they consistently request more regular distribution schedules.

Second, the vast majority of parents say they would like to receive more detailed information about how their child is doing in school. They are quick to add, however, that they want that information in a jargon-free form that they can understand (see Million, 1999). This appears to be the reason why many parents prefer letter grades on reporting forms. It's not that they are convinced of the merits of letter grades in comparison to other reporting methods but, rather, because they experienced letter grades in their educational backgrounds they believe they understand what letter grades mean. To most parents, letter grades possess two highly desirable qualities: They communicate information clearly, and they are easy to interpret.

We also discovered that the resistance many parents express to change in reporting methods is due to confusion caused by the language that educators use in newly developed reporting forms. Certain words and phrases that educators perceive to be clear and precise are either mysterious or meaningless to parents. In some cases, this confusion causes parents to misinterpret completely the message that educators are hoping to communicate.

The word "emerging," for example, is used in many reporting forms to describe a skill or understanding that students have just begun to develop. To most parents, however, the word "emerging" suggests a creature crawling out of a dark swamp. "Emerging literacy" implies simply that the creature is carrying books. Similarly, many teachers use the phrase "developmentally appropriate" to describe activities that are well suited to students' level of cognitive, physical, and emotional maturation (Galen, 1994). Yet to many parents, "developmental" means "remedial." They equate such activities with those offered in "developmental" courses in high schools and colleges. At these levels, "developmental" is the label attached to the remedial work that students must complete before they can be considered "on level" or "on track." To many parents, a child engaged in "developmentally appropriate" activities is in serious trouble and at risk of failure—clearly not the message that teachers want to convey. In choosing the words and phrases used in reporting to parents, educators must avoid such "educationese" to ensure that what they mean is accurately communicated.

The third thing parents reveal is that they need practical suggestions about how they can help their children. We found that most parents dearly love their children and sincerely want them to succeed in school (see Henderson & Berla, 1995). At the same time, however, they are uncertain of teachers' specific expectations and precisely what they can do at home to help (Hoover-Dempsey & Sandler, 1997). This "formative" aspect of reporting is very important to parents but is frequently neglected or ignored by educators (Cattermole & Robinson, 1985; Kreider & Lopez, 1999).

## Parents' Perceptions of Teachers

As part of our informal interviews and discussion sessions with parents, we also asked "What do you most want to know about your child's teacher?" and "What teacher characteristics are most important to you?" Although parents' answers varied slightly from the elementary to secondary level, overall they were surprisingly consistent.

Two items topped the list of things parents wanted to know about their child's teacher. First, they want to know that *the teacher is competent.* They want to be assured that their child's teacher is well trained, knowledgeable, and well prepared to teach (Million, 1999). They also stressed, however, that they don't want a "know-it-all, unapproachable clinician." Instead, they want their child's teacher to be capable and highly skilled, yet personable (see Rich, 1998). While a few parents expressed reservations about having their child placed in the classroom of a beginning teacher, most indicated that the number of years' teaching experience matters little to them.

Second and equally important, parents want to know that *the teacher cares about their child.* They hope the teacher will take the time to get to know their child as an individual and, in doing so, will recognize their child's positive attributes as well as the faults. The vast majority of parents see their child as a special and highly unique person and want their child's teacher to share that perception (see Watts, 1996).

---

**What Parents Most Want to Know
About Their Child's Teacher**

1. The teacher is competent.

2. The teacher cares about their child as an individual.

---

Parents also described certain actions related directly to these two items that diminish their perceptions of teachers. One recounted an experience that occurred during a school open-house session early in the school year. To a group of parents attending the session, the teacher announced that she had never before taught at that grade level, was unprepared for the change in assignment and, therefore, would probably be learning right along with the children. Although this admission was undoubtedly truthful and sincere, it did little to convince parents of the teacher's competence. How much better it would have been had the teacher indicated that while this was her first year teaching at this level, she had spent a major portion of the summer preparing for the new assignment, had attended several professional development sessions on teaching students of this age, and was truly excited about working with this particular group of students.

Similarly, subtle actions on the part of teachers often lessen parents' estimation of them. The teacher who must glance at the grade book before saying anything to parents about the performance of their child, for example, communicates to many parents a profoundly negative impression. Although this may be an unconscious act on the part of the teacher, to parents it communicates that the teacher knows very little about their child personally and doesn't care about their child as an individual. It's far better for the teacher to begin the conversation by mentioning something positive about the child or perhaps relate a personal experience shared with that child. Then later in the conversation the grade book can be turned to for more specific information about the child's learning progress.

Teachers must be ever mindful of not only the direct ways in which they communicate with parents but also the many indirect and subtle ways in which parents gain information from them and about them. Small things can make a very big difference.

## Summary

Perceptions of grading and reporting vary widely among teachers, students, and parents. To fulfill the primary communication purposes of grading and reporting, these drastic differences must be met and resolved. Multifaceted reporting systems that include a collection of reporting tools to satisfy the diverse information needs of teachers, students, parents, and other interested persons present the best and most practical solution to these challenging communication problems.

# CHAPTER 2

# Exploring the History of Grading and Reporting

When we began our investigation of grading and reporting practices, we were surprised to find how much had been written on the topic. A computerized literature search yielded a reference list that included more than 4,000 books, articles, essays, and research studies. Most of these references are essays about problems in grading and what should be done about them. The research articles consist mainly of teacher surveys (Haladyna, 1999).

Even a cursory review of this vast literature reveals four things. First, we know a great deal about grading and reporting student learning. Second, much of what we know we've known a very long time. Third, for various reasons a lot of what we know has not found its way into practice. And fourth, our knowledge and understanding with regard to some aspects of grading and reporting (e.g., the use of technology) are only now beginning to develop (Guskey, 1994, 1996b).

One of our initial discoveries as we explored this literature was that educators have struggled with the problems associated with grading and reporting for many years. We found, for example, a report prepared by Warren Middleton, who was charged with the task of leading a committee that would revise his school's grading and reporting system. He described the work in this way:

> The Committee on Grading was called upon to study grading procedures. At first, the task of investigating the literature seemed to be a rather hopeless one. What a mass and a mess it all was! Could order be brought out of such chaos? Could points of agreement among American educators concerning the perplexing grading problem actually be discovered? It was with considerable misgiving and trepidation that the work was finally begun. (p. 5)

Few educators would consider the difficulties encountered by Middleton and his colleagues to be particularly surprising. In fact, their dilemmas sound quite similar to those faced by most grading and report card committees today. Most are shocked to discover, however, that this quote is taken from a report published in 1933!

Clearly, the issues related to grading and reporting student learning have confounded educators for a long time. Yet, despite all the debate about grading and the multitude of studies that have been conducted, coming up with prescriptions for best practice remains a daunting task.

# Early Developments

Although student assessment has been a part of teaching and learning for centuries, grading and reporting are relatively recent phenomena. The ancient Greeks used assessments in their teaching, but these were not formal evaluations of student achievement. Instead, their purpose was primarily formative. Examinations provided students the opportunity to demonstrate, usually orally, what they had learned. They also gave teachers a clear indication of what topics required additional work or instruction.

In the United States, grading and reporting were virtually unknown in schools before 1850. Back then, most schools grouped students of all ages and backgrounds together with one teacher. The teacher reported students' learning progress orally to parents, usually during a visit to the student's home. At that time, few students went beyond the elementary education offered in these one-room schoolhouses.

As the number of students increased in the late 1800s, however, schools began to group students in grade levels according to their age, and new ideas about curriculum and teaching methods were tried (Edwards & Richey, 1947). One of these new ideas was the use of formal progress evaluations of students' work. In these evaluations, teachers would simply write down the skills each student had mastered and those on which additional work was needed. This was done primarily for students' benefit, since they were not permitted to move on to the next level until they demonstrated their mastery of the current one. It was also the earliest example of a narrative report card.

With the passage of compulsory attendance laws at the elementary level, the number of students entering high schools increased rapidly. Between 1870 and 1910, the number of public high schools in the United States increased from 500 to 10,000 (Gutek, 1986). As a result, subject area instruction in the high schools became increasingly specific and student populations became more diverse. While elementary teachers continued to use written descriptions and narrative reports to document student learning, high school teachers began to employ percentages and other similar markings to certify students' accomplishments in different subject areas. This was the beginning of the grading and reporting systems we know today (Kirschenbaum, Simon, & Napier, 1971).

## Problems With Subjectivity in Grading

The shift to percentage grading was gradual, and few American educators questioned it. The practice seemed a natural by-product of the increased demands on high school teachers, who now faced classrooms with growing numbers of students. But in 1912, a study was published that seriously challenged the reliability of percentage grades as accurate indicators of students' achievement.

Starch and Elliott (1912) set out to determine the extent to which the personal values and expectations of teachers influence their grading standards. In other words, they were interested in how much subjectivity was involved in the grades that teachers assigned to their students. To test this, they made copies of two English-language examination papers that had been written by two students at the end of their first year in high school. These papers were then sent to 200 high schools where the teacher who typically taught first-year English was asked to mark the papers according to the practices and standards of the school. Of the 200 schools contacted, 142 returned the papers graded.

Both papers were graded on a percentage scale on which scores could range from 0 to 100. A score of 75 was considered passing. For one paper, the scores varied from 64 to 98. The other paper received scores ranging from 50 to 97. One of the papers was given a failing mark by 15% of the teachers, while 12% gave the same paper a grade of more than 90 points.

Starch and Elliott found that many teachers, in addition to their subjective feelings about the papers, were influenced by neatness, spelling, and punctuation. While some teachers focused on elements of grammar and style, others considered only how well the message of the paper was communicated. With more than 30 different scores assigned to a single paper and a range of over 40 points, it is easy to see why this report caused a stir among educators. It also shows that our current problems regarding the reliability of the writing sample and portfolio scores are nothing new.

Starch and Elliott's (1912) study was immediately criticized by those who claimed English teachers were naturally prone to be more subjective in their assessments of students' work. Some even argued that good writing is, after all, a highly subjective judgment. To counter this criticism, Starch and Elliott (1913) repeated their study the following year using geometry papers submitted to high school mathematics teachers. When they analyzed these results, they found *even greater variation* in the percentage grades assigned by the mathematics teachers than had been shown by the English teachers. Among the 138 returns, scores on one of the papers ranged from 28 to 95: a 67-point difference! While some teachers deducted points only for a wrong answer, many others took neatness, form, and spelling into consideration.

# Modern Grading and Reporting Systems

These demonstrations of wide variation in teachers' grading practices led to a gradual move away from percentage scores to scales that had fewer and larger categories. One was a three-point scale that employed the categories of *Excellent, Average,* and *Poor.* Another was the familiar 5-point scale of *Excellent, Good, Average, Poor,* and *Failing,* or *A, B, C, D,* and *F* (Johnson, 1918; Rugg, 1918). This reduction in the number of score categories served to reduce the variation in grades, but it did not solve the problem of teacher subjectivity. The requirements for an *A, B,* or *C* in any course of study varied widely from teacher to teacher.

To ensure a fairer distribution of grades among teachers and to bring into check the subjective nature of scoring, the idea of "grading on the curve" became increasingly popular. By this method, students were simply rank ordered according to some measure of their performance or proficiency. The top percentage was then assigned a grade of *A,* the next percentage a grade of *B,* and so on (Corey, 1930). Some advocates of this method even specified the precise percentages of students that should be assigned each grade. One example was the 6-22-44-22-6 system (Davis, 1930).

Grading on the curve was believed to be appropriate at that time because it was well known that the distribution of students' intelligence test scores approximated a normal probability curve. Since innate intelligence and school achievement were thought to be directly related, such a procedure seemed both fair and equitable (Middleton, 1933). Grading on the curve also relieved teachers of the difficult task of having to identify specific learning criteria. Fortunately, educators today have a better understanding of the flawed premises behind this practice (see the discussion of "grading on the curve" in Chapter 3) and its many negative consequences (Bloom, Madaus, & Hastings, 1981; Bracey, 1994; Wood, 1994).

In the years that followed, the debate over grading and reporting intensified. A number of schools abolished formal grades altogether, believing they were a distraction in teaching and learning (Chapman & Ashbaugh, 1925). Some schools returned to using only verbal descriptions and narrative reports of student achievement. Others advocated pass-fail systems that distinguished only between acceptable and failing work (Good, 1937). Still others advocated a "mastery approach," in which the only important factor was whether or not the student had mastered the content or skill. Once mastered, that student would move on to other areas of study (Heck, 1938; Hill, 1935).

Today, lack of consensus about what works best has led to the implementation of widely varied grading and reporting practices, especially at the elementary level (Lake & Kafka, 1996). Many elementary schools continue to use the traditional letter grades of *A, B, C, D,* or *F,* and record a single grade on each student's reporting form for each subject area. Others use numbers or descriptive categories as proxies for letter grades. They might, for example, record a *1, 2, 3,* or *4,* or describe a student's achievement as *Beginning, Developing, Proficient,* or *Distinguished.* Some elementary schools have developed "standards-based" reporting forms that note students' learning progress on specific skills or learning goals (see Chapter 6). Most of these also include separate sections for teachers to evaluate students' work habits or behaviors, and many provide space for teachers to write brief narrative comments.

Grading practices tend to be much more consistent and much more traditional at the secondary level where letter grades still dominate reporting systems. Many high schools attempt to enhance the discriminatory function of letter grades by adding a plus or a minus to them or by pairing letter grades with percentage indicators (see Chapter 5). Because most secondary school reporting forms allow only a single grade to be offered for each course or subject area, most teachers feel compelled to combine a variety of factors into that single symbol. The result is a "hodgepodge grade of attitude, effort, and achievement" (Brookhart, 1991, p. 36; Cross & Frary, 1996) that is extremely difficult to interpret. A few secondary schools have begun using multiple grades in each course or subject area in an attempt to separate achievement grades from marks related to learning skills, work habits, or effort (see Bailey & McTighe, 1996), but such practices are not widespread.

## The Effects of Grading on Students

Over the years, researchers have also been interested in how grades and the comments teachers inscribe on students' papers might affect students' achievement. An early investigation by Page (1958) focused specifically on this issue. In this now classic study, 74 secondary school teachers administered a test to the students in their classes and scored it in their usual way. A numerical score was assigned to each student's paper and, on the basis of that score, a letter grade of *A, B, C, D,* or *F.* Next, teachers randomly divided students' papers into three groups. Papers in the first group received only the numerical score and letter grade. The second group, in addition to the score and grade, received these standard comments:

*A:*  Excellent! Keep it up.

*B:*  Good work. Keep at it.

*C:*  Perhaps try to do still better?

*D:*  Let's bring this up.

*F:*  Let's raise this grade!

For the third group, teachers marked the score, letter grade, and then wrote on each paper a variety of individualized comments. Page asked the teachers to write anything they wished on these papers but to be sure their comments corresponded with their personal feelings and instructional practices. Papers were then returned to students in the customary way.

Page evaluated the effects of the comments by considering students' scores on the very next test or assessment given in the class. Results showed that the students who received the standard comments with their grade achieved *significantly higher* scores than those who received only a score and grade. Those students who received individualized comments did even better. This led Page to conclude that grades can have a beneficial effect on student learning but only when accompanied by specific or individualized comments from the teacher. Studies conducted in more recent years confirm Page's results (e.g., Stewart & White, 1976).

Page's study is important for two reasons. First, it illustrates that while grades may not be essential for teaching or learning, grading can be used in positive ways to enhance students' achievement and performance. Second and perhaps more important, it shows that these positive effects can be gained with relatively little effort on the part of teachers. Stamps or stickers with standard comments such as these could be easily produced for teachers to use. Yet something as simple as this can have a significant, positive effect on students' performance.

Keep in mind, however, that the nature of the comments that teachers offer is important as well. Note, for example, that all of the comments included in Page's study emphasize the teacher's high expectations for students, the importance of students' effort, and the teacher's willingness to work with students to make improvements (i.e., "Let's . . .). The message teachers communicate in their comments to students is vital to its effects on students.

## Summary

Education is a dynamic profession with an ever-expanding knowledge base. This is especially true in the area of grading and reporting student learning. To advance as a profession, however, we must understand that knowledge base and build on it. This means we must know the history of ideas and practices and understand what was learned in those early efforts (Guskey, 1999a). We also must become discriminating consumers of research evidence so that we can make better and more thoughtful decisions about what is best for students (Guskey & Huberman, 1995). If we do not, we are indeed doomed to repeat that history, committing the same mistakes again and again (Cuban, 1990), and will never realize our true potential as educators.

CHAPTER 3

# Laying a Foundation for Change

As we saw in Chapter 2, grading and reporting student learning has been a favorite topic for education writers and researchers for many years. But what have we learned from all this writing and research? Is it still the mass and mess that Middleton and his colleagues described in 1933, or are there points of agreement in this vast collection of evidence?

Although the debate over grading and reporting continues, today we know more than ever before about which practices benefit students and encourage learning, and which ones do not. In some areas, of course, the current research evidence remains inconclusive. But in other areas, results are highly consistent and offer clear prescriptions for better practice. These areas are the focus of this chapter.

Each section of this chapter describes an aspect of grading and reporting for which we have strong and consistent evidence. The prescriptions for better practice described in each section and the accompanying recommendations we offer provide a basis for improvement efforts. They also establish the foundation from which the ideas set forth in later chapters will build.

## Grading and Reporting Are Not Essential to Instruction

Although this particular finding causes some teachers to gasp, strong research evidence shows that grading and reporting are not essential to the instructional process. Teachers do not need grades or reporting forms to teach well, and students can and do learn many things quite well without them (Frisbie & Waltman, 1992). We must recognize, therefore, that the primary purpose of grading and reporting is other than facilitation of teaching or learning.

At the same time, we must keep in mind that regularly *checking* on students' learning progress *is* an essential aspect of successful teaching. To facilitate learning, teachers must provide students with regular and specific feedback on their learning progress. Equally important, that feedback must be paired with explicit guidance and direction for making improvements when needed. Checking, however, is different from grading. Checking implies finding out how students are doing, what they have learned well, what problems or difficulties they might be experiencing, and what corrective measures may be necessary. The process is primarily a diagnostic and prescriptive interaction between teachers and students (see Bloom, 1968; Guskey, 1997). Grading and reporting, on the other hand, typically involve judgment of the adequacy of students' performance at a particular point in time. As such, it is primarily descriptive and evaluative (Bloom et al., 1981).

When teachers do both checking and grading, they must serve dual roles as both advocate and judge for students—roles that, as we mentioned earlier, are not necessarily compatible (Bishop, 1992). Ironically, this incompatibility is usually recognized when administrators are called upon to evaluate teachers (Frase & Streshly, 1994) but generally ignored when teachers are required to evaluate students. As might be expected, finding a meaningful compromise between these dual roles is discomforting to many teachers, especially those with a child-centered orientation (Barnes, 1985).

We believe that much of this discomfort can be resolved by distinguishing the formative and summative purposes of grading and reporting. As we describe in Chapter 4, most of a teacher's grading and reporting tasks are actually *formative* in nature; that is, they are designed to offer students prescriptive feedback on their performance. Only occasionally must teachers combine that information in order to assign a cumulative, *summative* grade to students' achievement and performance (Bloom, Hastings, & Madaus, 1971). By keeping this distinction in mind and by using more thoughtful ways to combine the various sources of information in order to determine summative grades, teachers can emphasize their role as an advocate for students while still fulfilling their evaluation responsibilities.

*Recommendation*

Teachers must seek an appropriate balance between the formative, instructional purposes of assessments of student learning, and the summative, evaluative purposes required in grading. Not every piece of evidence on student learning needs to be included as part of the grade. Nevertheless, most students need to be shown the explicit benefits of putting forth appropriate effort on formative assessment devices.

An increasing number of teachers accomplish this through the use of mastery learning strategies. In mastery learning classes, students who perform poorly on regular formative assessments (quizzes) are required to engage in structured, teacher-directed corrective activities immediately following each assessment. When their corrective work is completed, students have the opportunity to retake an alternative form of the assessment to gauge the improvements they have made. Completion of the corrective activities, however, is a necessary prerequisite to having the second chance on the assessment.

Once students understand the important advantages they derive from these formative assessments and how such checks help improve their performance on larger tests and other summative evaluations, teachers find students take them quite seriously. For more information on mastery learning and the use of formative assessments as learning tool, see Guskey (1997).

## Grading and Reporting Require Subjective Judgments

Regardless of the method used, assigning grades and reporting on student learning is an inherently subjective process. As we described in Chapter 1, it is an exercise in professional judgment that involves one person making evaluative decisions about the achievement or performance of another person. For this reason, efforts to develop completely objective grading or reporting systems are largely in vain. Even in schools with specific grading policies, individual teachers usually have great latitude when it comes to deciding what components go into the grade, how each component will be evaluated or scored, how those various components will be weighted, and how they will be combined in determining the grade. In most instances, individual teachers also choose the procedures used to assess student learning, how rigorous or challenging those assessments will be, and what level of performance will be expected for each grade category. Even though clarifying these decisions and making them explicit may help students understand each teacher's particular grading procedures, it doesn't make the process of grading any less subjective.

Confounding matters further is the fact that the more detailed and analytic the grading procedures become, the more likely that subjective elements will influence the results (Ornstein, 1994). Highly detailed and keenly analytic reporting procedures simply allow more opportunities for the unique personal opinions and perceptions of individual evaluators to come into play. That is why, for example, analytic scoring procedures for performance assessments are typically much less reliable than holistic scoring procedures. Although two evaluators may find it relatively easy to agree on the general classification of a student's performance, they generally find it much more difficult to reach consensus in their judgments of each specific aspect of that performance.

At the same time, however, we must remember that more detailed and analytic reporting procedures yield better learning tools (Bloom et al., 1981). Students seeking ways to improve their achievement or performance get little direction from holistic scoring, just as they get little guidance from a single grade written at the top of their paper. To make improvements, they need detailed and analytic information paired with specific suggestions for correction (Guskey, 1997). The challenge for teachers, therefore, is to find purposeful

ways to balance these vital instructional purposes with the reporting requirements they must meet. Specific suggestions as to how this can be accomplished are presented in Chapter 4 in our discussion of the formative and
summative purposes of grading and reporting.

Finally, we must keep in mind that subjectivity in the process of grading
and reporting isn't always bad. Being subjective doesn't mean that grades lack
credibility or are indefensible. Because teachers know their students, understand various dimensions of students' work, and have clear notions of the progress made, their subjective perceptions can yield very accurate descriptions
of what students have learned (Brookhart, 1993; O'Donnell & Woolfolk, 1991).

*Recommendation*

Valid grading is not a mechanical process. And as we will see in later chapters,
it's also not a process that can be made more valid with mathematical precision or through the use of sophisticated technology. Teachers at all levels must
be clear about their grading standards, the various components that will be
considered in determining grades, and the criteria that will be used to evaluate
those components. But while clearly articulated standards and grading criteria
can enhance the validity of grades as accurate reflections of students' achievement and performance, the process of grading still involves thoughtful, reasonable, but imperfect human judgment and should be recognized as such.

# Bias Must Be Avoided in Grading and Reporting

Subjectivity in grading becomes detrimental to students when it translates to
bias. This occurs when factors apart from students' actual achievement or
performance affect their grades. Studies have shown, for example, that cultural differences among students, as well as their appearance, family backgrounds, and lifestyles can sometimes result in biased evaluations of their
academic performance (Scott, 1995; Thomas, 1987). Teachers' perceptions of
students' behavior also can significantly influence their judgments of scholastic achievements (Hills, 1991). Students with behavior problems, for example,
seldom receive a high grade regardless of what they demonstrate because
their behavioral infractions overshadow their performance. These effects are
especially pronounced in judgments of boys because their conduct typically
is perceived as less adequate than that of girls (Bennett, Gottesman, Rock, &
Cerullo, 1993).

The neatness of students' handwriting has been shown to significantly
affect teachers' judgments of their work (Sweedler-Brown, 1992), and gender
appears to play a role in this case as well. Illegible handwriting is more

frequently attributed to boys than to girls, and boys' grades tend to suffer as a result (Sprouse & Webb, 1994). Gender bias appears less prevalent in teachers' judgments of students' mathematics performance (Wiles, 1992), however, and seems to be less common in college instructors' evaluations of students' work (Eames & Loewenthal, 1990).

Even the order of the papers a teacher reviews can sometimes influence the grade assigned. Research has demonstrated, for instance, that good work is evaluated much more favorably when it follows poorer quality work than when it precedes it. If the good paper follows two or more papers of poor quality, the biased advantage is even greater (Spear, 1997). Knowing this, students who wish to enhance their grade could simply make sure they place their paper beneath that of a poorer performing classmate.

### Recommendation

Training programs can help teachers identify and reduce these negative bias effects and can lead to greater consistency in teachers' judgments (Afflerbach & Sammons, 1991). Unfortunately, as we noted earlier, few teachers receive adequate training in grading or reporting as part of their preservice experiences (Barnes, 1985; Boothroyd & McMorris, 1992; Schafer & Lissitz, 1987). Also, few school districts provide teachers with adequate guidance or assistance to ensure consistency in their grading or reporting practices (Austin & McCann, 1992). Well-designed professional development programs that help teachers clarify their grading criteria and make them aware of these tendencies toward bias can help alleviate these problems, however, and should become part of every teacher's professional development experiences. Such programs also could help teachers at all levels become more conscientious in their grading practices and ensure that the grades they assign are truly accurate descriptions of students' achievement and performance.

## Grades Have Some Value as Rewards, But No Value as Punishments

Although educators would undoubtedly prefer that motivation to learn be entirely intrinsic, the existence of grades and other reporting methods are important factors in determining how much effort students put forth (Cameron & Pierce, 1994, 1996; Chastain, 1990; Ebel, 1979). Studies show that most students view high grades as positive recognition of their success, and some work hard to avoid the consequences of low grades (Feldmesser, 1971).

At the same time, no studies support the use of low grades or marks as punishments. Instead of prompting greater effort, low grades more often cause students to withdraw from learning. To protect their self-images, many regard the low grade as irrelevant and meaningless. Other students may blame themselves for the low grade but feel helpless to make any improvement (Selby & Murphy, 1992).

Sadly, some teachers consider grades or reporting forms their "weapon of last resort." In their view, students who do not comply with their requests must suffer the consequences of the greatest punishment a teacher can bestow: a failing grade. Such practices have no educational value and, in the long run, adversely affect students, teachers, and the relationship they share. Rather than attempting to punish students with a low grade or mark in the hope it will prompt greater effort in the future, teachers can better motivate students by considering their work as incomplete and then requiring additional effort.

Recognizing this, some schools have initiated grading policies that eliminate the use of failing grades altogether. Teachers at Beachwood Middle School in Beachwood, Ohio, for example, record students' grades as *A, B, C,* or *I* (Incomplete). Students who receive an *I* grade are required to do additional work in order to bring their performance up to an acceptable level. This policy is based on the belief that students perform at a failure level or submit failing work in large part because teachers accept it. If teachers no longer accept substandard work, however, they reason that students will not submit it and, with appropriate support, will continue to work until their performance is satisfactory.

Beachwood Middle School teachers strongly believe that giving a failing grade to students who have not performed well, despite their ability to do so, offers them an easy way out. If, on the other hand, teachers insist that all assignments designed to demonstrate learning eventually be completed and done well, then students will choose to do their work in a timely fashion and at a satisfactory level of quality. The guiding maxim of the teachers at Beachwood Middle School is "If it's not done well, it's not done!"

Implementing grading policies such as this requires additional funding for the necessary support mechanisms, of course. Students who receive an *I* grade, for example, typically are required to attend after-school, make-up sessions or special Saturday school programs staffed by teachers, volunteer parents, and older students. Those who are unable or unwilling to do the make-up work during the school year must attend required summer school sessions designed to help them bring their performance up to an acceptable level (Kuehner, 1998). Although these support mechanisms demand commitment and additional funding, schools implementing such programs generally find them highly successful (Bernetich, 1998). Many also discover that in the long run they actually save money. Because this regular and ongoing support helps students remedy their learning difficulties before they become major problems, less time and fewer resources need to be spent in major remediation efforts later on.

*Recommendation*

At all levels of education, we need to think seriously about the use of failing grades. Although honesty must prevail in assessments and evaluations of student learning, we also must consider the negative consequences of assigning failing grades to students' work or level of performance (see Roderick & Camburn, 1999). Especially in the early years of school, the negative consequences of failing grades are quite serious and far outweigh any benefits. Even in upper grades, the fear of failure is a questionable motivation device. Better and more effective alternatives to failing grades need to be found. The use of *I*'s or incomplete grades present one meaningful alternative, especially if the necessary policies and resources are put in place to support those students who need additional assistance.

## Grading and Reporting Should Be Done in Reference to Learning Criteria

Grading and reporting should *always* be done in reference to specific learning criteria rather than in reference to normative criteria or "on the curve." It is certainly true that using the normal probability curve as a basis for assigning grades will yield consistent grade distributions from one teacher to the next. In other words, the classes of every teacher will have the same percentage of *A*'s, *B*'s, *C*'s, and so on. But the consequences of this practice are overwhelmingly negative. Strong evidence shows that it is detrimental to the relationships among students and to the relationships between teachers and students (Krumboltz & Yeh, 1996).

Grading "on the curve" makes learning a highly competitive activity in which students compete against one another for the few scarce rewards (high grades) distributed by the teacher. Under these conditions, students readily see that helping others become successful threatens their own chances for success (Gray, 1993; D. Johnson, Skon, & Johnson, 1980; R. Johnson, Johnson, & Tauer, 1979). High grades are attained not through excellence in performance but simply by doing better than one's classmates. As a result, learning becomes a game of winners and losers, and because the number of rewards is kept arbitrarily small, most students are forced to be losers (Haladyna, 1999; Johnson & Johnson, 1989).

The majority of students, as well as most adults, can relate horror tales based on their experiences in classes where they were graded "on the curve." Many recall the anger they felt toward the high-scoring student in their class who "inflated the curve" and, in their minds, caused other class members to receive a low grade. Some remember being the object of their classmates'

---

**On "Grading on the Curve"**

John Bishop of Cornell University recently related an interesting story about education in Ireland that is relevant here. In Ireland there are national educational standards against which all students are evaluated. Ireland considered changing this policy and leaving evaluation criteria to local educational units and teachers. When teachers were polled to assess their reaction, they opposed the change. Why? Because they felt the proposed change would pit them against their students and their students against one another. When there is a common standard, it is the goal of every teacher to have all students achieve this standard, and it is a common goal of all students to help their classmates make the grade. The competition is against the standard, not against one another.

Contrast this with our system, in which any teacher who dared to give the whole class grades of *A* because all students had reached mastery would at best be criticized for lacking standards and contributing to grade inflation. Contrast this with our system, in which the principal of an affluent suburban Philadelphia high school recently remarked that group learning activities were difficult to arrange in his school because students could not get beyond worrying about how they were to be graded in comparison to others in their group. The idea that they could all excel together was alien to them.

SOURCE: Gray (1993, p. 374)

---

anger because they were that high-scoring student. Stories also abound of students hiding books in the library so that their classmates could not use them or removing equipment needed in projects or experiments in order to enhance their chance for a high grade. Furthermore, grading "on the curve" denies students the opportunity to work together and to help each other attain valuable, shared learning goals.

Perhaps most important, grading "on the curve" communicates nothing about what students have learned or are able to do. Rather, it tells only a student's relative standing among classmates, based on what are often ill-defined criteria. Students who receive the high grades might actually have performed very poorly but simply less poorly than their classmates. Differences between grades, therefore, are difficult to interpret at best and meaningless at worst (Bracey, 1994).

If the purpose of grading is to reflect what students have learned and are able to do, then grading "on the curve" falls far short. As Bloom and his colleagues (1981) so succinctly put it,

There is nothing sacred about the normal curve. It is the distribution most appropriate to chance and random activity. Education is a purposeful activity, and we seek to have students learn what we have to teach. If we are effective in our instruction, the distribution of achievement should be very different from the normal curve. In fact, we may even insist that our educational efforts have been *unsuccessful* to the extent that the distribution of achievement approximates the normal distribution. (pp. 52-53)

Other unintended but equally adverse consequences for students can result from grading "on the curve." A study by Wood (1994), for example, found the percentage of students receiving *A*'s, *B*'s, *C*'s, and so on in an urban high school remained virtually the same from the sophomore through senior years. At first glance this appears to show that teachers throughout the school were remarkably consistent in their grading. However, Wood also found that each year there were fewer students in the school. Since students who leave are generally those with the lowest grades, this consistency in grade percentages means that as one group of unsuccessful students drops out, it is replaced by a succession of newly created low grade students who were formerly successful. In other words, additional students are at risk of failing each year. Some students who got *C*'s as sophomores will get *D*'s as juniors, and so on.

Furthermore, modern research has shown that the seemingly direct relationship between aptitude or intelligence and school achievement depends on instructional conditions, *not* a normal probability curve (Engel, 1991). When the instructional quality is high and well matched to students' learning needs, the magnitude of this relationship diminishes drastically and approaches zero (Bloom, 1976; Bloom et al., 1981). Moreover, the fairness and equity of grading "on the curve" is a myth.

## Recommendation

In any educational setting where the central purpose is to have students learn, grading and reporting should always be done in reference to specific learning criteria rather than in reference to normative criteria. Because normative criteria or "grading on the curve" tell nothing about what students have learned or are able to do, they provide an inadequate description of student learning. Plus, they promote unhealthy competition, destroy perseverance and other motivational traits, and are generally unfair to students (Haladyna, 1999). At all levels of education, therefore, teachers should identify what they want their students to learn, what evidence they will use to verify that learning, and what criteria will be used to judge that evidence. Grades based on specified learning criteria have direct meaning and serve well the communication purposes for which they are intended.

## Alternative Strategies for Selecting Valedictorians

Although many teachers today understand the negative consequences of grading "on the curve" and have abandoned the practice, most fail to recognize other common school practices that yield similar negative consequences. One of the most prevalent is the way in which schools select class valedictorians. There is nothing wrong, of course, with recognizing excellence in academic performance. But in selecting the class valedictorian, most schools operate under the traditional premise that there can be *only one*. This commonly results in severe and sometimes bitter competition among high-achieving students to be that "one." Early in their high school careers, top students figure out the selection procedures and then, often with the help of their parents, find various ingenious ways to improve their standing in comparison to classmates. Again, to gain that honor a student must not simply excel; he or she must outdo the other students in the class. Sometimes the difference among these top students is as little as one-thousandth of a decimal point in a weighted grade point average (GPA).

An increasing number of high schools have resolved this problem simply by moving away from the policy of having just one valedictorian and, instead, name multiple valedictorians. This is similar to what colleges and universities do in naming graduates *magna cum laude* and *summa cum laude*. West Springfield High School in Fairfax County, Virginia, for example, typically graduates 15 to 25 valedictorians each year (Smith, 1999). Every one of these students has an exemplary academic record that includes earning the highest grade possible in numerous honors and Advanced Placement (AP) classes. Instead of trying to distinguish among these exceptional students, the faculty at West Springfield High School decided that all should be named valedictorians. In other words, rather than creating additional, arbitrary criteria in order to discriminate among these top students (considering, for example, their academic record from middle school or even elementary school), the faculty decided to recognize the excellent achievement and performance of the entire group. And because they believe their purpose as teachers is not to *select* talent but, rather, to *develop* talent, they take great pride in these results. All of the valedictorians are named at the graduation ceremony, and one student, selected by his or her fellow valedictorians, makes a major presentation.

Some might object to a policy that allows multiple valedictorians, arguing that colleges and universities demand such selection and often grant special scholarships to students who attain that singular distinction. But current evidence indicates this is not the case. In processing admission applications and making decisions about scholarships, colleges and universities are far more interested in the rigor of the curriculum students have experienced (Bracey, 1999). In fact, an index composed of the number of AP courses taken, the highest level of math studied, and total number of courses completed has been shown to be a much stronger predictor of college success than standardized test scores, GPA, or class rank (Adelman, 1999). The rigor of the academic program experienced by the valedictorians from West Springfield High School has helped them gain admission and win scholarships to many of the most selective colleges and universities in the nation.

### Recommendation

The process by which class valedictorians are selected is yet another example of a practice that we continue, not because we have thought about it deeply, but simply because "we've always done it that way." Better understanding of the consequences of such practices allows us to implement improved and more appropriate policies that benefit students and teachers alike. Recognizing excellence in academic performance is a vital aspect in any learning community. But such recognition need not be based on arbitrary standards and deleterious competition. Instead, it can and should be based on clear models of excellence that exemplify our highest standards and goals for students and for ourselves. If many students meet these high standards of excellence, all the better.

## Clarifying Learning Criteria

When grading and reporting relate to learning criteria, teachers are able to provide a clearer picture of what students have learned and are able to do. Students and teachers alike generally prefer this approach because they consider it both fairer and more equitable (Kovas, 1993). The types of learning criteria typically used for grading and reporting purposes fall into three broad categories: *product, process,* and *progress.*

- *Product criteria* are favored by advocates of standards-based and performance-based approaches to teaching and learning. These educators believe the primary purpose of grading and reporting is to communicate a summative evaluation of student achievement and performance (Cangelosi, 1990). In other words, they focus on *what* students know and are able to do at a particular point in time. Teachers who use product criteria often base their grades or reports exclusively on final examination scores, final products (reports or projects), overall assessments, and other culminating demonstrations of learning.

- *Process criteria* are emphasized by educators who believe product criteria do not provide a complete picture of student learning. From their perspective, grading and reporting should reflect not just the final results but also *how* students got there. Teachers who consider effort or work habits when reporting on student learning are using process criteria. So too are teachers who count regular classroom quizzes, homework, class participation, or attendance.

- *Progress criteria* are used by educators who believe it is most important to consider how much students have gained from their learning experiences. Other names for progress criteria include "learning gain," "improvement scoring," "value-added learning," and "educational growth." Some educators draw distinctions between "progress," which they measure backward from a final performance standard or goal, and "growth," which is measured forward from the place a student begins on a learning continuum (e.g., Wiggins, 1996). We believe, however, that if learning is assessed using a well-defined set of credible learning standards that include graduated levels of performance, then progress and growth criteria can be considered synonymous.

Teachers who use progress criteria typically look at how far students have come over a particular period of time rather than just where they are at a given time. As a result, scoring criteria may be highly individualized among students. Currently, most of the research evidence on the use of progress criteria in grading and reporting comes from studies of students involved in differentially paced instructional programs (Esty & Teppo, 1992) and those enrolled in special education programs (Gersten, Vaughn, & Brengelman, 1996).

> **Types of Learning Criteria Used in Grading and Reporting**
>
> 1. *Product* criteria
> 2. *Process* criteria
> 3. *Progress* criteria

Because teachers are concerned with student motivation, self-esteem, and the social consequences of giving grades, they rarely use product criteria solely in determining grades. Instead, teachers routinely base their grading procedures on some combination of these three types of learning criteria (Brookhart, 1993; Frary, Cross, & Weber, 1993; Friedman & Manley, 1992; Nava & Loyd, 1992; Stiggins, Frisbie, & Griswold, 1989). Most also vary the criteria they employ from student to student, taking into account individual circumstances (Natriello, Riehl, & Pallas, 1994; Truog & Friedman, 1996). Although this is usually done in an effort to be fair, the result is a "hodgepodge grade" (Brookhart, 1991; Cross & Frary, 1996) that includes elements of achievement, effort, and improvement. Interpreting the grade or report thus becomes exceptionally difficult not only for parents but also for administrators, community members, and even the students themselves (Friedman & Frisbie, 1995; Waltman & Frisbie, 1994). A grade of *A*, for example, may mean the student knew what was intended before instruction began (product), did not learn as well as expected but tried very hard (process), or simply made significant improvement (progress).

Recognizing these interpretation difficulties, most researchers and measurement specialists recommend the use of product criteria exclusively in determining students' grades. They point out that the more the process and progress criteria come into play, the more subjective and biased the grades are likely to be (Ornstein, 1994). How can a teacher know, for example, how difficult a task was for students or how hard they worked to complete it?

Many teachers, on the other hand, point out that if product criteria are used exclusively, some high-ability students receive high grades with little effort while the hard work of less talented students is seldom acknowledged. Take, for example, the case of two students enrolled in a physical education class. The first student is a well-coordinated athlete who can perform any task the teacher asks without even putting forth serious effort—and typically does not. The second student is struggling with a weight problem but consistently tries hard, exerts extraordinary effort, and also displays exceptional sportsmanship and cooperation. Nevertheless, this student is unable to perform at the same level as the athlete. Few teachers would consider it fair to use product criteria exclusively in determining the grades of these two students.

Teachers also point out that if only product criteria are considered, low ability students and those who are disadvantaged—students who must work hardest—have the least incentive to do so. These students find the relationship between high effort and low grades unacceptable and, as a result, often express their displeasure with indifference, deception, or disruption (Tomlinson, 1992).

## Recommendation

A practical solution to the problem of these diverse learning criteria, and one that increasing numbers of teachers and schools are using, is to establish clear indicators of the product, process, and progress criteria, and then to report them separately (Bailey & McTighe, 1996; Stiggins, 2001; Wiggins, 1996). In other words, grades or marks for learning skills, effort, work habits, or learning progress are separated from assessments of achievement and performance. The key to success in doing so, however, rests in the clear specification of those indicators and the criteria to which they relate. This means that teachers must clearly describe the criteria they will use to evaluate students' achievement, effort, and progress, and must clearly communicate these criteria to students, parents, and others. Several examples of reporting forms in which this is done appear in later chapters.

## Summary

Although a great deal remains to be learned about the process of grading and reporting, significant evidence is available to guide us in our improvement efforts. We know, for example, that grading and reporting are not essential to instruction and that the process will always involve subjective judgments on the part of teachers. We also know that grades have some value as rewards but no value as punishments. Furthermore, considerable evidence shows that for the benefit of teachers and students alike, grading and reporting should always be done in reference to clearly specified learning criteria and never in reference to normative criteria or "on the curve." These understandings form the basis for the points we make in subsequent chapters. They also are the foundation of the guidelines we then offer for building better reporting systems.

# Building a Grading and Reporting System

In Chapter 3 we described several areas of grading and reporting for which strong evidence offers us clear prescriptions for better practice. In this chapter we build on that evidence to show how our knowledge base can be used to construct better grading and reporting systems.

## Problems in Grading and Reporting Reform

A great deal of time, money, and energy has been spent in recent years on attempts to reform grading and reporting procedures. The educators leading these reform efforts recognize the many inadequacies in current policies and practices and are convinced of the need for change. But as we described in the Introduction, most of their well-intentioned attempts at improvement are met with unexpected controversy and firm resistance (Olson, 1995). As a result, many change efforts have proved to be sad and costly failures.

Several reasons have been suggested to explain the difficulties encountered in these reform efforts. We believe, however, that three factors offer the clearest explanation. First, change initiatives too often have focused on *form* rather than *function*. In other words, they have concentrated on the structure of a single reporting device and ignored the primary purpose of reporting. Enamored by the appeal of new reporting formats, educators involved in these efforts have neglected vital dimensions of the communication process. In particular, they have failed to consider what message they want to communicate and who is the primary audience for that message. Furthermore, most have been unaware of critical shortcomings in these new grading and reporting formats, and of the interpretation problems they often create. As a result, predictable difficulties arise that thwart even the most dedicated attempts at reform.

Second, leaders in these initiatives frequently haven't understood the dynamics of the change process, particularly in so public an arena as grading and reporting student learning. They neglect the powerful influence of tradition and the importance of communicating fully with the broad range of stakeholders in the grading and reporting process. Consequently, they proceed in a politically charged environment with little more than vague conventional wisdom to guide their efforts. The problem with this approach is that while conventional wisdom and common sense are important, they often turn out to be wrong or at least simplistic, especially when it comes to grading and reporting (Guskey, 1999a).

The third factor contributing to the difficulties experienced in grading and reporting reforms is that most of these efforts center exclusively on report card reform. Everyone recognizes, of course, that report cards are an indispensable component in grading and reporting at any level. But far too often educators try to accomplish too much and serve too many purposes with this single reporting device. This usually leads to a series of compromises with which no one is completely satisfied and results in a reporting form that serves no purpose particularly well. It also makes the report card a clear target of discontent and a lightning rod for controversy.

Our goal in this chapter is to help resolve these difficulties by providing a framework for successful reform. We hope to do this by (1) offering a detailed description of the critical dimensions of effective communication, (2) expanding awareness of those aspects of the change process that are particularly relevant in grading and reporting, and (3) emphasizing the importance of developing of a *multifaceted reporting system.* Although we cannot guarantee that such an understanding and emphasis will ensure success in all reform initiatives, we are convinced that these are vital tools in the improvement process that can greatly enhance the chances of success.

---

**Factors Contributing to the Difficulties
in Grading and Reporting Reform**

1. Changes focus on *form* rather than *function.*

2. Leaders lack understanding of the change process.

3. Efforts center exclusively on report card reform.

---

## The Basis of Good Reporting Is Good Evidence

One of the points we emphasized in the Introduction was that the primary goal of grading and reporting is *communication.* We stressed that regardless of the format, grading and reporting should provide high-quality information to interested persons in a form they can understand and use. The basis of that high-quality information is good evidence on student learning. Evaluation experts stress that if you are going to make important decisions about students that have broad implications, such as the decisions involved in grading, then you must have good evidence (Airasian, 1994; Linn & Gronlund, 2000; Stiggins, 2001). In the absence of good evidence, even the most detailed and sophisticated grading and reporting system is useless. It simply cannot serve the basic communication functions for which it is intended.

Three qualities contribute to the goodness of the evidence that we gather on student learning: *validity, reliability,* and *quantity.*

## Validity

Validity is a crucial issue in all assessments of student learning, regardless of the type of learning outcome considered. It is also one of the most frequently misunderstood concepts in education today.

Frequently, we hear someone refer to a particular assessment device or a particular procedure used to gather information on student learning as "valid" or "invalid." But validity actually refers not to assessments or information-gathering procedures themselves. Rather, it refers to the appropriateness and adequacy of interpretations made from that information (Linn & Gronlund, 2000). For example, if an assessment is to be used to describe students' reading comprehension, we would like our interpretations to be based on evidence that actually reflects reading comprehension and not other irrelevant factors, such as students' gender or background characteristics. In this way, validity is always specific to a particular interpretation or use.

No assessment is valid for all purposes. The results of an arithmetic test, for instance, may have a high degree of validity for indicating students' computational skill, a low degree of validity for indicating their mathematical reasoning, and essentially no validity for predicting success in reading or writing. When appraising or describing the validity of a particular assessment or information-gathering method, therefore, we always must consider the specific interpretation or use to be made of the results.

Particularly important in assessments of student learning is "construct validity." Reading, mathematics, and social studies achievement are examples of constructs. So too are personal attributes such as responsibility, diligence, and effort. We address construct validity by asking questions such as these: Does this procedure, intended to measure problem solving, actually reflect higher order abilities rather than recall? Does this set of questions on scientific concepts provide a sound basis for generalizing about students' understanding of the domain of science? How much do difficulties with the English language impair performance of some pupils on mathematics assessment? (Baker, Linn, & Herman, 1996).

The construct validity of an assessment or information-gathering procedure is frequently undermined by construct-irrelevant influences. These occur when students' performance is affected by knowledge, skills, or traits other than those the assessment is intended to measure (Haertel & Wiley, 1993). Such ancillary attributes can have either positive or negative effects. Testwiseness (knowing how to take a specific type of test) and neatness of writing, for example, can inflate scores and confound interpretations of results. Students' inability to understand the language used in the assessment is perhaps the most common example of a negative effect along with personal characteristics such as test anxiety and impulsivity (Baker et al., 1996).

In addition to its use with assessments and information-gathering procedures, validity can describe the appropriateness and adequacy of interpretations made from grades or other reporting methods. For example, if grades are to represent students' achievement in a subject area over a specified period of time, we must ensure that the grade is based on evidence that actually reflects achievement and not other irrelevant factors, such as students' effort or their punctuality in turning in assignments. To include these construct-irrelevant factors diminishes the validity of our interpretation of the grade as a descriptor of achievement.

Similarly, if grades are to represent students' current level of achievement or performance, we must ensure that they are based on evidence of what students can do now and not what they were able to do last week or last month. This means that including scores from assessments administered weeks or months earlier lowers the validity of our interpretation of the grade as a descriptor of students' current level of accomplishment or proficiency. We consider this idea in greater depth in Chapter 8 when we review the practice of "averaging" to obtain a final grade.

We must always remember, therefore, that validity refers to the interpretation of an assessment or grade, and it is a matter of degree. Validity does not exist on an all-or-none basis. Consequently, we should avoid thinking of assessment results or grades as valid or invalid. Validity is best considered in terms of categories such as high validity, moderate validity, and low validity, depending on the use or interpretation of the information (Linn & Gronlund, 2000).

## Reliability

Reliability refers to the consistency of assessment results. If, for example, we attain very similar scores when the same assessment procedures are used with the same students at two different times, we would conclude that our results have a high degree of reliability. Similarly, if two different teachers independently rate students' performance on the same task and obtain similar scores, we would say the results are highly reliable from one rater to another, or that they have a high degree of "interrater" reliability. The same is true in terms of grading. If two different teachers independently look at the same collection of evidence on a student's achievement and assign the same grade, we would say that the grading process is highly reliable. In each of these cases our major concern is with the consistency of results.

Sometimes, reliability and validity are confused, especially by those new to the areas of assessment and evaluation. Reliability is necessary for assessment results to be valid, but results can also be reliable and not valid. In other words, certain measures may be highly consistent and yet provide the wrong information or be interpreted inappropriately. Results from a standardized assessment composed of multiple-choice items dealing with grammar and punctuation, for example, might be highly reliable and yet have very low validity as a measure of students' writing skills. A valid assessment of writing skills is likely to require students to do some writing. Similarly, a grading procedure that outlines the specific elements to be included in the grade, and describes how those elements will be weighted and combined, may yield consistent results. But this doesn't make the grade a valid indicator of students' level of achievement and performance, especially if some of those elements have low validity as measures of student learning. Nor does this make the grading process any more objective. Teachers still subjectively decide what elements are included in determining the grade and how those elements will be combined. In all areas of assessment and grading, reliability is concerned with the consistency of results, whereas validity is concerned with the appropriateness of the interpretations made from the results (Linn & Gronlund, 2000).

## Quantity

Validity and reliability relate primarily to the quality of the evidence we gather on student learning and the interpretations we make of that evidence. But the quantity of evidence considered is important as well. Any single source of evidence on student learning can be flawed or misinterpreted. Even the most carefully designed assessments can, under certain conditions, yield imprecise measures of what students have learned or are able to do. It is not uncommon, for example, for some unusual occurrence in a student's life to impinge on his or her performance on that particular day and adversely affect assessment results. Perhaps the student felt ill at the time of the assessment or had an experience earlier in the day that had an enduring emotional impact. Because of the potential fallibility of any single indicator, it is essential that we use multiple sources of evidence in grading and reporting student learning. In other words, more evidence is usually better evidence.

Grading and reporting are largely decision-making processes that involve professional judgment. Teachers gather evidence from a variety of sources and then decide what evidence best reflects students' achievement and level of performance. Generally, the more evidence that teachers have available in making those decisions, the better and more accurate those decisions will be.

In gathering evidence on student learning, however, a critical balance must be struck between evidence collected for instructional purposes and that compiled for use in grading and reporting. Teachers frequently gather evidence from students to diagnose learning problems and to plan corrective strategies. Such "formative" evidence is typically collected while teaching and learning are in progress and used primarily to remedy learning errors, improve instructional procedures, and enhance learning outcomes. Other evidence, however, is gathered to summarize students' achievement and to certify their competence. This "summative" evidence provides the basis for grading and reporting. Although most types of evidence can be used for either formative or summative purposes, rarely can a single source of evidence be used appropriately for both.

Teachers must decide, therefore, what purpose each source of evidence is to serve and then tailor their assessment practices to fit that purpose. In particular, they must be careful in their efforts to increase the quantity of evidence available for grading and reporting that they don't use formative information for summative purposes (Bloom et al., 1981). It would be inappropriate, for example, to use the results from formative quizzes constructed to check on students' learning progress and prescribe corrective activities, or from homework assignments designed to offer additional practice on difficult concepts or skills, in determining students' summative grade in a subject area or course. To do so would be detrimental to the teaching and learning process. It also compromises the relationship between teachers and students.

Some teachers express the fear that assessments, observations, or assignments that are not counted as part of the grade will not be taken seriously by students. In other words, they believe that if it "doesn't count," students won't be motivated to put forth their best effort. In their classes, therefore, no source of evidence on student learning is ever used solely for formative purposes. Instead, everything counts in determining the grade.

The problem with this approach is that it not only imposes severe limitations on the learning process, it also restricts students' creativity and limits their expression. Instead of experimenting with new ideas or trying new approaches to problems or tasks, most students "play it safe" and do what they believe the teacher wants. Other students will do nothing when confronted with a problem or difficult assignment and simply will wait for the teacher to offer additional directions or to tell them more precisely what is required. Experimenting, taking a chance, or trying something new is to risk failure, and that would drastically reduce their chances for a high grade.

Many teachers have found, however, that when students understand the purposes of formative assessments and see the direct payoff they derive from the feedback offered by such assessments, motivation is no longer a problem. Teachers who use mastery learning strategies, for example, in which regular formative assessments are used as an integral part of the instructional process, find that students welcome these opportunities to receive diagnostic feedback on their learning progress (Guskey, 1989, 1997). Formative assessments in mastery learning classes generally take the form of short quizzes that teachers administer about every two weeks. In most cases, these assessments are not counted as part of the grade but, instead, are used to offer students specific feedback on what they have learned well and what they need to spend more time learning. This feedback is then paired with guidance and direction on how identified learning errors can be remedied prior to the administration of more comprehensive "summative examinations," which are used primarily for grading and evaluation purposes. Evidence shows this mastery learning process typically results in dramatic improvements in student learning (Guskey & Piggott, 1988).

In later chapters we consider various techniques for helping students distinguish these formative and summative purposes of grading and reporting, as well as different strategies for combining summative information into single symbols that represent students' achievement or level of performance.

## The Purposes of Grading and Reporting

The first and most important question that must be addressed when we consider the issues of grading and reporting is "What is its purpose?" In other words, "Why do we use reporting devices and assign grades or marks to students' work?" Researchers have asked teachers and school administrators these questions and generally find that their answers can be classified in six broad categories (see Feldmesser, 1971; Frisbie & Waltman, 1992; Linn, 1983). The major purposes they identify include the following:

1. *To communicate the achievement status of students to parents and others.* Grading and reporting provide parents and other interested persons (e.g., guardians) with information about their child's progress in school. To some extent, it also serves to involve parents in educational processes.

2. *To provide information students can use for self-evaluation.* Grading and reporting offer students information about the level or adequacy of their academic achievement and performance in school.

3. *To select, identify, or group students for certain educational paths or programs.* Grades are a primary source of information used to select students for special programs. High grades are typically required for entry into gifted education programs, whereas low grades are often the first indicator of learning problems that result in students' placement in special needs programs. Grades are also used as a criterion for entry into colleges and universities.

4. *To provide incentives for students to learn.* Although some may debate the idea, extensive evidence shows that grades and other reporting methods are important factors in determining the amount of effort that students put forth and how seriously they regard any learning or assessment task (Cameron & Pierce, 1994, 1996; Chastain, 1990; Ebel, 1979).

5. *To evaluate the effectiveness of instructional programs.* Comparisons of grade distributions and other reporting evidence are frequently used to judge the value or effectiveness of new programs and instructional techniques.

6. *To provide evidence of students' lack of effort or inappropriate responsibility.* Grades and other reporting devices are frequently used to document unsuitable behaviors on the part of certain students, and some teachers threaten students with poor grades in an effort to coerce more acceptable behaviors.

---

**Major Purposes of Grading and Reporting**

1. To communicate the achievement status of students to parents and others

2. To provide information that students can use for self-evaluation

3. To select, identify, or group students for certain educational paths or programs

4. To provide incentives for students to learn

5. To evaluate the effectiveness of instructional programs

6. To provide evidence of students' lack of effort or inappropriate responsibility

---

Educators generally agree that all of these purposes may be legitimate, but they seldom agree on which purpose is most important. In workshops and seminars on grading and reporting, for example, we frequently ask participants to rank order these six purposes. In almost every case some portion of the group ranks each one of the six purposes as first—even when the group consists of teachers from the same school. And that is precisely the problem. Because we don't agree on what purpose is most important, we often attempt to address *all* of these purposes with a single reporting procedure, usually a report card, and typically end up achieving none very well (Austin & McCann, 1992). The simple truth is that no single reporting device can serve all of these purposes well. In fact, some purposes are actually counter to others.

Suppose, for example, that the educators in a particular school or school district strive to have all students learn well. Suppose, too, that these educators are highly successful in their efforts and, as a result, nearly all of their students attain high levels of achievement and earn high grades. These wonderful results pose no problem if the purpose of grading and reporting is to communicate students' achievement status to parents or to provide students with self-evaluation information. The educators from this school or school district can be proud of what they've accomplished and can look forward to sharing those results with parents and students.

This same outcome poses major problems, however, if the purpose of grading and reporting is to select students for special educational paths or to evaluate the effectiveness of instructional programs. Selection and evaluation demand variation in the grades. They require that the grades be dispersed across all possible categories in order to differentiate among students and programs. How else can selection take place or one program be judged better than another? But if all students learn well and earn the same high grades, there is no variation. Determining differences under such conditions is impossible. Thus while one purpose was served very well, another purpose was not.

### Recommendation

Reform initiatives that set out to improve grading and reporting procedures must begin with inclusive, broad-based discussions about purpose that involve various stakeholders. The major focus of these discussions should be what message is to be communicated through grading and reporting, who is the audience or audiences for that message, and what is the intended goal of the communication. Once decisions about purpose are made, other critical issues about form and structure will be much easier to address and resolve.

## The Importance of a Reporting System

Grading and reporting procedures *must* be tailored to fit very specific purposes. Expecting any grading procedure or device to satisfy multiple purposes is extremely dangerous. As we mentioned earlier, that is why so many report card reform initiatives fail miserably. Either they attempt to serve too many purposes with a single reporting device, or they expect that device to serve purposes for which it is ill suited (Allison & Friedman, 1995; Pardini, 1997).

At the same time, we must recognize that reporting procedures need to serve multiple purposes. At the very least it should accommodate both formative and summative intents (Reedy, 1995). But because no single reporting device can serve all purposes well, it is essential that reform initiatives focus on developing a *multifaceted reporting system.* A reporting system includes multiple reporting tools, each with its own specific and well-defined purpose. The specified purpose of each tool guides its development, determines its format, and establishes the criteria by which its effectiveness will be judged. For example, a particular school or school district's reporting system might include a report card, standardized assessment reports, planned phone calls to parents, monthly progress reports, school open-houses, newsletters to parents, portfolios or exhibits of student' work, and student-led conferences. The integrated combination of these various reporting tools, each designed to serve a specific purpose, would comprise that school or school district's comprehensive reporting system.

Surveys of parents' perspectives on reporting consistently show that they would like to have report cards distributed more frequently. If given the choice between having report cards sent home every 6 weeks or every 9 weeks, for instance, the vast majority of parents indicate they want to receive them every 6 weeks (Wemette, 1994). As we indicated in Chapter 1, however, our surveys and interviews with parents revealed that parents don't necessarily want report cards sent home more often. Rather, they simply want more information that they can understand on how their child is doing in school, and they want to receive that information on a more regular basis. Because they perceive report cards as the primary and sometimes only source of such information, most parents indicate they want to receive them more often. A reporting system that includes multiple reporting tools can address this parental concern and, if well designed, can offer parents precisely the kind of information they want and can use.

The key to success in selecting the tools to be included in a reporting system is first to determine what purpose or purposes we want to serve. In other words, we must decide what information we want to communicate, who is the primary audience for that information, and how would we like that information be used. Then, having decided on the specific purposes, we can select the tool or tools that best serve those purposes. Different tools can and should be designed to serve different purposes. And since most reporting systems are designed to serve multiple purposes, most need to include multiple reporting tools.

Some of the reporting tools frequently included in schools' and school districts' reporting systems are listed in the following box. Each of these tools is described in detail in later chapters.

Too often in recent years educators have become enamored with specific reporting tools and move ahead in their development and implementation

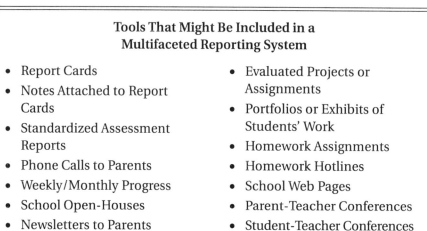

**Tools That Might Be Included in a
Multifaceted Reporting System**

- Report Cards
- Notes Attached to Report Cards
- Standardized Assessment Reports
- Phone Calls to Parents
- Weekly/Monthly Progress
- School Open-Houses
- Newsletters to Parents
- Personal Letters to Parents
- Evaluated Projects or Assignments
- Portfolios or Exhibits of Students' Work
- Homework Assignments
- Homework Hotlines
- School Web Pages
- Parent-Teacher Conferences
- Student-Teacher Conferences
- Student-Led Conferences

without considering thoroughly the purpose that tool is to serve. They start off by saying "Let's change our report card" or "Let's have students develop portfolios" without ever considering why that should be done or what purpose they hope to accomplish. Efforts that focus on particular tools without first considering their purpose inevitably fail. As we stressed earlier, form must always follow function. Purpose must always precede process or format. For these reasons, decisions about purpose must always come first.

If, for example, a school staff decides that the primary purpose of its report card is to communicate to parents information about students' achievement status, then parents must be able to understand that information, interpret it correctly, and make appropriate use of it. This also means that parents must be involved in the development of the report card and must be given opportunities to offer suggestions and feedback on its implementation. If, on the other hand, the report card is too complex for parents to understand or if it offers information they cannot interpret, then that report card has failed its purpose.

Similarly, if a school staff decides that the primary purpose of its report card is to provide students with information they can use for self-evaluation, then students need to be involved in the development and implementation of the report card. Not only must they understand the information the report card includes, they also must be given guidance and direction on how to use that information. If the information is ambiguous to students or nonprescriptive, then the report card won't serve its intended purpose.

## Recommendation

Efforts to reform grading and reporting procedures should focus on the development of multifaceted reporting systems. Such systems should be designed to include multiple reporting tools that serve different but well-defined purposes. They should permit different types of information to be shared with different audiences in order to enhance instructional processes and improve student learning outcomes.

# Statements of Purpose

To help clarify the intended purpose of each reporting tool included in a reporting system, we recommend that the purpose be written directly on each reporting device or included as part of the reporting procedure. In other words, the purpose of the report card should be printed directly on the card for everyone to see. Similarly, the purpose of a monthly progress report or a school newsletter should be stated on the top of that form. Even student portfolios should include a statement of purpose printed on the portfolio cover or in an introductory statement prepared collaboratively by teachers and students. As we mentioned earlier, different reporting tools typically serve different purposes. An explicit statement of purpose for each tool included in the reporting systems helps clarify that tool's intent, the information it includes, and the intended audience. Miscommunication and misinterpretation are far less likely when the purpose of each tool is clearly spelled out and printed directly on the form.

Statements of purpose can be as widely varied as the reporting tools themselves. A highlighted box on the front of the report card might include a statement such as the following:

> "The purpose of this report card is to describe students' learning progress to their parents and others, based on our school's learning expectations for each grade level. It is intended to inform parents about learning successes and to guide improvement efforts when needed."

This statement tells the specific aim of the report card, for whom the information is intended, and how that information might be used. The purpose of a newsletter for parents, on the other hand, might be stated as follows:

> "The purpose of this newsletter is to inform parents of the topics students will be exploring during the next month, the learning activities we have planned, and how those activities can be supported at home."

The set of reporting tools that is most appropriate and most effective in a reporting system will vary depending on the context. Differences from grade to grade are not uncommon, and elementary reporting systems tend to differ from middle school and high school systems. At all levels, however, it is essential that the purpose of each tool be made clear to all who are involved in the grading and reporting process: administrators, teachers, parents, and students.

### Recommendation

Each reporting tool included in a reporting system should have a well-defined purpose stated directly on that reporting device or included as part of the reporting procedure. Explicitly stating each reporting tools' purpose clarifies its intent and helps avoid misinterpretation.

## Sources of Grading and Reporting Evidence

Earlier we described the importance of using multiple indicators when grading and reporting student learning. We stressed that because any single source of information may be flawed and may not represent a valid depiction of students' true achievement or level of performance, it is essential that multiple sources of evidence be considered.

Research confirms that most teachers use multiple sources of information in determining students' grades, but they vary widely in the particular evidence they consider and in the procedures they use to combine or summarize that evidence (Cizek et al., 1996; McMillan et al., 1999). Studies also show that the evidence teachers use typically represents a combination of product, process, and progress criteria (Brookhart, 1993, 1994). Some of the major sources of evidence used by teachers in determining students' marks or grades include the following.

### Major Exams or Compositions

Especially at the middle school and high school levels, most teachers use the scores students obtain on major examinations and on major papers or compositions as an important component in determining students' grades. Although individual teachers prepare the majority of these examinations and assign the compositions, increasing numbers of teachers today make use of assessment devices that are included as supplements to their textbook series. To accurately reflect students' achievement or level of performance, such assessment devices must be well aligned with established achievement targets and have clear scoring procedures. Scores from these examinations or compositions can be tallied and weighted in a variety of ways and generally reflect product grading criteria. When both pre- and postassessments are considered, however, they also can be used as progress grading criteria.

## Class Quizzes

Class quizzes are shorter assessment devices that teachers use on a regular basis to check on students' learning progress. Quizzes are best suited for formative purposes to help identify students' learning problems and plan subsequent remediation strategies. As such, they represent process grading criteria but are still used by many teachers in determining students' grades.

## Reports or Projects

Teachers at all levels have students prepare major reports or projects to demonstrate what they have learned. Although most reports and projects are individual endeavors, some are designed to involve students in cooperative learning teams. Reports and projects allow students to demonstrate higher levels of learning and permit alternative forms of expression that often cannot be shown in exams and compositions. When accompanied by clear scoring criteria or rubrics (Andrade, 2000) that articulate the qualities of good work on a descriptive continuum, reports and projects represent definite product grading criteria.

## Student Portfolios

Portfolios are collections of students' work. Although typically used to gather examples of students' writing, portfolios can be incorporated in any subject area. They might include samples of students' mathematics activities, science reports or projects, or social studies papers. Most portfolios are used for summative purposes and represent product grading criteria. Certain kinds of portfolios are purely formative, however. They are developed to serve process criteria by giving students opportunities to reflect on their own work and to try to improve it (Arter & Spandel, 1992). Still others are designed to reflect students' progress over a period of time by showing both early and later work samples.

## Exhibits of Students' Work

Some teachers use exhibits of students' work as a basis for grading. The most common examples include science projects and art or technology exhibits.

While these typically represent product grading criteria, they can be valuable learning tools that help students articulate the qualities of good work and learn to recognize those qualities in their own work. Students also benefit through the process of selecting examples to exhibit, articulating the reasons for their selection, and finally assembling those examples in the exhibit (Brookhart, 1999).

## Laboratory Projects

Science and technology teachers frequently build their classes around a series of laboratory experiments or projects that students are expected to complete. When incorporated within instructional activities, these projects allow students to demonstrate higher levels of learning and offer valuable information on process criteria. Like reports, however, laboratory projects typically are evaluated in terms of specific product grading criteria.

## Students' Notebooks or Journals

Many teachers require their students to keep notebooks or journals as part of a course. Although generally considered an instructional device that is used to facilitate student learning, some teachers evaluate students' notebooks or journals and include these scores or marks as process grading criteria.

## Classroom Observations

Especially in the early elementary grades, many assessments of student learning are based on teachers' classroom observations of students. When related to specific criteria that are clearly communicated to students through the instructional process, classroom observations yield product grading criteria information. Many teachers also use observations for formative purposes in which they reflect process or progress criteria.

## Oral Presentations

Students' oral presentations can take many forms. They include assessments of students' answers to the questions raised in class discussions, their explanations of solutions to complex mathematics problems, or their oral responses in a foreign language class. They also include evaluations of oral presentations of projects or reports. Again, when directed toward clear achievement targets and accompanied by specific scoring criteria or rubrics, oral presentations denote product grading criteria.

## Homework Completion

Many teachers keep track of whether or not students complete their homework assignments and include this as part of the grade. As we will see in Chapter 8, however, the way in which most teachers consider homework in determining students' grades does not actually reward students for completing assignments. Rather, it punishes students for not completing them. If homework is assigned to aid students' learning, then it's difficult to justify lowering the grade of otherwise high-performing students for assignments not completed. Similarly, researchers suggest that missing assignments for poor performing students are more a symptom than a cause of learning difficulties (Cooper, 1994). Homework completion clearly reflects process grading criteria.

## Homework Quality

Some teachers thoroughly check homework assignments, assess the quality of students' work, and use those assessments in determining students' grades. But like class quizzes, homework is best suited for formative purposes to help identify and then remedy students' learning problems. And like homework completion, assessments of homework quality represent process grading criteria.

## Class Participation

In some classes, teachers keep formal records of students' participation in class and consider these participation rates when assigning grades. They might, for example, keep a runnng tally of the number of times each student contributes to class discussions. Other teachers use class participation in less formal ways, usually to give a break to those students whose other achievement or performance results might be just below a certain grade cut-score (Truog & Friedman, 1996). Class participation is another clear example of process grading criteria.

## Work Habits and Neatness

Some teachers give students special credit if their work is exceptionally neat and well organized, and penalize other students for work that appears sloppy or careless. Although it is certainly possible to develop specific performance criteria for work habits and neatness, this is rarely done. Hence, such assessments typically represent highly subjective judgments by the teacher. Work habits and neatness also represent process grading criteria.

## Effort

To enhance motivation and recognize students' hard work, many teachers include assessments of effort in determining students' grades. In some cases, teachers consider effort to be an expression of students' attitude toward learning or their work ethic. Because explicit criteria for evaluating effort are rarely identified, however, these assessments also tend to be highly subjective judgments on the part of the teacher. Evidence indicates, too, that teachers generally use effort to give a break to only those students who would otherwise receive a low grade, such as a *D* or *F* (Truog & Friedman, 1996). Effort is another example of process grading criteria.

## Attendance

Recognizing that class attendance is usually highly related to students' academic achievement and performance, some teachers consider attendance in their grading procedures. Other teachers consider attendance important because students learn from each other during class sessions and they want to draw attention to these important interactions. In some cases, students receive credit for attending class regularly, but more often they are penalized for being tardy or missing class completely. Attendance also reflects process grading criteria.

## Punctuality of Assignments

In an effort to encourage responsible behavior on the part of students, many teachers consider punctuality of assignments in grading. Typically, the scores of students who turn in assignments late are lowered, regardless of the quality of that work or the level of performance it reflects. Punctuality is another example of process grading criteria.

## Class Behavior or Attitude

As we described in Chapter 3, students' behavior and the attitudes they display in class sometimes influence teachers' judgments in determining grades.

Some teachers include specific behavior indicators among their grading criteria, such as "Remain attentive during class sessions" or "Show appropriate respect for the teacher and other class members." More often, however, behavior and attitude assessments tend to be ill-defined and inconsistently applied. Behavior and attitudes generally represent process grading criteria.

## Progress Made

Many teachers consider the improvements that students have made in their performance over a particular period of time when determining grades. Assessing progress generally requires multiple measures that can be used to demonstrate what has been gained or the degree of improvement. It also requires articulation of clear indicators of progress along a descriptive continuum. In all cases, these are indicators of progress grading criteria.

---

### Typical Sources of Grading and Reporting Evidence

- Major Exams or Compositions
- Class Quizzes
- Reports or Projects
- Student Portfolios
- Exhibits of Students' Work
- Laboratory Projects
- Students' Notebooks or Journals
- Classroom Observations
- Oral Presentations

- Homework Completion
- Homework Quality
- Class Participation
- Work Habits and Neatness
- Effort
- Attendance
- Punctuality of Assignments
- Class Behavior or Attitude
- Progress Made

---

## Relating Evidence to Purpose

In workshops and seminars, we frequently ask participants to indicate which and how many of these indicators they use in grading and reporting student learning. Typically, we find that some portion of the group uses each one of these sources of evidence. But more surprising is the tremendous variation we find among teachers in the number of indicators they include. Some teachers base grades on as few as 2 or 3 of these indicators, whereas others incorporate evidence from as many as 15 or 16—and this is true even when the group consists of teachers from the same school.

We are convinced that the reason for this tremendous variation among teachers is a lack of clarity regarding the purpose of grading and reporting. When the purpose is unclear, decisions about what evidence is most appropriate and most valid are extremely difficult to make. And because each of these sources of evidence varies in its appropriateness and validity depending on the identified purpose, decisions about purpose must always be made first, before the decisions about what sources of evidence to include.

If, for example, the expressed purpose of the grades or marks included in a reporting form is to communicate students' achievement status, then the evidence used in determining those grades should represent an accurate depiction of students' achievement or level of performance. Those sources of evidence that clearly reflect process grading criteria; such as homework, class participation, and effort; should not be included in determining that grade. This doesn't mean, of course, that process grading criteria cannot or should not be reported. These are important criteria that have a clear place in reporting procedures. It implies only that these criteria must be reported separately and not included as part of a grade or mark that is to represent an accurate and valid depiction of students' achievement status.

All of these sources of evidence vary in their importance depending on the reporting purpose and context. Each represents a different aspect of the learning process, and each constitutes a different form of product, process, or progress criteria. Although each can be used appropriately, the use of any one also can be corrupted. Most important, while each can be informative on its own, serious communication problems result when these various types of evidence are combined to yield a single grade or mark. As we emphasized earlier, such "hodgepodge grades" (Brookhart, 1991; Cross & Frary, 1996) are exceptionally difficult to interpret and can be challenged on the grounds of both validity and reliability.

## Recommendation

In later chapters we will take up the issues of combining evidence on student learning for the purposes of grading and reporting. We will argue, however, that the solution to our grading and reporting dilemmas rests not in the development of better or more sophisticated ways to summarize and combine evidence. Mathematical solutions simply will not solve these complex communication problems. We will suggest, instead, that the solution lies in using multiple reporting methods that include multiple grades or marks. We will show how reporting results separately from various sources of evidence greatly facilitates the communication process and can enhance both teaching and learning (see Brookhart, 1999). The biggest challenge we face is finding ways to help teachers develop the good judgment and the good written, oral, and interpersonal communication skills that such multifaceted reporting systems require.

# Summary

We are convinced that most of the problems experienced in efforts to reform grading and reporting procedures stem from attempts to do too much with a single reporting device. Clearly, there is a need for better quality and more detailed communication about student learning. But no single reporting device, such as report card, can adequately serve all of these diverse communication needs.

We believe that the solution rests in the development of comprehensive, multifaceted reporting systems. Such systems will include multiple reporting tools, each with a clearly specified purpose. These purposes will vary depending on what we want to communicate and to whom. The reporting tools included in the system should be designed to provide high-quality information to interested persons in a form they can understand and use effectively. The result will be stakeholders with a deeper and more reflective understanding of the various aspects of grading and reporting, who are better prepared to work as partners in the teaching and learning process to help improve the learning of all students.

# CHAPTER 5

# Grading and Reporting Methods I

*Letter Grades, Percentage Grades, and Other Categorical Grading*

In the previous chapter we emphasized the importance of developing multi-faceted reporting systems. We stressed that no single reporting device such as a report card can serve all of the diverse purposes we typically want to accomplish in grading and reporting student learning. Therefore, reform efforts need to focus on developing multifaceted reporting systems that include multiple reporting tools, each serving a specific and well-defined purpose.

A vital aspect of any reporting tool is the grading method used with that tool. Grading methods bring meaning to the information included in reporting forms and facilitate interpretation. They serve both formative and summative functions. In essence, they provide the key to understanding the message being communicated. This is especially true with report cards and similar reporting forms, although it can be equally important with test scores, portfolios, and other exhibits of students' work.

Simple measures of student learning have little meaning in themselves. Knowing that a student attained a score of 60 on a particular assessment, for example, tells us nothing about the quality of that performance. This measure gains meaning only when it is compared to something else. If we knew, for example, that a score of 60 translates to a letter grade of *B*, to a level 3 performance on a 4-point standards-based rubric, to a "Proficient" but not "Exceptional" performance criterion, or to a passing mark, then we would know more precisely just what that number meant. These bases of comparison are examples of grading methods. They provide information about the quality of that performance as judged by the teacher or another competent person.

Like the reporting tools themselves, grading methods vary widely. Each method has its unique advantages and its distinct shortcomings. Each also varies in its appropriateness depending on the context and the purpose of the reporting tool.

In this chapter, we focus on four different grading methods. They are (1) letter grades, (2) plus and minus letter grades, (3) other categorical grades, and (4) percentage grades. We describe each method, how it is typically applied, its major advantages and principal shortcomings, and how it can be used most effectively. We also explore some of the common fallacies and misunderstandings regarding each of these methods. Then in Chapter 6 we turn our attention to several of the most common alternative grading methods, including (5) standards-based grading, (6) pass/fail grading, (7) mastery grading, and (8) narratives. Although grading methods other than these can be found, most are adaptations of these eight major types.

---

### Major Grading Methods

1. Letter Grades

2. Plus and Minus Letter Grades

3. Other Categorical Grades

4. Percentage Grades

5. Standards-Based Grading

6. Pass/Fail Grading

7. Mastery Grading

8. Narratives

---

Our goal in this chapter and the next is not to advocate one particular grading method or set of methods. Rather, it is to help educators at all levels become more knowledgeable about the different grading methods so that they can thoughtfully select and use those that best suit their reporting purposes. We also will show how different grading methods can be combined to enhance their communicative value. While no one grading method is appropriate under all conditions, we are convinced that a better understanding of the various grading methods will lead to more appropriate reporting decisions and far more effective communication.

## Letter Grades

Letter grades are undoubtedly the most common and best known of all grading methods. In most instances, letter grades compose a 5-level grading scale,

| Subject | Marking Period | | | | |
|---|---|---|---|---|---|
| | 1 | 2 | 3 | 4 | Final |
| Language Arts | B | A | | | |
| Mathematics | C | C | | | |
| Science | B | B | | | |
| Social Studies | C | B | | | |
| Health | A | A | | | |

**Figure 5.1.** Typical Letter Grade Reporting Form

labeled by the first five letters of the alphabet. The grade of *A* represents the highest level of achievement or performance, *B* the next level, then *C, D,* and finally *E* or *F* for the lowest level. In the earliest applications of letter grades, the letter *E* designated the lowest level of performance. But because the letter *E* was occasionally misinterpreted to mean "Excellent," educators gradually dropped its use and instead began using the letter *F* to represent the lowest grading-scale level, typically indicating "Failure."

As we described in Chapter 2, letter grades have been used in schools since the early part of the 20th century. They remain the most prevalent grading method today in high schools, colleges, and universities. Teachers at these levels assign letter grades to all forms of students' work, including quizzes, compositions, projects, experiments, and even homework assignments. They also use letter grades to designate the results of their summative evaluations of students' achievement or performance in a subject area or course over a specific period of time. That time period might be a 6- or 9-week marking period, a semester, or an entire academic year. Reporting forms that record letter grades usually look similar to the one shown in Figure 5.1. In this form, a single letter grade is recorded for each subject area at the conclusion of each reporting period.

In many reporting forms, one set of letter grades is used to summarize students' achievement and performance in academic areas such as language arts, math, science, and social studies, while another set is used to report evaluations of their work in art, music, and physical education. The grade categories for these latter subject areas typically are restricted to three levels. For example, *E, S,* and *N* might be used to designate *Excellent, Satisfactory,* and *Needs Improvement.* Teachers' judgments of students' learning skills, work habits, or class behavior are commonly represented with similar three-level, letter grade categories.

## Letter Grades Descriptors

Despite their apparent simplicity, the true meaning of letter grades isn't always clear. What teachers wish to communicate with a particular letter grade and what parents interpret that grade to mean often are not the same (Waltman & Frisbie, 1994). Therefore, to further clarify the meaning of letter grades, most schools and school districts include a key or legend on the reporting form in which each letter grade is paired with an explanatory word or phrase. These descriptors are provided to ensure parents' accurate interpretation of the grades or marks. Such descriptors must be carefully chosen, however, to avoid additional complications and misunderstanding.

In one particular school that we know, the reporting policy states that "report card grades reflect students' progress on grade level learning goals." To us, this clearly implies that the grades are criterion referenced. In other words, they are intended to describe students' learning progress in terms of specific criteria that have been defined for that grade level. But the words used to describe each letter grade in the legend on the report card include the following:

---

**KEY**
*(Less Desirable)*

*A* = Outstanding
*B* = Above Average
*C* = Average
*D* = Below Average
*F* = Failing

---

At least three of these five descriptors (Above Average, Average, and Below Average) reflect norm-referenced comparisons rather than criterion-referenced standards. That is, they compare each student's progress to that of other students, not to specific learning goals. Most parents rightly interpret "average" to mean "in the middle of the group." However, this tells us nothing about "students' progress on grade level learning goals." An "average" grade of *C* might be pretty good if most of the other students are making excellent progress. On the other hand, it might be quite dismal if the majority of students are struggling. And even if a norm-referenced interpretation is intended, we have no way of knowing what group of students is the referent. Is it this particular class of students, other students in the school, or perhaps all students at this grade level?

In this example, and in many others, the descriptors used to clarify the meaning of each letter grade do not match the stated intent of the reporting form. If, indeed, letter grades are to represent progress on "grade level learning goals," then more appropriate descriptors might be the following:

> **KEY**
> *(More Appropriate)*
>
> *A* = Excellent
> *B* = Good
> *C* = Satisfactory
> *D* = Poor
> *F* = Unacceptable

These evaluative descriptors communicate the teacher's criterion-related judgments of students' achievement or level of performance. Ideally, these descriptors would be paired with specific performance indicators that identify the qualitative differences between each grade category. Such information helps parents make sense of the grade and understand more fully the teacher's summative judgments. They also avoid the many negative effects associated with norm-referenced comparisons.

## Advantages and Shortcomings

Letter grades offer parents and other interested persons a brief description of students' achievement and level of performance along with some idea of the adequacy of that performance (Payne, 1974). Furthermore, because most parents have experienced letter grades in their own educational backgrounds, they believe they understand what letter grades mean. For this reason, many parents express a preference for letter grades on papers, quizzes, report cards, and other reporting devices (Libit, 1999).

Despite their simplicity and ease of interpretation, however, letter grades also have their shortcomings. First and probably most important, their use requires the abstraction of a great deal of information into a single symbol (Stiggins, 2001). When so many measures of student learning are combined into this single symbol, interpreting what that symbol means is exceptionally difficult. As we described earlier, many teachers integrate a combination of product, process, and progress criteria into a single grade, and thus the grade becomes a confusing amalgamation rather than a meaningful summary.

Second, despite educators' best efforts, letter grades tend to be interpreted by parents in strictly norm-referenced terms. Probably because the letter grades most parents received while they were in school reflected their standing in comparison to classmates, they assume the same is true for their children. To them, a *C* doesn't represent achievement at the third level of a 5-level performance scale, similar to a middle-level belt in a karate class. Instead, a *C* means "average" or "in the middle of the class." Helping parents make this adjustment and see letter grades in criterion-referenced terms represents a significant challenge for educators.

A third shortcoming of letter grades is that the cutoffs between grade categories are always arbitrary and difficult to justify. If the teacher decides that the scores for a grade of *B* will range from 80 to 89, for example, the student with a score of 80 receives the same grade as the student with a score of 89, even though there is a 9-point difference in their scores. But the student with a score of 79—a 1-point difference—receives a grade of *C*. Why? Because the teacher set the cutoff for a *B* grade at 80. While cutoffs between grade categories are absolutely necessary in any multilevel grading method, we must always recognize their arbitrary nature.

Finally, letter grades lack the richness of other more detailed reporting methods, such as standards-based grading, mastery grading, or narratives. Although letter grades offer a brief description of the adequacy of students' achievement and performance, they provide no information that can be used to identify students' unique accomplishments, their explicit learning strengths, or their specific areas of weaknesses.

## *Recommendation*

Because of their long tradition of use and their general acceptance among teachers at the high school and college levels, it is likely that letter grades will continue to be one of the most popular methods of grading. But as we stressed in Chapter 3, letter grades should always be based on explicit learning criteria and not norm-referenced criteria. Furthermore, educators must be able to clearly communicate these criteria to students, parents, and other interested persons. Defining these criteria needs to become part of the instructional planning process and should include specific performance indicators for judging the quality of students' accomplishments.

In addition, to avoid the dilemma of having to integrate so much information into a single symbol, we recommend that teachers use multiple grades to represent their evaluations of different aspects of students' achievement or performance in each subject area. An example of such a reporting form is shown in Figure 5.2 and additional examples are given in Chapter 9. In forms such as these, teachers record separate grades for various aspects of learning in that particular subject. The subject area of language arts, for instance, is broken down in this form into reading, writing, speaking, and listening.

Using multiple grades relieves teachers of the difficult task of having to combine so many diverse sources of information into a single symbol. It also provides more detailed information to students and to parents about each student's achievement and performance. Many school reporting forms also allow teachers to offer separate marks for learning skills, work habits, and

| Subject | Marking Period | | | | |
|---|---|---|---|---|---|
| | 1 | 2 | 3 | 4 | Final |
| **Language Arts** | | | | | |
|   Reading | *B* | *A* | | | |
|   Writing | *B* | *A* | | | |
|   Speaking | *C* | *B* | | | |
|   Listening | *A* | *A* | | | |
| **Mathematics** | | | | | |
|   Computations | *C* | *B* | | | |
|   Problem Solving | *C* | *B* | | | |
|   Geometric Principles | *B* | *B* | | | |
|   Graphic Representations | *B* | *A* | | | |

**Figure 5.2.** Reporting Form With Multiple Grades for Each Subject Area

class behavior in each subject area. Although this makes the reporting form somewhat more complex, it permits teachers to separate product from process and progress criteria. It also offers parents information that is much more interpretive and far more prescriptive.

## Plus and Minus Letter Grades

To provide more precise descriptions of students' level of achievement or performance, some educators add a plus (+) or a minus (–) to letter grades. This allows a single grade category to be divided into three levels. The *B* category, for example, is divided into *B+* designating the high level, *B* for the middle level, and *B–* for the low level. Most systems that use plus and minus grades keep *A* as the highest grade, although some include an *A+*. And most maintain the single failing grade of *F.*

Like many grading issues, the appropriateness of plus and minus grades is hotly debated. Advocates stress that the wide variation in achievement among students in a single grade category demands finer discrimination (Abou-Sayf, 1996). They insist there are real differences between a "high *B*" and a "low *B*," and that plus and minus grades allow them to communicate these obvious differences. Furthermore, some survey data indicate that parents favor the use of plus and minus grades on report cards (Schulz, 1999). Opponents counter that the criteria by which these distinctions are made are typically so fuzzy that such fine discrimination is inherently invalid (see Dwyer, 1996). They point out that in the absence of clearly articulated learning standards and well-refined assessment instruments based on those standards, such minute distinctions are dubious at best. The process is akin to cutting pudding with a razor.

## Advantages and Shortcomings

The seriousness of arguments over plus and minus grades contrasts sharply with the simplicity of the issue involved. Basically, the issue comes down to whether it is better to have a 5-category grade system (*A, B, C, D,* and *F*), or a 12-category grade system (*A, A–, B+, B, B–, C+, C, C–, D+, D, D–,* and *F*). But if more categories are better, one might ask, "Why stop at 12?" There's nothing sacred or particularly special about using 12 categories. Instead, we might consider a scale similar to the one used to express grade point average: 0.0 to 4.0. If we limited ourselves to only one decimal point, that would yield 41 grade categories (see Farley, 1995). Or we might move to percentage grades, a major grading method discussed later in this chapter, which yields 101 categories. Increasing the number of grade categories, however, does not come without its costs.

Research on rating scales shows that increasing the number of rating categories from 4 to just 6 generally lowers both the reliability and validity of the measures (Chang, 1993, 1994). Other studies indicate that scales of 5 to possibly 9 categories are about as many as any qualified judge can reliably distinguish (Hargis, 1990, p. 14). Moreover, as the number of potential grades or grade categories increases, especially beyond 5 or 6, the reliability of grade assignments decreases. This means that the chance of two equally competent judges looking at the same collection of evidence and coming up with exactly the same grade is drastically reduced. Furthermore, as the number of grade categories increases, the potential influence of subjective elements becomes greater. In other words, the subtle influence that subjective elements exert on teachers' judgments as they assign grades is more likely to show up when teachers are required to identify very fine differences in student performance.

Hence the added precision of plus and minus grades is far more imaginary than real, especially when the criteria by which the grades are assigned are not well defined or clearly specified. Even when they are, the use of plus and minus grades requires articulating 11 cutoffs between 12 distinct grade categories—an ominous challenge for even the most skilled teacher. For these reasons, we cannot recommend the use of plus and minus grades at any level of education.

In addition, parents' preferences for plus and minus grades are likely an expression of their desire for better and more detailed information. Most parents simply want to know more from teachers about the adequacy of their child's progress. There are far better ways of providing this information, however, than by adding more categories to the grading system. As we mentioned above, teachers might offer more than a single grade in each subject. Instead of abstracting all the information they gather on student learning into a single grade, teachers could give multiple grades on different components of the course, different subtopics of study, or different aspects of performance. They could, for instance, give different grades for achievement, for process elements like work habits and participation in class, and for progress made during that marking period. Instead of giving a single grade for physical education, they could assign separate grades for concepts, skills, effort, and improvement.

If the reporting form did not permit multiple grades, teachers could supplement the reporting form with a more detailed description of the learning standards defined for the course and each student's progress with regard to those standards. Such information gives parents better insights into how well students are doing in terms of specified expectations for their learning. It also helps parents understand that grades stand for something credible, clear, honest, and fair.

## Statistically, Plus and Minus Grades Are Less Reliable

Although some might argue the point, adding the plus and minus to letter grades also diminishes their statistical reliability. Many educators assume that the more classification categories you have, the less likely you are to be inaccurate. More categories mean greater precision and greater reliability. Otherwise, the reasoning goes, one would advocate a test with fewer items over a longer one because of the smaller range of potential test scores. But as we know, longer tests are almost always more reliable than shorter ones.

In the case of grades, however, the issue is not the number of potential scores but the number of categories. These are two quite different things. When it comes to categories, statistical error is generally associated with misclassification. Setting more cutoffs in a distribution of scores (category demarcations) necessitates that more cases will be vulnerable to fluctuations across those boundaries (Dwyer, 1996). In other words, with more cutoffs, more cases fall close to those cutoffs and, therefore, are more likely to be misclassified. As the number of categories increases, so do the number of classification errors. One might argue, of course, that these errors are of lesser magnitude; that is, moving from an A– to B+ is less of a difference than moving from an A to B. Still, there will always be a greater absolute number of errors.

For example, when you have 5 grade levels determined from 4 cutoffs on a score scale, you get a layout like this:

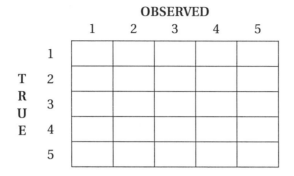

Let's assume that the scores and accompanying grades are meant to be measures of what students learned. Each of these cells represents ranges of "true" scores (scores reflecting what students actually learned) versus "observed" scores (scores they obtained that will be used to determine their grade). In a perfect world, the "true" and the "observed" scores would be exactly the same. But because of the measurement error that exists in our imperfect world, often they are not.

The "observed" scores have been put into discrete grades or "grade categories." In this example, if a "True 1" gets an "Observed 2," then a misclassification has occurred. The student learned more than was reflected in the score he or she obtained. In this configuration, therefore, 20 of the 25 cells represent misclassifications. The Total Correct Classifications = Sum of Diagonal Cells (5 cells), which in statistical terms is

$$\text{Correct Classifications} = p11 + p22 + p33 + p44 + p55.$$

When you collapse these 5 grading categories down to 2 categories by considering a single cutoff (e.g., pass/fail grading) you get

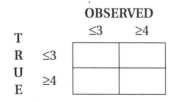

Now, if a "True 1" gets an "Observed 2," it will not show up as a misclassification, since 1 and 2 are both less than 3. In this case, the Total Correct Classifications = Sum of Diagonal Cells (13 cells). Misclassifications occur in only 12 of the 25 cells. Again, in statistical terms, this is

$$\begin{aligned}
\text{Correct Classifications} \ = \ & p11 + p22 + p33 + p44 + p55 \\
& + p12 + p13 + p23 + p21 + p31 + p32 \\
& + p45 + p54.
\end{aligned}$$

The actual errors don't decrease in this example, because we still have the same number of cells. But because we have only a single cutoff, what we categorize as error does! Fewer scores are vulnerable to fluctuations across category boundaries. And the important point to remember is that in cases such as this, reliability has to do with classification errors, not with precision per se. Hence with just two categories there is a smaller absolute number of classifications considered erroneous, and reliability is drastically improved.

By extending this reasoning, we can see that the reliability of a 5-category grade system with 4 cutoffs will be far superior to that of a 12-category system with 11 cutoffs. Hence increasing the number of grade categories actually lowers the reliability of the assigned grades, which is a further reason for our opposition to the use of plus and minus grades.

### Recommendation

As we saw above, use of the plus and minus does not add to the precision of grades, nor does their use improve reliability. In the absence of clearly articulated performance criteria, adding more categories to the grading system actually diminishes the reliability of grades. A far better way to communicate students' level of achievement or performance is to limit the number of grade categories to 4 or 5 but offer separate grades on different components of the course or different aspects of the performance. In particular, achievement indicators should be separated from process elements such as effort and progress components related to improvement. As we will see in Chapter 6, providing a supplemental narrative description or component checklist can further add to the communicative value of the grade. When policies dictate that only a single grade can be reported, as is true of many college or university grading systems, the performance criteria used to determine the grade should be spelled out in detail and clearly articulated to students from the outset of the course.

## Other Categorical Grades

In recent years, letter grades have been the focus of many heated debates. Some educators argue that letter grades label students and damage their sense of self-esteem, especially those students whose achievement or performance is assigned a low grade. Others suggest that the negative connotations of low letter grades stigmatize students and destroy their motivation to learn (Willis, 1993).

For these and other reasons, numerous schools and school districts have abandoned the use of letter grades altogether, especially at the lower elementary levels. In their place they use categorical grading methods with category labels they believe to be more affirming. In Kentucky, for example, many elementary schools discontinued the use of letter grades in reporting forms after passage of the Kentucky Education Reform Act and adopted the same category labels used in the statewide assessment system: *Novice, Apprentice, Proficient*, and *Distinguished*. In Nebraska, a similar 4-category system is used with the labels *Beginning, Progressing, Proficient*, and *Advanced*. The *Terra Nova* testing program of CTB/McGraw-Hill reports students' scores in 5 performance levels labeled *Starting Out, Progressing, Nearing Proficiency, Proficient*, and *Advanced*. Some systems use "educationese" terms such as *Pre-Emergent, Emerging, Developing, Acquiring*, and *Extending* to describe student performance, although such labels often make little sense to parents. Still other schools and school districts substitute more neutral symbols for letter grades. For example, the use of ✔–, ✔, and ✔+ is quite popular on elementary-level reporting forms, as are numerals such as *1, 2, 3*, or *4*.

| Examples of Categorical Grading Labels | | | |
|---|---|---|---|
| **Kentucky** | **Nebraska** | **Terra Nova** | **Other** (Less Desirable) |
| Distinguished | Advanced | Advanced | Extending |
| Proficient | Proficient | Proficient | Acquiring |
| Apprentice | Progressing | Nearing Proficiency | Developing |
| Novice | Beginning | Progressing Starting Out | Emerging Pre-Emergent |

## Advantages and Shortcomings

Categorical grades composed of verbal labels are generally more descriptive than letter grades. Verbal category labels also eliminate the need for a key or legend explaining what each grade category means. This is not the case, however, with categorical methods that use symbols such as ✔s or numerals, which still require verbal descriptors to clarify their meaning.

Whether or not categorical grades are more affirming and have fewer negative connotations than letter grades remains uncertain. Results from our surveys and informal interviews with parents indicate, however, that in many instances parents simply translate these category labels to the letter grades they understand. In other words, to most parents *Advanced* is an *A, Proficient* is a *B*, and so on. We also suspect that many students do exactly the same, especially those who have had prior experience with letter grades. So while educators might believe these more affirming category labels soften the blow of being assigned to a particular grade category, the message they communicate to parents and to students may be little different from what was conveyed by the assignment of a letter grade. Further research on this aspect of categorical grades is clearly needed.

---

### Categorical Grading

An old joke tells of the child who brings home a paper from school with the grade "Super" written across the top. The parents, of course, are well pleased and praise the child mightily.

Then one parent asks, "Is 'Super' the best you can get?"

"Oh no," proclaims the child. " 'Outstanding,' 'Extraordinary,' and 'Stupendous' are all better. 'Super' is just OK."

If parents' interpretation of a grade is not the same as what we as educators are trying to convey, then it's our responsibility to find better ways to communicate that information.

---

Categorical grading methods also have many of the same drawbacks as letter grades. When a single grade is assigned to students' achievement or performance in a subject area or course, a great deal of information must be abstracted into that single categorical label. In addition, parents frequently interpret categorical grades in norm-referenced terms, and the cutoffs between the various categories are often quite arbitrary. Like letter grades, categorical grades also lack the richness of other more detailed reporting methods, such as standards-based or mastery grading. So while categorical grading methods provide a brief description of the adequacy of students' achievement and performance, they don't offer the kind of information that can be used to diagnose students' learning errors or prescribe remediation strategies.

## Recommendation

Although to our knowledge no research evidence to date confirms that more affirming grade-category labels reduce the stigma attached to low grades, we remain optimistic that this may be true. Certainly the connotation of *Novice* or *Beginning* is far less negative that that of *Failing*. Furthermore, we find the use of "failing" grades at the lower elementary level indefensible under any conditions. Sufficient evidence convinces us that assigning a failing grade to any student's work at this level does much more harm than good. Therefore, we encourage teachers at these early grade levels to eliminate the use of failing letter grades altogether and, instead, use more affirming, verbal grade-category labels such as those described above. Not only are these labels more optimistic and hopeful, they avoid the connotation of finality typically associated with a failing grade.

At more advanced grade levels, we also believe that it is much more advantageous to assign a grade of *I* or *Incomplete* to students' work and expect additional effort than it is to assign a letter grade of *F* (see the discussion of "Grades as Punishments" in Chapter 3). Granted, this practice may require additional resources and specific support mechanisms along with cooperation from parents. Nevertheless, tentative evidence indicates its implementation can have a very positive impact on student learning and be highly cost-effective in the long run (Bernetich, 1998).

In developing categorical grades, educators must take care to ensure that the category labels they select are clear and meaningful to parents as well as to students. This means avoiding labels such as "Emerging," "Developing," "Acquiring," or "Fluent" because few parents understand what these terms really mean (Libit, 1999). If the purpose of the grade is primarily communication, then category labels must be selected that make sense to parents and can be easily interpreted.

To ensure accuracy in the message they are trying to communicate, teachers should also clarify the specific learning criteria that each grade category or level represents. Carefully articulated learning criteria paired with clear grade-category labels can greatly enhance the communicative value of any reporting tool.

# Percentage Grades

Percentage grades are the ultimate multicategory grading method. Percentage grades can range from 0 to 100 and thus offer 101 grade categories. Some schools and school districts use percentage grades alone to express teachers' summative judgments of students' achievement or performance in a particular subject area or course. In most schools, however, percentage grades are paired with letter grades using a common translation table. The translation most frequently employed is this:

> **Grading Scale**
>
> 90%  –  100% = *A*
> 80%  –   89% = *B*
> 70%  –   79% = *C*
> 60%  –   69% = *D*
>         < 59% = *F*

Percentage grades are generally more popular among middle school and high school teachers than they are among teachers at the elementary level. Like letter grades, they have a long history of use in schools and are second only to letter grades in their prevalence on reporting forms.

## Advantages and Shortcomings

By including so many grade-level categories, percentage grades allow for maximum discrimination in evaluations of students' achievement and performance. Even when the percentages are translated to letter grades, teachers can still distinguish between a "high B," a "solid B," and a "low B." The use of percentage grades also maximizes the variation among students, making it easier to choose students for individual honors or determine which students should be assigned to special programs. Thus, if selection and classification are the major purpose of grading, percentage grades serve that purpose well.

Similar to the other grading methods presented above, however, percentage grades require the abstraction of lots of information into a single grade. This in turn makes accurate interpretation of the meaning of a percentage grade extremely difficult. Along with the increased number of grade categories comes an increased number of arbitrary cutoffs between those categories. In other words, the cutoffs are no less arbitrary; there are just a lot more of them. Furthermore, the large number of grade categories and the fine discrimination required in determining the differences between categories allow for the greater influence of subjectivity and greatly diminish the reliability of the grade. Therefore, as was true of plus and minus grades, the increased precision of percentage grades is far more imaginary than real.

## Setting Cutoffs

A widely debated issue with regard to percentage grades and particularly their translation to letter grades is how to set appropriate cutoffs between grade categories. In the example above, for instance, the cutoff for the grade of A was set at 90%, for the B at 80%, and so on. Although most educators find this reasonable, others contend that higher standards should be set, especially for the highest grade category. In their classes, therefore, they might set the cutoff for the grade of A at 92% or even 95%, believing that by increasing the cutoff by these additional percentage points they have raised both their standards and their expectations for students' performance.

What these individuals fail to recognize, however, is the relative and very arbitrary nature of these decisions. Raising the particular cutoff percentage set for each grade category may increase the challenge for students to some degree. But a much more significant consideration is the difficulty of the tasks that students are asked to perform or the complexity of the assessment questions they are required to answer. The cutoff percentage representing an excellent level of performance on an extremely challenging task or very difficult set of questions might be quite different from what would be considered excellent on a relatively simple task. This does not imply that the challenge is determined by how well other students perform (norm-referenced). Rather, it means only that tasks or items designed to assess the same learning goal can vary widely in their intricacy and complexity (criterion referenced).

Consider the following simple example developed by Professor Jeffrey K. Smith of Rutgers University. Suppose we were interested in assessing students' basic knowledge about the presidents of the United States. We could ask a question in an open-ended, constructed-response format, also known as "short answer" or "completion" items, such as

---

1. Who was the 17th President of the United States?

---

For most students, this is an extremely difficult item that fewer than 10% are able to answer correctly. Its high level of difficulty is actually rather odd because most people know that Abraham Lincoln was the 16th president and they know that Andrew Johnson succeeded him. Putting these two pieces of information together, however, along with the necessary mathematics skills, proves quite difficult for the vast majority.

We might then consider asking the same question in a different format, this time as a multiple-choice, selected-response item. For example,

---

2. Who was the 17th President of the United States?

   A. Abraham Lincoln
   B. Andrew Johnson
   C. Ulysses S. Grant
   D. Millard Fillmore

---

This remains a fairly difficult item for most students. But because of the multiple-choice format, about 30% are able to answer correctly. Of course, if all students simply chose an answer at random, the limited response, multiple-choice format would allow 25% to select the correct response.

Suppose we next adjust the possible responses, making the distinctions a bit easier for students:

---

3. Who was the 17th President of the United States?

   A. George Washington
   B. Andrew Johnson
   C. Jimmy Carter
   D. Bill Clinton

---

Now identifying the correct response is much easier for students and about 60% are able to answer correctly. We could probably assume that those who are still unable to identify the correct response have very limited knowledge of United States presidents.

Of course, we could make a final adjustment to the possible responses in order to make the item easier still:

---

4. Who was the 17th President of the United States?

   A. The War of 1812
   B. Andrew Johnson
   C. The Louisiana Purchase
   D. A Crazy Day for Sally

---

About 90% of students are able to answer this item correctly. Those who don't are usually drawn to the response "A Crazy Day for Sally" because they recognize it as the one response that doesn't belong with the others.

Some might argue that knowing who was the 17th president of the United States is a rather trivial learning outcome—and that might be true. The point is that although each of these items assesses the same learning objective, same goal, or same achievement target, each varies greatly in its difficulty. Suppose that items similar to each of these four types were combined in a larger assessment designed to measure students' learning in an instructional unit. Those four assessment devices would present vastly different challenges to students, and the scores students attained on such assessments undoubtedly would reflect those differences. Would it be fair to set the same grade percentage cutoffs for each of those four assessments?

Focusing only on a percentage cutoff is seductive but very misleading because tests and assessments vary widely in how they are designed. Some assessments include items that are so challenging that students who answer a low percentage of items correctly still do very well. For example, individuals who answer only 50% of the questions correctly on the Graduate Record Examination (GRE) Physics test perform better than more than 70% of those who take the test. For the GRE Mathematics test, 50% correct would outperform approximately 60% of the individuals who take the test. And among those who take the GRE Literature test, only about half get 50% correct (Gitomer & Pearlman, 1999). From this information, should we conclude that the prospective graduate students in physics, mathematics, and literature are a bunch of "failures"? Of course not. Percentage cutoffs, without careful examination of the questions or tasks, are just not that meaningful.

Researchers suggest that an appropriate approach to setting cutoffs must combine teachers' judgments of the importance of concepts addressed and consideration of the cognitive processing skills required by the items or tasks (Nitko & Niemierko, 1993). Using this type of grade assignment procedure shifts teachers' thinking so that grades on classroom assessments and other demonstrations of learning reflect the quality of student thinking instead of simply the number of points that students attain. It incorporates the value the teacher places on successful performance and the teacher's perception of the level of thinking that students must use to answer a question or perform a task.

Furthermore, the challenge or difficulty of any assessment task is also directly related to the quality of the teaching. Students who are taught well and provided ample opportunities to practice and demonstrate what they have learned are likely to find a well-aligned performance task or set of assessment questions much easier than students who are taught poorly and given few practice opportunities. Hence a 95% cutoff might be relatively easy to meet for students who are taught well, whereas an 80% cutoff might prove exceptionally difficult for those students who experience poor-quality teaching.

Our point in this discussion is not that cutoff percentages are unimportant. We believe that they are vital and necessary in nearly all teaching situations. But setting cutoffs is a more complex process than most educators anticipate and typically much more arbitrary than most imagine. What we must keep in mind is that mathematical precision in setting cutoffs is not a substitute for sound professional judgment. Raising standards or increasing expectations for students' learning is not accomplished by simply by raising the cutoff percentages for different grades. It requires thoughtful examination of the tasks students are asked to complete and the questions they are asked to answer in order to demonstrate their learning. It also requires consideration of the quality of the teaching students experienced prior to the assessment.

### Recommendation

As was true with plus and minus letter grades, the increased number of grade categories provided by percentage grades does not improve precision, objectivity, or reliability. In fact, in the absence of clearly articulated performance criteria, the large number of ill-defined categories included in percentage grades actually serves to diminish all of these qualities. Even when reporting policies require that only a single grade be assigned, these negative attributes make percentage grades difficult to justify.

By limiting the number of grade categories to 4 or 5 and offering separate grades for different aspects of performance, educators can provide better and far more useful information. Providing a supplemental narrative description or standards checklist describing the learning criteria used to determine the grade for each aspect of the subject further enhances the meaningfulness of this information. We must recognize that parents' requests for more and better information cannot be satisfied simply by adding more categories to the grading scale. Instead, we need to consider the quality of the information offered and its usefulness to parents, students, and other interested persons.

## Summary

Grading methods communicate teachers' evaluative appraisals of students' achievement and performance. In the process of grading, teachers convert different types of descriptive information and various measures of students' performance into grades or marks that summarize their assessment of students' accomplishments. Grades therefore provide parents, students, and other interested persons with the means to interpret the teachers' professional judgments. When grades are referenced to specific criteria or learning standards, they identify students' specific strengths as well as areas where improvement is needed.

Letter grades, categorical grades, and percentage grades all offer brief descriptions of the adequacy of students' academic performance. If only a single grade is reported for each subject area or course, however, many varied sources of information must be combined into that single symbol or category label. This makes the grade a hodgepodge of information that is impossible to interpret. To remedy this problem, we recommend the use of multiple grades, each one representing a different aspect of the subject area or course, or a different dimension of students' performance. When grading policies stipulate that only a single grade can be reported, we recommend that the performance criteria or learning standards used to determine the grade be described in detail and clearly articulated to parents and to students. If a written description of each student's performance in reference to these criteria accompanies the reporting form, then the grade has clearer meaning, more practical significance, and serves as a better communication tool.

CHAPTER **6**

# Grading and Reporting
# Methods II

## *Standards-Based, Pass/Fail, Mastery Grading, and Narratives*

In Chapter 5 we described four widely used grading methods: letter grades, plus and minus letter grades, other categorical grades, and percentage grades. In this chapter, our focus turns to four of the most common alternative grading methods. These include standards-based grading, pass/fail grading, mastery grading, and narratives. Recent emphasis on educational standards and performance-based assessments of student learning has prompted educators to recognize the inadequacies of many of their traditional grading and reporting methods. Consequently, many have turned to alternative methods such as these in hopes of building greater consistency among instruction, assessment, and grading and reporting processes.

Although the alternative grading methods described in this chapter are different from the more traditional methods presented in Chapter 5, it would be inaccurate to refer to them as "nontraditional." In some cases, the use of these alternative methods actually predates that of letter grades or other categorical grading methods. Mastery grading and narrative reports, for example, represent two of the earliest forms of grading used in formal school settings. Nevertheless, these alternative methods represent very different ways to communicate teachers' appraisals of students' achievement and performance.

As we did in Chapter 5, we first describe each of these alternative grading methods and how it is typically applied. Next, we outline the major advantages and principal shortcomings of each method along with some of the common fallacies and misunderstandings associated with each. Finally, we discuss how these alternative grading methods can be used most effectively and propose specific recommendations for implementation.

## Standards-Based Grading

In an effort to bring greater clarity and specificity to the grading process, many schools and school districts have initiated standards-based grading procedures and reporting forms. This typically involves a 4-step process. First, teams of educators identify the major learning goals or standards that students are expected to achieve at each grade level or in each course of study. Second, performance indicators of those learning goals or standards are established. In other words, educators decide what evidence best illustrates students' attainment of each goal or standard. Third, graduated levels of quality for assessing students' performance are determined. This step involves the identification of incremental levels of attainment (sometimes referred to as "benchmarks") that can be noted as students make progress toward achievement of the learning goals or standards (see Andrade, 2000; Wiggins & McTighe, 1998). Finally, educators develop reporting tools that communicate teachers' judgments of students' learning progress and culminating achievement in relation to the learning goals or standards.

---

**Steps in Developing Standards-Based Grading**

1. Identify the major learning goals or standards that students will be expected to achieve at each grade level or in each course of study.

2. Establish performance indicators for the learning goals or standards.

3. Determine graduated levels of quality (benchmarks) for assessing each goal or standard.

4. Develop reporting tools that communicate teachers' judgments of students' learning progress and culminating achievement in relation to the learning goals or standards.

---

## The Challenge of Identifying Standards

Identifying the specific learning goals or standards on which grades are to be based is probably the most important but also the most challenging aspect of implementing standards-based grading. These learning goals or standards stipulate precisely what students should know and be able to do as a result of their learning experiences. In earlier times they might have been referred to as "cognitive skills," "learning competencies," or "performance outcomes" (Guskey, 1999b). Often, teachers are asked to list these learning goals in their lesson plans, make note of them on assignments and performance tasks, and include them in monthly or weekly progress reports that go home to parents.

A vital consideration in identifying learning goals or standards is determining their degree of specificity. Standards that are too specific make reporting forms too cumbersome for teachers to use and too complex for most parents to understand. Standards that are too broad or general, on the other hand, make it difficult to identify students' unique strengths or particular areas of weakness. Most state-level standards, for example, tend to be quite broad and need to be broken down or "unpacked" by educators into more homogeneous categories or topics in order to be useful to classroom teachers (Marzano, 1999).

For grading and reporting purposes, the identified standards must be broad enough to allow for efficient communication of student progress, yet specific enough to provide information that is useful to students, parents, and others. Several modern volumes offer educators guidance on developing standards that meet this critical balance (e.g., Gronlund, 2000; Wiggins & McTighe, 1998). One of the best resources available, however, is the classic work by Ralph W. Tyler (1949) titled *Basic Principles of Curriculum and Instruction.*

Another vital issue related to specificity that educators must consider is the differentiation of standards across marking periods or grade levels. Most schools or school districts using standards-based grading develop reporting forms that are based on *grade-level learning goals or standards.* To interpret a reporting form based on grade level standards from the perspective of a single grade level, however, parents must assume either:

(a) Each standard has *one* level of difficulty or complexity that has been set for that grade level, and students are expected to meet the standard at that level before the end of the academic year; or

(b) Each standard *increases* in its difficulty or complexity each marking period during the academic year, and students are expected to meet a new, more complex level each time.

Unfortunately, most standards-based reporting forms are developed by educators based on assumption (a), but most parents interpret those reporting forms on the basis of assumption (b). For example, if the standard states "Students will write clearly and effectively," many parents believe their child should be doing this each marking period, not simply moving toward being able to do it by the end of the academic year. This is especially true of parents who encourage their children to attain the highest mark in all subject areas every marking period.

To the educators using such forms, students who receive a mark of *1* or *2* on a 4-point grading scale during the first or second marking period of the school year are making appropriate progress and are on track for their grade level. To parents, however, a report card filled with *1*'s and *2*'s, when the highest mark is a *4,* is cause for great concern. To them, this gives the impression that their child is failing. While including a statement on the reporting form such as "Marks indicate progress toward end-of-the-year learning standards" is helpful, it may not be enough to alleviate parents' concerns.

This dilemma is compounded if reporting forms list the same identical standards for multiple grade levels—a frequent practice among schools and school districts seeking to simplify their standards-based reporting procedures. In such cases, the standards listed on the reporting form for first grade are the same as those listed for second grade, and so on. This eliminates the need for a different reporting form with different learning goals or standards for every grade level. To accurately interpret such forms, however, parents must make different assumptions within a grade level than they make across grade levels. Interpretations within a grade level are to be based on assumption (a). But since exactly the same standards are listed on the reporting form for multiple levels, interpretations across grade levels are to be based on assumption (b). In other words, each standard maintains the same level of complexity across marking periods within a grade level but increases in complexity from one grade level to the next. Helping parents understand this difference can prove exceptionally challenging for teachers and school leaders.

## Facilitating Interpretation

The problem for reporting form developers thus becomes how to facilitate appropriate interpretation. The typical response of parents when they first view a standards-based reporting form filled with various marks and numbers is to turn to the teacher and say, "This is great. But tell me, how is my child doing, *really?*" Or often they ask, "How is my child doing compared to the other children in the class?" The reason why parents ask these questions is that they are uncertain about how to interpret the information in the reporting form. Furthermore, most parents' personal educational experiences were in classes that used comparative, norm-based reporting systems instead of criterion- or standards-based systems. As a result, they are more familiar with reports that compare students to their classmates than they are with those that compare students' progress to established learning standards and performance criteria.

What parents truly want is a way to make sense of the information provided on the reporting form. Their fear is that their child will reach the end of the school year and will not have made sufficient progress to be promoted to the next grade. To ensure this does not happen, parents want accurate information that they can use to judge the adequacy of their child's progress, and they want that information as early as possible.

To remedy this problem and ensure more accurate interpretations, several school districts have begun to use a *two-part marking system*. With this system, each student receives two marks for each standard every marking period. The first mark indicates the student's level of progress with regard to the standard. In this case, that mark might be a *1, 2, 3,* or *4,* indicating *Beginning, Progressing, Proficient,* or *Exceptional.* The second mark indicates the relation of that level of progress to established expectations for progress at this point in the school year. For example, a "++" might indicate "Advanced for grade level expectations," a "+" might indicate "On target" or "Meeting grade level expectations," and a "–" would indicate "Below grade level expectations" or "In need of improvement." An example of such a reporting form is shown in Figure 6.1. This form is adapted from one used in the Bellevue School District in Bellevue, Washington. All names appearing on all forms are fictitious.

The advantage of this two-part marking system is that it helps parents make better sense of the information on the reporting form for each marking period. It also helps alleviate their concerns about what they perceive as low grades and lets them know if their child is progressing at a rate considered appropriate for the grade level. In addition, it helps parents take a standards-based perspective in viewing their child's progress. Their question is no longer "Where is my child in comparison to his or her classmates?" but, rather, "Where is my child in relation to the learning goals and expectations set for this level?" It may be, for example, that all students in the class are doing exceptionally well and progressing at a rate considered "Advanced" in terms of grade-level expectations. This would not be possible, of course, in a norm-referenced system where even those students who are "Advanced" in relation to their classmates might be doing poorly in relation to grade level expectations. Schools and school districts that use the two-part marking system generally find that parents like the additional information and believe it adds to the communicative value of reporting forms.

## Performance-Level Descriptors

As was true with letter grades, standards-based grades that employ numerical grading scales also require a key or legend that explains the meaning of each numeral. The descriptors used in the key are typically words or phrases that help parents and others understand what each numeral means. But just as we described in our discussion of letter grades, these descriptors must be carefully chosen to avoid misinterpretation.

One of the most common sets of descriptors used on standards-based reporting forms matches performance levels *1, 2, 3,* and *4* with the achievement labels *Beginning, Progressing, Proficient,* and *Exceptional.* If the standards reflect aspects of students' performance that are stated in behavioral rather than cognitive or achievement terms, then descriptors such as *Seldom, Sometimes, Usually,* and *Consistently/Independently* are more frequently used.

Many reporting forms include a fifth level of *Not Applicable* or *Not Evaluated* to designate standards that have not yet been addressed or were not

| Elementary Progress Report | | | | |
|---|---|---|---|---|

**Student:** *T. Nedutsa* — **Grade:** *1*

**Teacher:** *Ms. Rotnem* — **School:** *Bloom Elementary* — **Year:**

This report is based on grade-level standards established for each subject area.
The ratings indicate your student's progress in relation to the year-end standard.

**Evaluation Marks**

4 = Exceptional
3 = Meets Standard
2 = Approaches Standard
1 = Beginning Standard
N = Not Applicable

**Level Expectation Marks**

++ = Advanced
+ = On Level
-- = Below Level

**Social Learning Skills & Effort Marks**

E = Exceptional
S = Satisfactory
U = Unsatisfactory

| Reading | 1st | 2nd | 3rd | 4th |
|---|---|---|---|---|
| Understands and uses different skills and strategies to read | 1+ | 2++ | | |
| Understands the meaning of what is read | 1++ | 2+ | | |
| Reads different materials for a variety of purposes | 1+ | 2- | | |
| Reading level | 1++ | 2++ | | |
| Work Habits | S | S | | |

| Writing | 1st | 2nd | 3rd | 4th |
|---|---|---|---|---|
| Writes clearly and effectively. | 1++ | 2++ | | |
| Understands and uses the steps in the writing process | 1++ | 2++ | | |
| Writes in a variety of forms for different audiences and purposes | 1+ | 2- | | |
| Analyzes and evaluates the effectiveness of written work | N | 1+ | | |
| Understands and uses the conventions of writing: punctuation, capitalization, spelling, and legibility | 1- | 2- | | |
| Work Habits | S | S | | |

| Communication | 1st | 2nd | 3rd | 4th |
|---|---|---|---|---|
| Uses listening and observational skills to gain understanding | 1+ | 2- | | |
| Communicates ideas clearly and effectively (Formal communication) | 1- | 2+ | | |
| Uses communication strategies and skills to work effectively with others (Informal communication) | N | 1+ | | |
| Work Habits | U | S | | |

**Figure 6.1.** Example of a Double-Mark, Standards-Based Reporting Form

SOURCE: Adapted by Bellevue School District (Bellevue, WA) from a document created by Issaquah School (Issaquah, WA). Used by permission.

assessed during that particular marking period. Including such a mark is preferable to leaving the marking space blank, which parents often interpret as something that was missed or neglected by the teacher.

| Examples of Performance-Level Descriptors | | |
|---|---|---|
| Performance Level | Achievement Descriptors | Behavioral Descriptors |
| 4 | Exceptional | Consistently/Independently |
| 3 | Proficient | Usually |
| 2 | Progressing | Sometimes |
| 1 | Beginning | Seldom |

Descriptors such as *Exceptional* and *Advanced* are generally preferable to *Exceeds Standard* or *Extending* in designating the highest level of performance simply because their meaning is clearer. Specific performance criteria can usually be articulated for an "exceptional" or "advanced" level of achievement or performance. Descriptors such as *Exceeds Standard* or *Extending,* however, are much less precise and may leave students and parents wondering just what is required to "exceed" or "extend." As we described in Chapter 5, it is also best to avoid "educationese" terms that are meaningless or confusing to parents. Instead, the selected descriptors should be clear, concise, and directly interpretable.

## Continuous-Progress Scales

Some standards-based reporting forms use developmental, continuous-progress scales to describe students' achievement or performance with regard to each standard. Based on their observations and assessments of students' performance, teachers record a mark on each scale at a particular level or at some point between levels to represent what each student has achieved. An example is shown in Figure 6.2.

Advocates of continuous-progress scales emphasize that they show learning as an ongoing process in which students move ahead steadily, albeit at different rates. Although including such a scale with each standard tends to complicate and lengthen the reporting form, they stress that it allows teachers to note more incremental amounts of progress. As we pointed out in our discussion of plus and minus grades and percentage grades, however, such fine distinctions between grade categories tend to be unreliable and difficult to justify.

Furthermore, results from our surveys and interviews with parents reveal that most prefer a simple numerical rating that reflects the teacher's judgment

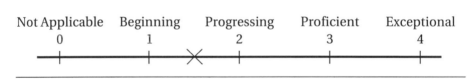

**Figure 6.2.** Example of a Continuous-Progress Grading Scale

of their child's achievement or performance to a mark on a developmental, continuous-progress scale. Many parents expressed uncertainty about how to interpret such scales. Several described their attempts to make sense of the scale marks by using a ruler to measure relative distances from one marking period to the next when both marks appeared between the same two levels. Others related that they would hold the two reporting forms up to a strong light to ensure that their child had made some amount of progress from the previous marking period.

We believe, therefore, that for most reporting purposes simple categorical or numerical level ratings are preferable to marks on a continuous-progress scale. Categorical or numerical ratings make the reporting process more efficient, simplify reporting procedures, and offer parents and others the important information they want in a form they can easily interpret and understand.

## Consistency in Reporting Forms

As we described earlier, educators implementing standards-based grading face a significant challenge in their efforts to maintain consistency on reporting forms across grade levels. Most schools and school districts involved in standards-based grading try to maintain a similar reporting format across grade levels to facilitate communication with parents. Most also use the same performance-level indicators at all grade levels. In this way, parents don't have to learn a new set of procedures for interpreting the reporting form each year as their child moves from one grade level to the next. Many parents also see consistency on reporting forms as an extension of a well-designed curriculum. It shows that the standards developed at each grade level build on and extend those developed at earlier levels.

While maintaining a similar reporting format across grade levels, however, most schools and school districts list different standards on the reporting form for each level. In other words, while the reporting format and performance indicators remain the same, the standards listed on the first grade reporting form are different from those on the second grade form, which are different from the standards included on the third grade form, and so forth. This approach requires the development of a different reporting form for each grade level. Nevertheless, it gives parents and others a clear picture of the increasing complexity of the standards at each subsequent grade level.

An alternative approach is to develop one reporting form that lists the same broad standards for multiple grades. The form from Bellevue, Washington, shown in Figure 6.1, is an example of this approach. To clarify the difference in the complexity of the standards at each grade level, reporting forms of this type are usually accompanied by a curriculum guidebook that describes precisely what the standard means and what criteria are used in evaluating the standard at each grade level. Most reporting forms of this type also include a narrative section where teachers can offer additional explanation. Although this approach to standards-based grading greatly simplifies the reporting form, it also requires significant parent training and a close working relationship between parents, teachers, and school and district leaders.

## Advantages and Shortcomings

When clear learning goals or standards are established, standards-based grading offers meaningful information about students' achievement and performance to students, to parents, and to others. If that information is sufficiently detailed, it also can be useful for diagnostic and prescriptive purposes. For these reasons, standards-based grading facilitates teaching and learning processes better than any other grading method.

At the same time, standards-based grading also has its shortcomings. First and perhaps most important, standards-based grading takes a lot of work. As we described earlier, not only must educators identify the learning goals or standards on which grades will be based, they also must decide what evidence best illustrates students' attainment of each goal or standard, identify graduated levels of quality for assessing students' performance, and develop reporting tools that communicate teachers' judgments of students' learning progress. These tasks can add significantly to the workload of teachers and school leaders.

Another shortcoming of standards-based grading is that the reporting forms educators develop are often too complicated for parents to understand. In their efforts to provide parents with "rich" information, educators sometimes go overboard in their "unpacking" tasks and describe learning goals in needless detail. As a result, reporting forms become cumbersome to handle, time-consuming for teachers to complete, and extremely difficult for parents to interpret.

A third shortcoming of standards-based grading is that it may not communicate the appropriateness of students' progress. Simply reporting a student's level of proficiency with regard to a particular standard communicates nothing about the adequacy of that level of achievement or performance. To make sense of the information included in a standards-based reporting form, parents need to know how that level of achievement or performance compares to the learning expectations that have been established for that particular grade level.

Finally, while standards-based grading can be used at any grade level and in any course of study, most current applications are restricted to the elementary level where there tends to be little curriculum differentiation among students. In the middle grades and at the secondary level, students usually pursue more diverse courses of study. Because of these curricular differences, standards-based reporting forms at the middle and secondary levels would need to vary from student to student. In other words, the marks included on the form would need to relate to each student's achievement and performance in his or her particular academic program. Although advances in modern technology would allow educators to provide such individualized reports, few middle and secondary schools have taken up the challenge. Thus standards-based grading at these levels tends to be restricted to the efforts of individual teachers rather than to a school- or districtwide initiative.

## Recommendation

As educators clarify the learning goals and standards they want students to meet as a result of their educational experiences, the advantages of standards-based grading will become increasingly evident. Most standards-based reporting forms list the specific learning goals or standards for each grade level on the form. The grades then provide students, parents, and others with an indication of each student's learning progress or achievement in relation to each learning goal or standard. Although this makes reporting forms more detailed and complex, most parents value the richness of the information provided, especially when it is expressed in terms they understand and can use.

We would encourage educators at all levels, therefore, to consider the use of standards-based grading. We would also encourage them, however, to use a two-part marking system with their standards-based reporting forms. As we indicated earlier, the first mark describes each student's level of progress with regard to the standard while the second mark indicates the relation of that level of progress to established grade level expectations. Such a system complicates the reporting form somewhat and requires additional explanation to parents. It also requires that expectations for learning progress be set not just for the grade level but for each marking period as well. Still, this system offers parents and others important information that can be used to facilitate students' learning.

The one drawback of the two-part marking system is that the detailed specification of marking-period expectations must take into account individual differences in children's development of cognitive skills. Because children in any class differ in chronological age and cognitive development, some might not meet the specified criteria during a particular marking period even though they are likely do so before the end of the year. This is especially common at the kindergarten level where students tend to vary widely in their entry-level skills but can make very rapid learning progress (Shuster, Lemma, Lynch, & Nadeau, 1996). These developmental differences must be taken into consideration by educators and thoroughly explained to parents in order to avert their concerns.

Later in this chapter we describe how including a narrative section on the reporting form is one way to offer such explanations. In a narrative, the teacher can indicate that although at this time a student may be a bit behind in terms of a particular standard, there is no reason for concern. The teacher should also explain that additional learning opportunities related to the standard will be provided in future learning units and that progress is assured before the end of the year. Finally, when appropriate, the teacher might offer specific suggestions with examples illustrating how parents might help the student at home.

Whether to use reporting forms that list different learning goals or standards for each grade level or to use a single form that includes a relatively small number of broadly defined standards that are identical across multiple grade levels appears to be a matter of individual preference. We know of no research or surveys that confirm one approach to standards-based reporting as superior to the other. The major advantage of listing the same standards for multiple grade levels is that it keeps the reporting form much simpler. As we noted, however, the use of such a form requires preparation of a curriculum guidebook that explains how the standards differ across the various grade levels. Such a guidebook helps parents understand that while the standards as stated on the reporting form remain the same, the criteria used to judge students' achievement and performance become increasingly more complex at each subsequent grade level.

Successfully implementing standards-based grading and reporting demands a close working relationship between teachers, parents, and school and district leaders. To accurately interpret the reporting form, parents need to know precisely what the standards mean at each marking period and at each grade level. Educators also must ensure that parents understand the language and terminology used in describing the standards. Well-organized meetings with parents to explain the standards and how to appropriately interpret the reporting forms will be essential in gaining parental acceptance and support.

## Pass/Fail Grading

One of the simplest alternative grading methods available to educators reduces the number of grade categories to just two—pass or fail. Pass/fail grading was originally introduced in college-level courses in the late 1800s as a way to get students to attach more importance to learning and less to the grades they attained (Durm, 1993). Many educators also believed that by lessening the emphasis on grades, students would be encouraged to take more challenging courses (Haladyna, 1999). The popularity of pass/fail grading continued to grow in colleges and universities through the 1970s, although its use has diminished somewhat in recent years. Still, current estimates indicate that the majority of public and private colleges offer the option of pass/fail grading in a wide variety of courses and programs (Weller, 1983). Fewer applications of pass/fail grading are observed in elementary and secondary schools.

To implement pass/fail grading, teachers typically select a minimum level of performance that they consider necessary to attain a passing grade. Those accustomed to using letter grades generally choose the cutoff between the *D* and *F* grades. Those students whose achievement or performance is evaluated above that particular cutoff then receive a grade of *Pass*, while those falling below receive a grade of *Fail*. Some applications include a third category of *Pass With Distinction* or *Pass With Honors* to recognize those students whose achievement or performance is exceptional.

As was true with letter grades, the selection of the cutoff between *Pass* and *Fail* is a fairly arbitrary process that may be either criterion referenced or norm referenced. However, norm-referenced cutoffs are particularly difficult to justify in pass/fail grading because they guarantee that a certain proportion of students will inevitably fail, regardless of the quality of their performance. For this reason, pass/fail cutoffs should always be criterion referenced.

Pass/fail grading can be implemented in two ways. In the first, the teacher sets a minimum level of performance for every component of the course or every source of grading and reporting evidence. To attain a *Pass* grade, students must achieve the passing level on each component. Teachers use this approach when every component of the course is considered important to students' overall performance or when they want to ensure full participation in all class activities and assignments. In a foreign language class, for example, the teacher might insist on a minimum level of performance in the areas of reading, writing, speaking, and listening. Not to do so, in the opinion of the teacher, would seriously limit students' knowledge and use of that language.

The major drawback of this approach is that undue emphasis may be given to relatively minor aspects of the course. Furthermore, because any single source of information on students' learning can be flawed, requiring a "pass" level on all sources of grading evidence may be unfair to students. In essence, it holds students accountable for design or assessment flaws over which they have no control.

The second approach to implementing pass/fail grading is for the teacher to tally various sources of evidence and then assign a *Pass* or *Fail* grade based on an overall, cumulative summary. This is the most common approach to pass/fail grading, especially at the college or university level. Its major advantage is that it allows students' weak performance in one area to be compensated by strong performance in another (Haladyna, 1999). And because the overall grade is based on multiple sources of information, it also provides a more reliable evaluation of students' achievement and performance in the course.

## Advantages and Shortcomings

Pass/fail grading offers many advantages. In particular, it greatly simplifies the grading process for teachers and for students. Clear performance criteria can be set for the single cutoff between *Pass* and *Fail* grades, and these can be clearly communicated to students, parents, and others. The use of a single, minimal cutoff and only two grade categories also generally improves the reliability of grade assignments. In addition, pass/fail grading has the potential to make learning environments more relaxed by focusing students' attention on learning rather than on the grade (Goldstein & Tilker, 1971). And finally, pass/fail grading is what students will face in many real-life situations. Driver's license examinations, college application procedures, and many professional certification examinations are all based on pass/fail criteria.

Using a single, minimal cutoff in determining students' grades also has its shortcomings, however. Even when a subject area or course of study is broken down or "unpacked" into multiple components on which students receive separate *Pass* or *Fail* grades, students gain very little prescriptive information from the grade. Furthermore, studies conducted at the college level show that students generally spend less time studying for pass/fail classes than they do for classes where a wider range of grades is offered (Thompson, Lord, Powell, Devine, & Coleman, 1991). Other investigations reveal that students in pass/fail classes study only enough to attain the minimum passing level and perceive little incentive to strive for excellence when it won't be recognized by the grade (Gatta, 1973; Stallings & Smock, 1971).

Still, a study involving medical school students yielded contradictory evidence. This investigation showed that pass/fail grading lessened student anxiety, improved motivation, and reduced competition among students while not altering achievement results (Robins et al., 1995). Perhaps pass/fail grading is optimally effective in settings such as medical school where students typically have both high ability and high motivation.

### Recommendation

Although pass/fail grading has an important place among grading methods, its value in most elementary and secondary school settings is limited. Setting a single level of performance or minimum competence is most appropriate when instruction focuses on relatively small increments of basic knowledge and skill, or when minimum standards of performance must be met. Some certification examinations and certain licensure criteria, for example, require a specific, minimum level of performance that cannot be waived. Nevertheless, these types of learning goals represent a relatively small portion of most school curricula.

In most teaching and learning environments, evaluating students' achievement on more graduated levels of performance provides important advantages. Specifically, it allows teachers to recognize incremental improvement so that students can see that progress is being made. It also provides more detailed information that can be used for diagnostic and prescriptive purposes. As we noted earlier, there is a limit to the number of grade-level categories that can be meaningful (see, for example, the discussion of plus and minus grades and percentage grades in Chapter 5). Still, providing only two categories appears overly restrictive.

We therefore advise teachers to use pass/fail grading sparingly and only when curriculum or instructional conditions warrant it. We further recommend that when using pass/fail grading, teachers add a third performance level of *Pass With Distinction* or *Pass With Honors* both as an incentive to encourage students to strive for excellence and as a means of recognizing those students whose performance is truly outstanding.

## Mastery Grading

Another simplified alternative grading method that overcomes many of the shortcomings of pass/fail grading is mastery grading. Like pass/fail grading, mastery grading also reduces the number of grade categories to just two. But mastery grading differs from pass/fail grading in two important ways. First, instead of setting a minimum level of performance or competence, mastery grading sets the cutoff between the *Mastery* and *Non-Mastery* grade at a high level of learning excellence. Teachers accustomed to using letter grades usually set the cutoff for *Mastery* at the *A* grade, or at least at the level of the *A* and *B* grades. In terms of percentages, this typically translates to the 80% to 90% level. The second difference is that with mastery grading, students are given multiple opportunities to meet the *Mastery* grade standard. In other words, students whose performance is initially below the *Mastery* level are given another chance (and sometimes more) to remedy their learning errors and improve their performance. Mastery grading taps students' internal and inherent motivation to succeed (Juarez, 1994). Kirschenbaum et al. (1971) describe it as not necessarily a new grading method but, rather, traditional grading done right.

## Mastery Grading and Mastery Learning

Mastery grading is usually associated with "mastery learning," an instructional process developed by Benjamin S. Bloom (1968, 1971). To use mastery learning, teachers first organize the content they are teaching into a series of learning units. After completing the teaching and learning activities planned for each unit, usually in a week or two of instructional time, students are administered a "formative assessment" designed to measure their attainment of the units' learning goals. This formative assessment may be a quiz composed of a combination of selected- and constructed-response items. It might also be an observation, composition, report, performance event, or learning exhibit. In essence, a formative assessment is any device or procedure used by the teacher to gain evidence on students' achievement or performance (Bloom et al., 1981).

The formative assessment doesn't represent the end of the unit, however, as is typical of most classroom assessments. Instead, it is considered part of the instructional process. Students who do not reach the *Mastery* level on the formative assessment are engaged in special "corrective" activities to help them correct their errors and remedy their learning problems. These corrective activities are specifically designed to be qualitatively different from the initial instruction. Typically they involve a different type of presentation and different form of involvement in learning so that students experience an alternative instructional approach. The corrective activities might, for example, tap different learning styles, learning modalities, or types of intelligence than were addressed in the initial instruction.

When students complete their corrective work after a class period or two, they are administered a second formative assessment. The second assessment is parallel to the first but not identical. In other words, it covers the same concepts and learning goals but is composed of different problems or questions. This ensures that students learn the important concepts from the unit rather than simply memorize the answers to specific questions.

This second formative assessment serves two major purposes in mastery learning classes. First, it verifies whether or not the corrective activities were successful in helping students overcome their individual learning difficulties. But second and more important, it offers students a second chance at success and hence has great motivational value.

It is likely, of course, that some students will perform excellently on the first formative assessment and demonstrate they've learned the unit concepts very well. The initial instruction was highly appropriate for these students and so there's no need for them to engage in corrective work. To ensure that their learning progress continues, however, Bloom recommended that these students be provided with special "enrichment" activities to broaden and extend their learning experiences. Enrichment activities incorporate exciting and

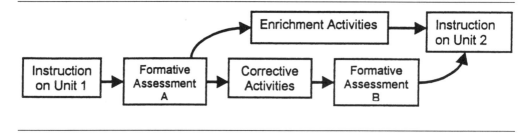

**Figure 6.3.** The Mastery Learning Instructional Process

challenging learning opportunities developed by the teachers or by the students themselves. They might involve special projects or reports, academic games, or any of a variety of complex learning tasks.

Through this process of formative assessment, combined with the systematic correction of individual learning difficulties, Bloom believed all students could be provided with a more appropriate quality of instruction than is possible under more traditional approaches to teaching. He recognized that, with careful planning, a teacher's initial approach to teaching is likely to be appropriate for many and perhaps even most of the students in the class. But because of individual differences among students, that approach also is likely to be inappropriate for some. Corrective procedures make other, hopefully more appropriate approaches available to those students so that a much larger portion of students learns well and reaches a high level of achievement and performance (Bloom, 1976, 1981).

## The Fairness of a "Second Chance"

When they first learn of mastery learning, some teachers express concern about the fairness of giving students a "second chance" on classroom assessments. From their perspective, it is unfair to offer the same privileges and high grades to students who require a "second chance" to demonstrate their mastery of the unit, as are offered to those students who achieve the *Mastery* level on the first formative assessment. According to these teachers, such students either simply did not prepare adequately for the first assessment or did not show appropriate responsibility.

Students who achieve *Mastery* on the first formative assessment certainly deserve distinct privileges along with the opportunity to extend their learning through the special enrichment activities. But those students who attain *Mastery* on the second formative assessment also learned the unit concepts and skills quite well. More important, perhaps the reason why they did not achieve *Mastery* on the first formative assessment was not their fault. Perhaps the teacher's initial instructional strategies were simply inappropriate for the way they learn. The correctives, on the other hand, proved more effective. If privileges and grades are determined on the basis of performance and these students have performed at the same high level, then they certainly deserve the same privileges and grades.

A comparable example is the driver's license examination. Many individuals don't "pass" their driver's license examination on the first attempt. On the second or third try, however, they reach the same high level of performance as others did on their first. Should these individuals be penalized for not being adequately prepared or not showing appropriate responsibility? Should they, for instance, be restricted to driving in fair weather only? During inclement weather, should they be required to pull their car over and park until the weather clears? Of course not! Because they eventually met the same high performance standards as those who passed on their initial attempt, they are granted the same privileges. The same should hold true for students who show that they, too, have learned well.

Other teachers raise the issue of the absence of a "second chance" in many professions. They describe how a surgeon doesn't get a second chance to perform an operation successfully. Likewise, a pilot doesn't get a second chance to land a jumbo jet safely. Because of the high stakes consequences involved, each is required to get it right the first time.

What we must remember in each of these cases, however, is the process used in training these professionals. The first operation performed by that surgeon was on a cadaver—a dead person—allowing a lot of latitude for mistakes. Similarly, the pilot was required to spend many hours in a flight simulator before ever attempting a landing from the cockpit. In both instances, it is recognized that mistakes are an inherent part of the learning process. These professionals developed their skills in a learning environment specifically structured to allow them to learn from their mistakes and then use that information to improve their performance. Nearly every professional endeavor uses similar training techniques. Only in schools do students face the prospect of "one shot—do or die," with no chance to demonstrate what they learned from their previous mistakes. Mastery learning offers students that opportunity (Guskey, 1997).

---

**Quote**

Spectacular achievement is always preceded
by unspectacular preparation.

—Roger Staubach, former Dallas Cowboys star quarterback
and MVP in Super Bowl VI win by the Cowboys

## Formative and Summative Assessments

Another unique feature of mastery learning is the distinction between formative and summative assessments (see Bloom et al., 1971). Formative assessments are brief checks on learning used throughout the instructional process to assess students' progress and to pinpoint any learning difficulties they may be experiencing. Teachers using mastery learning set a high level of performance or *Mastery* standard on each formative assessment and expect all students to meet that standard. Because the primary purpose of the formative assessments is to offer students feedback on their learning progress, most mastery learning teachers don't count them in determining students' course grades. Those who do typically disregard earlier marks and count only the highest level of performance that students attain.

Summative assessments, on the other hand, are larger assessments used in mastery learning classes to gather cumulative information on students' learning in order to assign grades or to certify competence. Like formative assessments, most summative assessments are composed of a combination of selected- and constructed-response items. However, they also can include observations, compositions, reports, performance events, learning exhibits, or any other procedure used by teachers to gather evidence on students' learning. Summative assessments tend to be broader in scope and usually cover a larger portion of the course than do the individual formative assessments. Still, nothing is included in a summative assessment of any form that students have not seen earlier in some type of formative assessment.

Since the purpose of summative examinations is to provide an overall evaluation of students' achievement or performance, most teachers assign the entire range of grades to the scores that students attain on these assessments. In other words, they might assign grades of *A, B, C, D,* and *F* or categorical grades such as *Beginning, Progressing, Proficient,* and *Advanced.* Because the use of formative assessments compels *all* students to meet high learning standards at regular intervals throughout the instructional sequence, however, mastery learning teachers generally find that students do exceptionally well on summative assessments and most attain the highest grade.

Although mastery learning teachers typically use summative assessment results as the primary source of information in assigning marks or grades, in most instances it's unwise to use the score from a single summative assessment as the *only* grading criterion. Most teachers administer two or three summative assessments during the marking period or term and count the results from all. Others use different types of summative assessments. For example, one assessment might be a traditional examination composed of multiple-choice and constructed-response items, another a special project or report, and the third an evaluation of students' portfolio entries. Some teachers vary the weight they attach to these various summative assessments, depending on the comprehensiveness of each or how much work each requires.

Using the results from a single summative assessment places undue emphasis on what might be a limited source of information about students' achievement and performance.

## Advantages and Shortcomings

Mastery grading offers many advantages. First, it is the only grading method based on a theory of student learning (Haladyna, 1999). The premise of mastery learning is that under appropriate instructional conditions *all students can learn well.* The classroom strategies, assessment practices, and grading procedures used by mastery learning teachers are all designed to provide students with these appropriate conditions. Most importantly, mastery learning strategies have a proven record of leading to significant improvements in students' learning and positive increases in students' attitudes at all educational levels (Guskey, 1987; Guskey & Piggott, 1988; Kulik, Kulik, & Bangert-Drowns, 1990a, 1990b)

Second, mastery grading is well aligned with most teachers' instructional purposes. By using formative assessments as an integral part of the instructional process, teachers are able to provide students with essential feedback on their learning progress. The single cutoff between *Mastery* and *Non-Mastery* helps teachers communicate their high expectations for all students. Having multiple opportunities to succeed allows students to venture into new areas and take risks without the fear of doing irreparable damage to their grade. And the use of summative assessments that incorporate the entire range of grades allows teachers to satisfy the reporting wants of many parents.

A third advantage of mastery grading is the clarity it brings to grade interpretation. Mastery grades must be based on well-defined learning criteria and specific levels of performance with regard to those criteria. Although mastery grading and mastery learning strategies are applicable to any level of instruction from basic skills to highly complex cognitive processes, their use requires clearly specified student learning goals.

Fourth, mastery grading is similar to what most students will face throughout their lives. Although most professional certification examinations are scored on a pass/fail basis, those who do not do well initially are given additional opportunities to improve their performance. Persons who do not score well on sections of the Medical Board Examinations or the Bar Examinations, for example, are given added chances to improve their score. Military training is based exclusively on the mastery model because of the dire consequences of poor performance. In essence, mastery grading teaches students the valuable lifelong learning skill that *you must learn from your mistakes.* Poor performance doesn't mark the end of learning. Rather, it can help point the way to improvements that are vital to success.

Mastery grading has its drawbacks, however. First and foremost, it requires extra time and work. To implement mastery grading and mastery learning, teachers must clearly specify the criteria by which student performance will be judged, prepare multiple formative assessments, set appropriate *Mastery* performance levels, develop corrective and enrichment activities, and develop well-aligned summative assessments. It also makes record keeping more complex as teachers keep track of students' performance on multiple assessments. Although the burden of many of these development tasks can be lessened if teachers have opportunities to work collaboratively, it still requires significant commitment on the part of teachers.

Furthermore, mastery grading requires essential management skills on the part of teachers. In particular, teachers must be able to manage the combination of corrective and enrichment activities going on simultaneously in the classroom. They also must vary the pacing of instructional units in order to maintain adequate content coverage. Most teachers find, for example, that more time is needed in early units to ensure students' involvement in the corrective process, but less time is required in later units because students are better prepared to learn more advanced concepts. In addition, teachers must find ways to motivate students to put forth serious effort on formative assessments knowing that they will have added opportunities to perform well. There are several valuable resources that provide teachers with practical guidance in addressing these concerns (see Block, Efthim, & Burns, 1989; Guskey, 1997), but they require serious consideration and advanced planning.

## Recommendation

The many advantages of mastery grading make it clearly superior to pass/fail grading in nearly all learning environments. By setting a high level of learning based on clear performance criteria and expecting all students to perform at that level, mastery grading encourages students to do their very best. Providing students with multiple opportunities to demonstrate what they have learned reduces the anxiety that students typically associate with assessments and allows greater freedom of expression. In addition, when mastery grading is used in conjunction with mastery learning instructional strategies, the effects on students' learning can be exceptionally positive.

The combination of mastery grading and mastery learning brings together many ideal instructional elements. Because it requires the specification of clear performance criteria for each learning unit, it incorporates many of the positive characteristics of standards-based grading. The formative assessments of mastery learning allow teachers to provide students with valuable feedback on their learning progress and to offer crucial guidance in correcting learning errors. The larger scale summative assessments, on the other hand, yield the cumulative evidence necessary for assigning grades and completing reporting forms.

These advantages make mastery grading ideal in nearly all teaching and learning settings. We recommend, therefore, that teachers at all levels give serious consideration to its implementation. If the issues with regard to classroom management and record keeping can be worked out, and if collaborative arrangements can be structured to help reduce the amount of work involved for an individual teacher, then mastery grading has much to offer teachers and students alike.

# Narratives

Narratives are open-ended, written descriptions of student achievement and performance prepared by the teacher. They represent the oldest of all grading methods. Narratives can be very general or highly specific, depending on the reporting policies of the school and the inclination of the individual teacher. Although most common at the elementary level, increasing numbers of middle and high schools have begun to incorporate some form of narrative grading on their reporting forms. Few schools or school districts, however, use narrative grading alone. Most combine narrative reports with other grading methods such as letter grades or standards-based grading as a way to clarify meaning or present additional explanation.

Reporting forms based on narrative grading are typically quite simple in structure. Most are composed of a series of boxes in which teachers record their descriptive evaluations of what students have accomplished and what areas need improvement. Early forms required teachers to write their comments on the reporting form by hand and were extremely time-consuming to prepare. An example of such a form is shown in Figure 6.4. In most schools today, however, student records are kept on computer files, making the recording process much easier. Teachers simply access each student's record and type in the comments they want to have printed on the reporting form.

Computerized reporting forms present teachers with additional advantages when using narrative grading. In particular, they allow teachers to offer more extensive and more detailed information. Some schools and school districts, for example, structure the narrative section of their reporting form in two parts. In the first part, the teacher enters one or two sentences that describe the major concepts addressed or the specific topics explored during that marking period. These sentences are printed on the reporting form of every student enrolled in that class. In the second part, the teacher adds a sentence or two about each student's individual accomplishments or learning progress. This two-part narrative reduces the work required of teachers in completing the narrative report while providing parents and others with specific and useful information. An example of such a form is illustrated in Chapter 9.

| York School District Elementary Reporting Form | | |
|---|---|---|
| Student: *T. Trebor* | | Grade: *2* |
| Teacher: *Ms. Yelaib* | School: **Tyler Elementary** | Year |
| **Reading**<br><br>*In reading our class has been working on perspective in works of fiction. Although Teresa contributes regularly to class discussions, her reading speed is slow and her comprehension skills need improvement. She could benefit from additional supervised reading time at home.* | **Writing**<br><br>*This marking period we concentrated on sentence structure in writing. Teresa can construct complex sentences that show deep understanding and creative expression. Her writing has shown significant improvement in recent weeks.* | |
| **Mathematics**<br><br>*This marking period we worked on basic addition and subtraction skills, along with problem solving. Teresa can solve double-digit addition and subtraction problems, and does exceptionally well with verbal problems applying these skills.* | **Science**<br><br>*In science we are currently investigating classification systems. Teresa works well with her classmates in cooperative assignments and did a great job on her independent class project.* | |

**Figure 6.4.** Traditional Narrative Reporting Form

Narrative grading is most effective when teachers' comments relate to clearly defined learning goals. In particular, comments should focus on students' strengths and what they've achieved during that marking period. When necessary, comments might also pinpoint students' weaknesses and offer suggestions as to how those weaknesses might be remedied. Such comments, however, should be helpful to students and should *never* include negative statements about students' behavior or character. Some teachers argue that referring to students as "lazy" or "uncooperative" is simply an honest appraisal. But above all else such comments are belittling and demeaning to students, and they have no place on a reporting form.

Teachers' narrative comments should be explicit, direct, free of jargon or complex technical language, and related to specific learning goals. For example, a comment such as "Lisa can locate, open, and search databases for relevant information" communicates a lot more than "Lisa understands databases." But even this latter comment is better than a general and nondescript comment such as "Lisa is a pleasure to teach and I enjoy having her in my class."

## Standardized Comment Menus

To simplify narrative grading, many schools and school districts have adopted computerized grading programs that allow teachers to select comments from a standardized comment menu (Friedman & Frisbie, 1995). In using such programs, teachers simply scan down a list of standard comments, click on the one or two they want to include, and these are then printed on the reporting form. Although most programs print the entire comment, some print only a comment number and then refer parents and others to a separate, numbered comment list.

Standardized comment menus represent the briefest form of narrative grading and are always used in conjunction with other grading methods such as letter grades or standards-based grading. Menus typically include both positive and negative comments that cover a wide range of achievement and nonachievement aspects of students' performance (see Figure 6.5). While the number of comments available to teachers normally ranges from 50 to 100, teachers tend to use only 15 to 20 different comments from the list. And while most programs allow teachers to offer a maximum of two comments per student per subject area each marking period, only rarely do teachers select more than a single comment for each student (Friedman, Valde, & Obermeyer, 1998).

Studies of standardized comment menus indicate that teachers vary widely in the comments they select. Some offer only positive comments while others assign negative comments to the majority of their students every marking period. Negative comments tend to be used to inform parents about what factors contributed to poor grades. But ironically, most of the comments offered to explain poor grades describe nonacademic factors such as students' level of effort, attitude, or classroom behavior rather than specific aspects of their academic performance (Friedman et al., 1998). As we described earlier, teachers routinely base grades on a combination of achievement and nonachievement factors that can vary from student to student (Friedman & Frisbie, 1995; Truog & Friedman, 1996). This evidence suggests, however, that nonachievement factors may be the primary contributors to the low grades that teachers assign.

Evidence gathered from teachers and parents shows that both believe it is important to provide more than just grades on reporting forms. But only a small portion of parents and teachers think that the menu-based comments are adequate (Friedman et al., 1998). Parents generally want more specific and more individualized comments. Others criticize the menu-based comments as too impersonal and imprecise.

Results from our surveys and interviews with parents reveal much the same. Few parents indicated that standardized, menu-based comments were helpful, and none found them prescriptive. Many of the parents with whom we spoke described such comments as "highly impersonal" and illustrated

| Type of Comment | Example |
|---|---|
| Positive Academic | "Asks appropriate questions" |
| Positive Behavioral | "Behaves appropriately in class" |
| Negative Academic | "Does not understand the subject" |
| Negative Behavioral | "Disturbs other students" |
| General | "Fails to bring instruments/materials" |

**Figure 6.5.** Examples of Standardized Computer Comments

SOURCE: Adapted from Friedman, Valde, and Obermeyer (1998).

their point by citing how different teachers, teaching different subject areas, oftentimes offered the same, word-for-word comment about their child. Listing only a comment number and then referring parents to a standard comment list was identified as the most impersonal of all. Hence, while teachers frequently want to give and parents frequently want to receive more information than grades alone provide, one would be hard-pressed to suggest that either group found standardized comment menu systems sufficient for this purpose.

## Advantages and Shortcomings

Of all grading methods, narratives have the potential to be the most specific and most personalized. Especially if teachers' comments are based on carefully articulated learning goals that students and parents understand, narratives can offer a clear description of achievement, performance, and learning progress. Depending on the nature of the information included, they also can be useful for diagnostic and prescriptive purposes. In narratives teachers can describe students' unique learning difficulties and recommend explicit strategies for improvement. When used in conjunction with other grading methods such as letter grades or categorical grades, narratives bring added clarity and richness to the information on the reporting form. Some research indicates, in fact, that many parents like narrative reports for these very reasons. They are more personal, less competitive, and convey more explicit information about students' learning progress (Hall, 1990).

At the same time, however, narrative grading also has its shortcomings. Among all grading methods, narratives show the greatest variation among teachers, especially in the absence of specific guidelines for their development. Some teachers offer detailed descriptions while others include only a brief statement or two. Good narratives are also extremely time-consuming to prepare, even with the help of computerized grading programs. Furthermore, as teachers complete more and more narratives, their comments tend to become increasingly standardized. That is why so many schools and school districts opt to use computer programs that incorporate standardized comment menus.

Perhaps the greatest drawback of narratives, however, is that they frequently do not communicate the adequacy of students' performance (Afflerbach & Sammons, 1991). Even parents who recognize the limitations of letter grades and other categorical grading methods generally prefer these methods to narrative reports because they consider them more accurate and more precise (Allison & Friedman, 1995). For this reason, schools and school districts that have experimented with reporting forms based primarily on narrative grading often are forced to return to letter grades or other categorical grades within a short period of time (see, for example, British Columbia Ministry of Education, 1994).

*Recommendation*

The flexibility, versatility, and richness of the information narratives can offer make them an important component in any grading and reporting system. Although many parents consider narrative grading insufficient when used alone, most welcome narrative comments as a supplement to other grading methods and believe they bring added precision to the grading process. When teachers receive special training on the development of narrative reports and focus their comments on specific learning goals, narratives greatly enhance the communicative value of reporting forms (Wiggins, 1994).

We recommend, therefore, that teachers at all levels give strong consideration to the use of narratives not only in reporting forms but with all procedures used to gather information on students' learning. Narratives give teachers the opportunity to clarify the marks or grades they record. Through narrative comments the teacher can offer additional explanation, describe unique aspects of students' learning experiences, emphasize special strengths, or point out specific weaknesses. Furthermore, by focusing their comments on specific learning goals teachers can prescribe solutions to identified learning problems. They might, for example, suggest ways for the parents and teacher to work together as a team to help the student. When appropriate, the teacher could also offer ideas on how parents could become more involved in their child's education at home.

To emphasize parents' roles as partners in the learning process, many narrative reporting forms include a section for the parents to complete. In other words, instead of just signing the reporting form before it's returned to school, parents are asked to add their comments to the teacher in this section. Here they might, for example, pose questions, comment on their child's progress, or request a conference. This helps facilitate two-way communication between home and school, illustrates the teacher's openness to parents' feedback, and gives parents the opportunity to become more involved in their child's education.

Finally, to guarantee realizing the positive benefits of narratives, we strongly recommend that schools and school districts provide professional development for teachers on the completion of narrative reports. The tremendous variation among teachers in the detail and quality of the comments they offer in narrative reports is undoubtedly due to the fact that few have any background or training in narrative grading. Such training can help teachers enrich the quality and focus of their comments, enhance their communicative and prescriptive value, and, perhaps, serve to improve student performance.

## Summary

As we emphasized in Chapter 5, grading methods communicate teachers' evaluative appraisals of students' achievement and performance. Through grading, teachers convert descriptive information and various measures of students' performance into grades, marks, or narrative reports that summarize their assessment of students' accomplishments. By its very nature, therefore, grading is a subjective process. But being subjective does not mean that grades lack credibility or are indefensible. Rather, it implies that grading is and will always be an exercise in professional judgment. Grades simply provide parents, students, and other interested persons with the means to interpret the professional judgments that teachers have made.

Standards-based grading, pass/fail grading, mastery grading, and narratives are all ways that teachers summarize the results of their evaluations of students' achievement and performance. What should be apparent in our discussion of these alternative grading methods, however, is that grading is much more a challenge in effective communication than simply a process of quantifying students' achievement. What matters most in grading is not what method we use or what symbols we employ but what message we want to communicate. When grades are referenced to specific criteria or learning standards that parents, students, and others understand, they become meaningful communication tools. They can identify students' specific strengths as well as areas where improvement is needed. When the message that teachers want to communicate is accurately interpreted by those for whom that message is intended, then grading has served its communicative purpose well.

CHAPTER 7

# Grading and Reporting for Students With Special Needs

Students with special needs present teachers with unique challenges when
it comes to establishing grading policies and reporting formats. In most
instances, these challenges involve three different groups of students. The
first is students with disabilities who are included or "mainstreamed" in general education classes. The second is students for whom English is not their
primary language and are therefore involved in English as a Second Language
(ESL), English Language Learner (ELL), or bilingual educational programs.
The third group includes students with exceptional skills or abilities who may
be considered "gifted" or "talented." Because the grading dilemmas associated with each of these groups of students are different, we consider each
group separately.

---

### Special Students in General Education Classes

1. Students with disabilities

2. Students who are English Language Learners (ELLs)

3. Students considered gifted or talented

---

## Students With Disabilities

Since the early 1980s, increased efforts have been made to integrate students
with special needs into regular education classrooms. Current estimates indicate that over 80% of students with disabilities spend the major portion of
their school day in general education classes (U.S. Department of Education,

1997). Before inclusion became part of the federal law, most students with disabilities were taught in separate classes, in part to avoid the humiliation they might experience because their level of academic performance was far below their age-level peers. The grades they received typically were based on progress in achieving the individualized learning goals set forth in an Individualized Education Program (IEP). The disadvantages of this practice were that it separated students from the socialization and other age-appropriate activities of their peers and sometimes led to educational expectations that were too low (Phillips, 1999).

Mainstreaming and inclusion programs seek to remedy this situation by including students with disabilities in the same educational experiences and classroom activities as regular education students. Most general education teachers welcome these students in their classes and, with the help of cooperating special education teachers, work hard to ensure their success. Using procedures outlined in a redesigned IEP, they make accommodations in their instructional practices and in the classroom environment to provide these students with favorable learning conditions (Hendrikson & Gable, 1997).

Inclusion efforts have been confounded in recent years, however, by the enactment of education accountability programs that typically embody demands for high, uniform learning standards for all students. In many states and school districts, these standards have been translated into rigid policies that dictate to teachers how student achievement should be assessed and how learning progress should be reported. Such policies present regular education teachers with unique problems when it comes to grading the performance of students with disabilities. In particular, teachers are faced with the dilemma of deciding how to make accommodations for students with disabilities so that their accomplishments can be recognized and, at the same time, be fair to the other students in the class.

Four different points of view currently prevail regarding grading policies for students with disabilities who are included in regular education classes. These include (a) applying the same grading standards to all students, (b) grading in terms of individual effort, (c) grading in terms of learning progress, and (d) making specific grading adaptations.

---

**Grading Policies for Students With Disabilities**

1. Applying the same grading standards to all students

2. Grading in terms of individual effort

3. Grading in terms of learning progress

4. Making specific grading adaptations

The advantages and relative shortcoming of each of these different perspectives are described below.

## Applying the Same Grading Standards to All Students

The first point of view holds that while adaptations in the procedures used to gather achievement or performance information from students with disabilities are permissible (e.g., reading the assessment to students or giving them more time to complete the assessment), grading standards should remain absolute. In other words, what is required for an *A* or *B* or *Proficient* should mean the same for all students. Thus, while teachers may alter testing or assessment procedures for students with special needs, all students should be held to the same standards in determining their grade.

On the surface, this approach seems reasonable. After all, students with special needs and their parents need to know where they stand in reference to clearly defined learning goals or standards (Wiggins, 1996). Furthermore, this is what inclusion means: being part of all regular classroom processes and practices, including the grading policies. But the consequences of this approach are also clear. Studies indicate that 60% to 75% of students with disabilities receive a grade of *D* or lower year after year in regular education classes (Donohoe & Zigmond, 1990). Similarly, more than half of all students with disabilities have GPAs below 2.24, 35% are below 1.74, and one third report receiving at least one failing grade (Valdes, Williamson, & Wagner, 1990). So although educators generally agree on the need to adapt educational practices for students with disabilities in general education classes, it is evident that these students are relatively unsuccessful when evaluated in terms of traditional grading practices.

The debilitating effects of such a system are not hard to imagine. Although most students with disabilities consider the traditional grading practices used in general education classes to be fair (Bursuck, Munk, & Olson, 1999; Vaughn Schumm, Niarhos, & Gordon, 1993), they feel helpless to achieve higher grades and yet blame themselves for their low grades (Selby & Murphy, 1992). The case of Joshua, described by Munk and Bursuck (1998a) in the adjoining box, provides just such an example. As a result, these students lose confidence in their abilities, tend to give up on academic pursuits, and are at high risk of dropping out of school (Zigmond & Thornton, 1985). More important, traditional grading systems that do not make reasonable accommodations for students with disabilities are inconsistent with the goals of the Education of All Handicapped Children Act (1975) and the Individuals with Disabilities Education Act (1990) (Mehring, 1995).

---

**Grading and Students With Special Needs: The Case of Joshua**

The problems associated with grading the achievement and performance of students with special needs are difficult for even the most skillful teachers. Munk and Bursuck (1998a, p. 44) capture the essence of this dilemma in their description of Joshua:

Joshua is a 6th grader with a learning disability in reading. At the beginning of the last grading period, Joshua was transferred into several content classes, including geography and science. His special and general education teachers worked cooperatively to adapt his lessons so that Joshua could finish on time and understand the material. Inclusion was proving to be a positive experience for him. He was excited about receiving his first report card since the change, but as he scanned the column of *C*'s and *D*'s, his spirits fell. Why did his teachers tell him he was doing well when he obviously wasn't? Could, or should, Joshua's teachers have done something to prevent his disappointment?

---

## Recommendation

The negative aspects of applying the same rigid grading standards to all students clearly outweigh the advantages of this method. It is inappropriate, unfair, and probably illegal. For these reasons we consider it the least defensible approach to grading the achievement and performance of students with disabilities.

## Grading in Terms of Individual Effort

The second point of view is diametrically opposed to the first and calls for students with disabilities to be graded primarily in terms of their individual effort. In other words, grades should recognize students' "potential" and identify those who are putting forth their best effort and trying their hardest. As humane as this approach might seem, however, there are numerous problems with it as well.

Many researchers consider it virtually impossible to accurately assess students' effort, especially when considered in relation to their "potential" (Hargis, 1990). How can a teacher judge, for example, if students are really trying their hardest? Furthermore, it is very difficult for teachers to determine the true reasons for students' actions or inaction. What appears to be a lack of initiative on the part of a student may actually be an indication of a profound learning problem. Judgments of effort are speculative at best and always highly subjective.

In an attempt to reduce the subjectivity of their assessments of effort, some teachers base effort grades on learning-related behaviors they can observe, such as handing in assignments on time, attendance, participation in class, and taking notes. While these behaviors are relatively easy to document, there are obvious problems with using them as criteria of effort. In addition, their use as a basis for the grade often indicates to students with disabilities that all the teacher requires of them is to stay out of trouble. Whether or not they learn anything is of little importance (Gersten et al., 1996). Students with special needs frequently report that "good behavior and good effort (not falling asleep!) . . . (are) the important criteria" when it comes to grades, and sitting quietly and doing their work are all that is necessary to get by (Calhoun & Beattie, 1984, p. 225). Although the majority of students with disabilities succeed in meeting these behavioral criteria, such practices subtly communicate teachers' low expectations for their academic performance.

### Recommendation

While it can be helpful to record teachers' judgments of students' effort on a reporting form, we believe it is inappropriate to base students' grades on effort alone. Accurate judgments about effort are difficult for teachers to make and tend to be highly subjective. More important, grades based solely on effort communicate to students with disabilities that all they need to do is to appear to be trying and that their actual achievement or performance is unimportant.

## Grading in Terms of Learning Progress

A third point of view is that grades for students with disabilities should be based on their individual growth rates. In other words, rather than trying to assess the elusive concept of effort, students' academic performance should be evaluated in terms of how much progress they make over a specified period of time (Gersten et al., 1996). This perspective does not discount the importance of assessing students' effort or learning-related behaviors. It simply recognizes that these are not sufficient for providing students with special needs or their parents with accurate information about how well these students are learning.

Grading in terms of learning progress requires that clear learning goals with specific performance criteria be established for all courses of study at every education level. Included with the performance criteria should be well-defined indicators of progress, or "benchmarks." These indicators describe the graduated levels of performance or developmental sequences that eventually will lead to successful achievement of the goal or standard. Learning is then recorded as progress along this developmental continuum. The adequacy of students' progress is defined individually, based on students' abilities and their starting point on the continuum. In most cases, these decisions about adequacy are outlined in advance within the IEP, along with the kinds of special help or assistance that students might need.

Grading according to learning progress offers many advantages. First, it emphasizes individual accomplishment and improvement. Regardless of where students begin on the learning continuum, their progress and growth can be recognized. This is similar to what weight lifters do when they chart their increases in poundage or what golfers do when they compare their scores to par. Second, it promotes individual responsibility. Students know in advance what is expected of them and what they must do to attain the grade they want. Third, by viewing all progress as positive it allows students to gain self-respect through their accomplishments (Haladyna, 1999). Fourth, and perhaps most important, grading according to learning progress is well aligned with the contractual aspects of the IEP. In designing an IEP, the student and teacher, in consultation with the parents and special educators, negotiate the learning tasks to be completed, the adaptations that will be made, the performance level expected on the tasks, a time frame for completion of the work, and the grade to be awarded. In essence, this aspect of IEP development represents a form of contract grading in which both instructional adaptations and criteria for grading are specified in advance (Retish, Horvath, Hitchings, & Schmalle, 1991).

As reasonable as it sounds, however, this process also has its drawbacks. Because interpretations of progress are based on individual standards, there is no guarantee the standards set will be completely appropriate or sufficiently challenging (Haladyna, 1999). Standards that are too low may promote slow or inadequate progress. This is reflected in the old joke about the student who divulges to a friend, "The best thing about my individualized instructional program is that I'm falling behind at my own pace." Standards that are too high, on the other hand, may lead to frustration, feelings of incompetence, and diminished motivation.

The most serious drawback of basing grades on learning progress, however, has to do with grade interpretation. When progress standards are individualized, the grade means something different for each student. We might decide, for example, that one student should master five skills or learning objectives during the marking period to obtain a grade of A, while another student with less ability or "potential" need master only three. If both students meet their individualized progress goals, both would receive the same high grade of A, even though that grade represents very different levels of learning and different amounts of progress. If the first student masters only three of the five specified skills or learning objectives during the marking period, that level of performance might translate to a grade of C for that student. However, this represents exactly the same amount of progress made by the second student who received a grade of A. Differences such as these greatly complicate the meaning of grades and lead to numerous interpretation problems (Gribbin, 1992). Furthermore, these interpretation problems can result in court battles similar to the one described in the accompanying box on "Legal Issues."

## Legal Issues in Grading the Performance of Students With Special Needs

Should students with special needs who receive *A*'s and *B*'s in special education classes graduate from high school with honors? The mother of a student with a learning disability raised this issue in Newport News, Virginia.

As described by Phillips (1998), the Newport News School District requires all honors graduates to maintain a cumulative 3.0 grade point average and to meet all state requirements for a high school diploma, including a passing score on the state literacy test. The district also uses a weighting procedure for calculating GPAs, which gives less weight for *A*'s and *B*'s in special education courses than for regular, honors, or Advanced Placement courses.

The student in question met neither local district GPA nor state diploma requirements and, therefore, was to receive a certificate of completion rather than a diploma. Although the student had qualified for the honor roll every year since fifth grade, her GPA was only 2.75 due to the lower weighting of her *A*'s and *B*'s in special education courses. Her mother asked the school board to modify its policy so that students with disabilities who are consistently named on the honor roll can qualify for graduation with honors. At issue was whether the Americans with Disabilities Act (ADA) requires the school board to change the standards for graduation with honors for students with disabilities.

According to Phillips (1998), the case raises several interesting questions:

- The "honors" designation is generally associated with high standards of achievement. But does "high standards" mean challenging content in the absolute sense of demonstrating specified knowledge and skills (e.g., algebra), or does it mean content that is challenging for that particular student?

- The use of the word "honor" appears to have different meaning for the honor roll than for graduation with honors. Although *A*'s and *B*'s in special education classes were discounted for honors graduation, they apparently were not weighted differentially when determining qualifications for the honor roll. If the mother and student did not understand this distinction, they could have reasonably assumed that maintaining honor roll status would result in graduation with honors.

- Should students with disabilities who receive *A*'s and *B*'s in lower level courses be eligible for the honor roll, or should the honor roll calculation be changed to use weighted grades so that students in special education classes do not qualify? Or should unweighted grades be used to calculate GPAs which are then used to determine who is on the honor roll and who will graduate with honors?

- Should students with disabilities who complete an Individualized Education Plan (IEP) that does not include all courses or assessments required for high school graduation receive a regular diploma or certification of completion? In other words, should state requirements for a high school diploma vary according to the status of the student as regular or special education?

According to Phillips (1998), the 1983 *Brookhart vs. Illinois State Board of Education* case provides some insight to these questions. In this case the court held that districts can deny diplomas to students with special needs who fail to meet academic requirements. However, it also held that parents must receive advance notice so that they might make a reasoned decision about whether their children should or should not take courses required for a diploma. While no absolute time frame was specified, the court did suggest that the complexity of making this decision within the IEP process might require more time than the notice given to regular education students.

## Recommendation

We believe that it is both reasonable and appropriate to provide some indication of students' learning progress in a reporting form, especially for students with disabilities. Procedures for judging the adequacy of these students' progress should be spelled out within the IEP and should include the type and quality of work to be completed, timelines for completion of the work, and clear guidelines for assessment and evaluation. Decisions about these procedures should be made prior to the beginning of instruction and should be clearly understood by everyone involved in the process, including the student, the parents, the regular classroom teacher, and the cooperating special education teacher.

As we noted, however, serious interpretation problems make it difficult to advocate learning progress as the sole criterion in determining grades for students with disabilities. Instead, we believe that a better approach is to supplement a learning progress grade with additional information about students' standing relative to the learning goals, standards, or expectations established for that grade level or course of study. One way to do this is to develop a learner "profile" that charts progress in relation to grade-level standards or learning expectations. Teachers, especially those who teach at the elementary level, consistently report that graphs documenting progress are far more comprehensible to students than are averages of scores or verbal descriptions in narrative reports (Gersten et al., 1996). Another approach would be to offer multiple grades, one for learning progress and another for the achievement of grade-level or course standards. A third approach would be to augment the class grade with a separate IEP evaluation report that would make special note of the progress made.

Each of these alternatives allows students' learning progress to be noted and appropriately recognized. More important, if we ensure that the information provided is clear and easily understood by students and their parents, the most serious interpretation problems mentioned earlier can be avoided.

## Making Specific Grading Adaptations

The fourth point of view regarding grading policies for students with disabilities in regular education classes is to make individualized adaptations in grading procedures. Grading adaptations are a relatively common practice among teachers, with as many as 50% indicating they make individualized adaptations when determining the grades of students with disabilities as well as regular education students (Bursuck et al., 1996). The adaptations that teachers consider most helpful include grading on improvement, basing a grade on meeting the objectives specified in an IEP, and assigning separate grades for product (achievement) and for process (effort and class behavior).

Most grading adaptations can be classified in the three broad categories illustrated in Table 7.1 (see Munk & Bursuck, 1998a, 1998b). The first category is changes in the criteria used to determine the grade. Some teachers, for example, vary the weights they assign to different activities or products considered in assigning grades. Others vary the curriculum expectations set for individual students based on their past achievement records or assessments of their current learning needs. A second category of adaptation involves the inclusion of supplemental information with the grade. This additional information might explain how the grade was derived or make special note of students' areas of improvement. The third category of adaptation includes changes in the types of grades used. This might entail moving from an overall summary grade to a checklist of skills, a standards-based reporting form, mastery grading, or even pass/fail reporting methods.

The grading adaptations that teachers use depend on school policies and on their judgment of the fairness and acceptability of specific practices. Because only about a third of all school districts have policies regarding grading procedures for students with disabilities, however, most teachers are left on their own in making these adaptation decisions (Polloway et al., 1994).

Students' perceptions of fairness also play a role in teachers' decisions about grading adaptations. But what complicates matters still further is the fact that students with disabilities and regular education students often differ

**Table 7.1**  Common Grading Adaptations for Students With Disabilities

| Adaptation | Example |
|---|---|
| **Change grading criteria** | |
| Vary grading weights assigned to different activities or products. | Increase credit for participation in classroom group activities and decrease credit for essay examinations. |
| Grade on improvement by assigning extra points. | Change a *C* to a *B* if the student's total points have increased significantly from the previous marking period. |
| Modify or individualize curriculum expectations. | Indicate in the IEP that the student will work on subtraction while the other students work on division. |
| Use contracts and modified course requirements for quality, quantity, and timelines. | State in the contract that student will receive a *B* for completing all assignments at 80% quantity, and timelines. accuracy, attending all classes, and completing one extra-credit report. |
| **Provide supplemental information** | |
| Add written comments to clarify details about the criteria used. | Write on the report card that the student's grade reflects performance on IEP objectives and not on the regular classroom curriculum. |
| Add information from student activity log. | Note that while the student's grade was the same this marking period, daily records show the student completed math assignments with less teacher assistance. |
| Add information about effort, progress, and achievement from portfolios or performance-based assignments. | State that the student's written language showed an increase in word variety, sentence length, and quality of ideas. |
| **Use other grading options** | |
| Use checklists of skills and show the number or percentage of objectives met. | Attach a checklist to the report card indicating that during the marking period, the student mastered addition facts, two-digit addition with regrouping, and counting change to one dollar. |
| Use pass/fail grades. | Students receives a "pass" for completing 80% of daily work with at least 70% accuracy, and attending 90% of class sessions. |

SOURCE: Adapted from Munk and Bursuck (1998a).

Table 7.2  Assessments of Grading Fairness

| Do I think it is fair for teachers to . . . | % Fair (No Disability) $n = 256$ | % Fair (Disability) $n = 14$ |
|---|---|---|
| 1. Give some students two grades for each subject (one for how hard they tried and one for how well they did). | 46 | 50 |
| 2. Give some students a higher report card grade when they do the best they can. | 44 | 50 |
| 3. Change how much certain things count toward the report card grades of some students (for example, making assignments worth more than tests). | 36 | 38 |
| 4. Grade some students on a pass/fail basis (without using number or letter grades). | 35 | 38 |
| 5. Pass some students no matter how poorly they do (as long as they try hard). | 24 | 46 |
| 6. Give some students a higher report card grade based on having to learn less material. | 19 | 29 |
| 7. Give some students a higher report card grade because they show improvement. | 14 | 64 |
| 8. Grade some students using a different grading scale (for example, 90-100 = $A$ rather than 93-100 = $A$). | 13 | 64 |
| 9. Give some students a passing report card grade no matter what. | 5 | 13 |

SOURCE: Adapted from Bursuck, Munk, and Olson (1999).

in what they consider fair. Table 7.2 shows the results of a survey study of high school students' perceptions of various grading adaptations and reveals some of the most striking differences. Table 7.3 displays the same students' perceptions of different strategies used to calculate students' GPA (Bursuck et al., 1999).

As can be seen in these figures, the majority of students without disabilities rate all grading adaptations as unfair. Although these students generally favor assessment adaptations involving extra help, extra time, or changes in student response mode (e.g., oral versus written homework or tests) (Polloway, Bursuck, Jayanthi, Epstein, & Nelson, 1996), the majority view grading adaptations as helping undeserving students get higher grades. Many also believe that making such adaptations does not prepare these students for the real world (Vaughn, Schumm, Klingner, & Saumell, 1995).

Table 7.3  Assessments of GPA Calculation Fairness

| Do I think it is fair for schools to . . . | % Fair (No Disability) $n = 254$ | %Fair (Disability) $n = 14$ |
|---|---|---|
| 1. Have grades count the same toward students' GPAs, no matter what the level of the class taken. (For example, a grade of A would be worth the same whether it was received in an Advanced Placement English, regular English, or special education English class.) | 35 | 71 |
| 2. Make grades in difficult classes count more toward students' GPAs. (For example, a grade of A in an Advanced Placement English class would be worth more than an A in a regular English class or special education English class.) | 70 | 47 |

SOURCE: Adapted from Bursuck, Munk, and Olson (1999).

Students with disabilities, on the other hand, differ significantly in their perceptions of two particular adaptations. They were much more likely to rate as fair (1) giving some students a higher report card grade for showing improvement, and (2) grading some students using a different scale. When asked about procedures for calculating students' GPAs, those with disabilities generally opposed the idea of weighted grades and were more likely to rate as fair counting all courses the same, regardless of difficulty (Bursuck et al., 1999). These findings reinforce the results from other studies, which show that grading adaptations represent an area of unique sensitivity for all students (Gersten et al., 1996).

## Recommendation

Making specific grading adaptations is both reasonable and appropriate in assigning grades to the achievement and performance of students with disabilities. We believe, however, that three essential conditions must be met in making such adaptations. First, input from the regular classroom teacher, the student, the parents, and the cooperating special education teacher should be considered in determining the adaptations made. Including input from all stakeholders in this process not only helps clarify grading procedures, it also improves the likelihood that the decisions will be perceived as fair (Cohen, 1983). Second, grading adaptations should be formalized and consistent. In other words, the procedures for making grading adaptations should be specifically described in students' IEPs and clearly communicated to everyone involved in the process prior to the beginning of instruction. This helps avoid interpretation problems and prevents unnecessary disappointments.

The third essential condition is that the grading adaptations should be applied fairly and conscientiously. This means that in cases where special circumstances exist, teachers may find it necessary to make adaptations in determining the grades of regular education students as well. Suppose, for example, that a particular student performs poorly on formal, objective tests because of inordinate test anxiety but does excellently on other types of performance tasks. Applying established grading procedures in this case might not yield a grade that correctly describes this student's level of knowledge and skill. Giving more weight to the performance tasks, on the other hand, allows the teacher to assign a grade that represents a much more valid reflection of what the student has learned.

Teachers must have the flexibility to make these kinds of grading adaptations. They also must have the skills needed to determine when such adaptations are appropriate. Most important, they must ensure that the adaptations they make are carefully specified and consistently applied. Adaptations that tend to draw the harshest criticism are those that are informal, capricious, or inconsistently applied (Munk & Bursuck, 1998a).

The grading adaptation considered fairest by the largest percentage of teachers and students, both with and without disabilities, is to give multiple grades—that is, to offer separate grades for product (achievement), process (effort and behavior), and progress (improvement). Multiple grades based on these different criteria allow teachers to make note of students' special accomplishments, even if their level of achievement or performance is not up to grade-level standards or expectations. Multiple grades also more accurately represent students' learning experiences in regular classrooms and better reflect how inclusion is working. Checklists of skills and standards-based reporting formats represent another form of multiple grades that can be highly effective in such instances.

When the grading format does not permit multiple grades, the most acceptable adaptation is to base the grades of students with disabilities on accomplishment of the learning goals set forth in the IEP. Typically this requires preparation of a supplemental report that contains descriptive information illustrating students' accomplishments and identifying areas where improvement is needed. As we mentioned earlier, procedures for judging the adequacy of students' accomplishments should be spelled out within the IEP and should include the type of work and quality of work to be completed, timelines for completion of that work, and clear guidelines for assessment and evaluation. These decisions should be made prior to the beginning of instruction and should be clearly understood by everyone involved in the process. Most important, school policies should make clear the implications of these decisions for honor roll status, honor society membership, class rank calculations, and graduation requirements in order to avoid misunderstandings and controversies similar to those we described earlier.

---

### Essential Conditions for Making Grading Adaptations

1. Input from the regular classroom teacher, the student, the parents, and the cooperating special education teacher should be considered in determining the adaptations made.

2. Grading adaptations should be formalized and consistent.

3. Grading adaptations should be applied fairly and conscientiously.

---

## Students Who Are English Language Learners (ELLs)

The second group of students with special needs who present unique grading challenges is English Language Learners (ELLs). Increasing numbers of students enter schools today with inadequate or nonexistent English language skills, principally because they come from homes where English is not the primary language. To help these students develop the English language skills they need, many are enrolled in English as a Second Language (ESL), English Language Learner (ELL), or bilingual educational programs.

The structure and format of these programs vary widely. Some place students in self-contained classrooms where they are taught using a combination of English and their native language. Others are similar to inclusion programs in which ELL students spend only a portion of the school day in a special class and most of their time in regular education classrooms. Regardless of their structure, however, the purpose of these programs is the same. All are designed to improve students' listening, speaking, reading, and writing skills in English so that they can communicate more effectively, do better in all school subjects, and function more efficiently in a predominately English language society.

The language difficulties encountered by ELL students make it hard to get an accurate picture of their learning progress. Recent research indicates, for example, that many tests and assessments underestimate ELL students' knowledge and skills (August & Hakuta, 1997; Garcia, 1991; LaCelle-Peterson & Rivera, 1994). In response, educators have begun using various forms of accommodation in order to obtain more accurate assessment evidence. Some of the most frequent accommodations are (1) modifying (simplifying) the English language used in assessment questions, (2) including a glossary that explains potentially unfamiliar or difficult words, and (3) providing extra time to complete the assessment (Abedi, 1999). While all of these accommodations help improve the performance of both ELL and non-ELL students, the only one shown to narrow the score difference between ELL and non-ELL students is modifying or simplifying the English language included in assessment items (Abedi, Lord, & Hofstetter, 1998).

The grading policies that teachers use for ELL students also vary widely. Some teachers allow assessment accommodations for ELL students but then apply the same grading standards to the work of all their students. Others use individual grading adaptations, the most common of which is to provide supplemental information with the grade to clarify its meaning, note specific improvements, and identify areas where additional work is needed. The challenge that remains, however, is how to communicate this information effectively to students, to their parents, and other interested adults who also may have limited English language skills.

To meet this communication challenge, more and more school districts are developing translations of their reporting forms. An example of one such form, and its Spanish translation, developed by educators from the Mesa Unified School District in Mesa, Arizona, are illustrated in Figure 7.1.

Reporting form translations such as this offer parents information they can understand about their child's achievement and performance in school. It also encourages a more direct line of communication between parents and teachers. Since the marks recorded on the English and Spanish versions of the reporting form are the same, the use of the translated version requires no extra work for teachers. Parents can be given the choice as to whether they would like to receive the English form, the Spanish form, or both.

### Recommendation

Specific adaptations in grading procedures may not be necessary for students who are English Language Learners (ELLs). Nevertheless, it is essential that (1) grades reflecting their achievement and level of performance be based on accurate and reliable evidence and (2) that information regarding teachers' appraisals of student' achievement and performance be clearly communicated. For this reason, accommodations are likely to be required in both assessment procedures and reporting devices.

We recommend, therefore, that schools and school districts develop policies that outline specific guidelines for teachers to use in making these necessary adaptations. Such policies should consider input from regular classroom teachers, ELL or ESL consulting teachers, ELL students, and their parents. The guidelines should describe a menu of acceptable adaptations, a process for selecting adaptations, and specific procedures for documenting the use of those adaptations. They also should delineate adaptations that are inappropriate and should never be used. An example might be promoting students to the next grade no matter what they do or accomplish. And as we emphasized

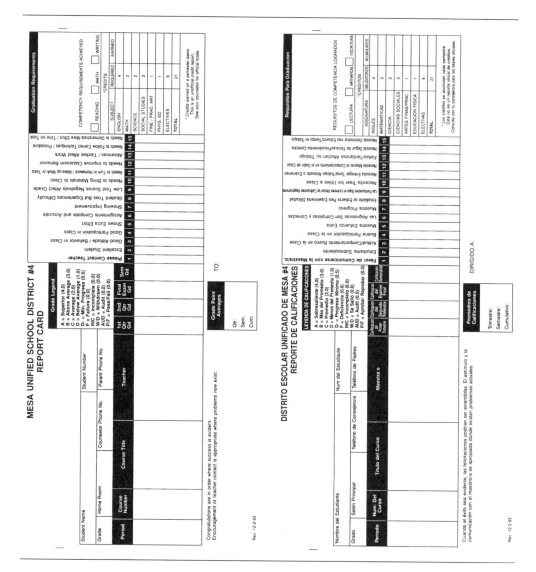

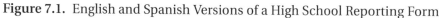

**Figure 7.1.** English and Spanish Versions of a High School Reporting Form

SOURCE: Report card of Mesa Public Schools (Mesa, AZ). Used by permission.
NOTE: For full reproduction of these forms, please see Resource A.

in the case of students with disabilities, these guidelines should discourage informal or inconsistent uses of adaptations.

We further recommend that these policies be clearly described in a school or school district handbook so that administrators, teachers, parents, and students have a resource to which they can refer should questions about adaptations arise. Policies should also be explained to teachers through formal professional development sessions and informally through individual meetings when necessary. Teachers should explain the policies to their students when they discuss their grading and reporting procedures. Although information about specific students who receive adaptations should be kept confidential, teachers should expect that other students will notice when adaptations are used and be prepared to explain their rationale.

Finally, we recommend that teachers monitor the progress of students who receive adaptations to determine whether the chosen adaptations are effective. By regularly reviewing their adaptation strategies, teachers can better individualize the adaptation process and begin to move students toward more complete involvement in regular classroom instruction and assessment procedures.

## Students Considered Gifted or Talented

The third group of students with special needs includes those students with exceptional skills or abilities who may be considered "gifted" or "talented." A grade of *A* or *Exceptional* on a standards-based reporting form may tell very little about what new knowledge these students have gained or what new skills they've acquired. Many gifted students master the learning goals or standards for a particular grade level or course of study one to three years prior to entering that grade or course (Peckron, 1996). Hence the high mark or grade they receive may reflect past achievements more than their current learning progress.

Like students with disabilities, gifted and talented students have unique learning needs that require special accommodations. In fact, many states currently mandate the development of an IEP for gifted students. Such a program typically specifies the curricular needs of the student, justifies placement in special classes based on those needs, and ensures special services appropriate to the student's unique learning characteristics. Many IEPs also specify alternative procedures for reporting learning progress (Dettmer, 1994).

In many schools and school districts, the educational needs of gifted and talented students are addressed through a three-step process. First, procedures are established that allow these students to show what they know and can do in reference to the curriculum. Because some gifted students may be able to demonstrate their mastery of grade-level standards before instruction actually begins, these assessment procedures let students verify the level of proficiency they've already attained. Second, curriculum alternatives are planned that allow gifted students to proceed to more advanced levels of learning. These alternatives might involve exploring topics in greater depth, developing special projects, or perhaps becoming involved in programs designed to accelerate their learning progress. Finally, the alternatives are implemented either as enrichment experiences within the regular classroom or as activities in specially assigned classes. In some cases, these alternatives are formalized through the development of independent study agreements or learning contracts (Peckron, 1996).

---

**Steps to Addressing the Needs of Gifted and Talented Students**

1. Establish procedures that allow gifted and talented students to demonstrate what they know and can do in reference to the curriculum.

2. Plan curriculum alternatives that permit these students to proceed to more advanced levels of learning.

3. Implement these alternatives as enrichment experiences within the regular classroom or as activities in specially assigned classes.

---

Because few reporting forms are designed to record information about gifted and talented students' achievement or level of performance with regard to these curriculum alternatives, a supplemental reporting form is typically required. An excellent example of one such form is included in Peckron (1996, p. 62). In most cases, this supplemental form accompanies the regular reporting form and offers evaluative information specific to an individual student's alternative program. Generally, it outlines the specific learning goals of the program and includes the marks or grades that students attain in reference to those goals. Most supplemental forms also have a narrative section that describes students' learning progress, special strengths, and areas where improvement or refinement might be needed. A portfolio containing samples of students' work is usually included to further illustrate students' accomplishments.

The principal advantage of a supplemental reporting form is that it provides more accurate and more detailed information on gifted and talented students' achievement and performance. But equally important, it allows teachers to set learning goals and expectations for these students that are more appropriate for their level of skill and ability (Johnsen, 1995). Furthermore, a supplemental report communicates vital information to parents to show that the school is providing for the special needs of their child.

## Recommendation

Parents of gifted and talented students generally believe that traditional grades and reporting forms do not provide an accurate description of what their child has learned or can do. Most parents also want teachers to recognize the special talents and abilities of their child, even when they are not noted on traditional reporting forms (Peckron, 1996). A supplemental report provides a way for teachers to offer parents this kind of information.

We recommend, therefore, that efforts be made to develop a supplemental reporting form to document teachers' appraisals of the achievement and performance of gifted and talented students. Such a form should accompany the traditional reporting form and should be based on specific learning goals. In most cases, however, these goals will involve more complex tasks and higher level skills than might be included in regular grade-level goals or standards. In addition, the students themselves often have input into the specification of these goals and the evaluation procedures.

We recognize, of course, that preparation of a supplemental reporting form for gifted and talented students requires additional work on the part of teachers. Not only must they coordinate the development of the specific learning goals on which the form is based, they also must perform the additional evaluation tasks involved in providing these students with feedback on their learning progress and coordinate the collection of students' work samples. Collaborative efforts involving district coordinators, specialists in gifted education, support personnel, and parents can help significantly reduce this workload, however, and generally enhance the quality of the products developed.

## Summary

Adaptations in grading and reporting policies and practices for students with special needs remain a complicated area. Although we continue to learn about grading adaptations as a way to meet the needs of special and general education students, important questions remain. Selecting appropriate adaptations would be a lot easier, for example, if we knew that certain ones are clearly superior. Furthermore, implementation efforts could be much more focused if we knew more specifically which adaptations teachers and students perceive to be fairer.

At this point, we do know that broad involvement in policy development and clear specification of implementation guidelines helps ensure that all stakeholders will consider the selected adaptations to be both appropriate and fair. By maintaining an open, honest, and flexible approach to adaptations in grading and reporting, we are likely to come up with policies and practices that serve well the diverse needs of the students, parents, and educators.

# CHAPTER 8

# Special Problems in Grading and Reporting

In the past few chapters we focused on many practical issues regarding grading and reporting. We considered the advantages and shortcomings of various grading methods and explored the complex issues involved in grading students with special needs. In this chapter we take practicality to another level by addressing some of the most troublesome problems educators face in developing grading and reporting policies and practices. Specifically, we consider technology and grading, weighted grades, grade inflation, and commonly employed grading practices that have potentially harmful effects on students.

Some educators may find our discussion of these issues a bit disturbing. Others might even be offended. Our purpose in bringing these issues to light, however, is not to offend. Rather, we want to help educators at all levels to view these issues from new perspectives and reflect on them with new knowledge. As we described earlier, educators persist in the use of many grading and reporting practices simply because they experienced these practices as students and never considered or learned about other alternatives. To grow as a profession and to do the best we can for our students, we must view these practices more thoughtfully and more critically. We also must use the knowledge base we have on grading and reporting to build better and more effective reporting systems.

## Technology and Grading

Throughout earlier chapters we've made reference to the use of technology in grading and reporting student learning. Computerized grading programs present educators with a wide range of grading and record-keeping options, and several have become extremely popular in recent years. Some of these programs simply help teachers keep more detailed records on students' learning progress (Eastwood, 1996). Others are more intricate and allow teachers to present evidence on students' achievement and performance in a variety of different formats, including computer displays, video report cards, and digital portfolios. Still other programs actually perform grading tasks. The simplest of these score, mark, and analyze assessments composed of true/false, matching, and multiple-choice items. In recent years, however, exciting advances have been made in the use of computers to evaluate and grade students' essays, compositions, and other writing samples (Page & Petersen, 1995; Wresch, 1993).

## Video Report Cards and Digital Portfolios

One of the most widely used alternative formats for communicating information about students' achievement and performance is the video report card. Since video technology first emerged, educators at many levels have recognized its potential as a medium for communicating with parents and others (Brown, 1972). Video recordings of individual students' performances present a dynamic record of what they have learned. More importantly, recording students' performance at several times during the school year yields a clear and authentic record of learning progress (Brewer & Kallick, 1996).

On the elementary level, for instance, many teachers record students reading orally, presenting a mathematics problem, discussing a class project, or performing a physical exercise at the beginning of the marking period and again at the end. This allows students, their parents, and others to see first-hand what improvements have been made (Greenwood, 1995). Similarly at the secondary level, video recordings of students' oral presentations, problem explanations, or musical performances provide a permanent record that can be reviewed and reexamined as a tool for further learning (Berg & Smith, 1996).

Some schools and school districts have formalized the video recording process by having students develop video portfolios of their work. Others with more advanced technology have developed digital portfolios that include a broad array of work samples and exhibits of students' accomplishments. Although video report cards and digital portfolios may not soon replace more standard types of reporting forms, they are a highly effective supplement to such forms and greatly enhance the meaningfulness of the information included in these and other reporting forms.

## Electronic Gradebooks

Computerized or electronic "gradebooks" also have become increasingly popular in recent years. These programs provide teachers with an organizing framework that simplifies their record-keeping tasks (Huber, 1997). The spreadsheet formats and database management systems included in these programs make it easy to enter and precisely tally numerical information (Vockell & Fiore, 1993). They are particularly well suited to the point-based grading systems of middle and high school teachers who often record numerical data on the performance of 100 or more students each week (Feldman et al., 1996).

For all their advantages, however, electronic gradebooks also have their shortcomings. Perhaps the most serious is that many educators believe the mathematical precision of computerized grading programs yields greater objectivity in grading. Others believe this increased precision enhances fairness in the grading process. Unfortunately, neither of these beliefs is true.

Computerized grading programs and electronic gradebooks yield neither greater objectivity nor enhanced fairness. At best, they offer teachers a tool for manipulating data. Although these programs may make record keeping easier, they do not lessen the challenge involved in assigning grades that accurately and fairly reflect students' achievement and level of performance.

Consider, for example, the data in Table 8.1. The scores on the left reflect the performance of seven students over five instructional units. The bold-face scores on the right side of the table represent summary scores for these students calculated by three different tallying methods. The first method is the simple arithmetic average of the unit scores, with all units receiving equal weight. The second is the median or middle score from the five units (Wright, 1994). The third method is the arithmetic average, deleting the lowest unit score in the group. This method is based on the assumption that no one, including students, performs at a peak level all the time (Canady & Hotchkiss, 1989). These are the three methods most frequently used by teachers and most commonly employed in electronic gradebooks and other computerized grading programs.

Consider, too, the following explanations for these score patterns:

*Student 1* struggled in the early part of the marking period but continued to work hard, improved in each unit, and performed excellently in Unit 5.

*Student 2* began with excellent performance in Unit 1 but then lost motivation, declined steadily during the marking period, and received a failing mark for Unit 5.

*Student 3* performed steadily throughout the marking period, receiving three *B*'s and two *C*'s, all near the *B–C* cutoff.

*Student 4* began the marking period poorly, failing the first two units, but with newfound interest performed excellently in Units 3, 4, and 5.

Table 8.1  Summary Grades Tallied by Three Different Methods

| Student | Unit 1 | Unit 2 | Unit 3 | Unit 4 | Unit 5 | Average Score | Grade | Median Score | Grade | Deleting Lowest | Grade |
|---|---|---|---|---|---|---|---|---|---|---|---|
| 1 | 59 | 69 | 79 | 89 | 99 | 79 | C | 79 | C | 84 | B |
| 2 | 99 | 89 | 79 | 69 | 59 | 79 | C | 79 | C | 84 | B |
| 3 | 77 | 80 | 80 | 78 | 80 | 79 | C | 80 | B | 79.5 | C |
| 4 | 49 | 49 | 98 | 99 | 100 | 79 | C | 98 | A | 86.5 | B |
| 5 | 100 | 99 | 98 | 49 | 49 | 79 | C | 98 | A | 86.5 | B |
| 6 | 0 | 98 | 98 | 99 | 100 | 79 | C | 98 | A | 98.8 | A |
| 7 | 100 | 99 | 98 | 98 | 0 | 79 | C | 98 | A | 98.8 | A |

**Grading standards:**

90% – 100% = A
80% –  89% = B
70% –  79% = C
60% –  69% = D
    –  59% = F

*Student 5* began the marking period excellently but then lost interest and failed the last two units.

*Student 6* skipped school (unexcused absence) during the first unit but performed excellently in every other unit.

*Student 7* performed excellently in the first four units, but was caught cheating on the assessment for Unit 5, resulting in a score of zero for that unit.

As can be seen, while all three of these tallying methods are mathematically precise, each one yields a very different pattern of grades for these 7 students. If the arithmetic average is used (Method 1), all 7 students would receive the same grade of *C*. If the median is used (Method 2), there would be only two *C*'s, one *B*, and four *A*'s. And if an arithmetic average is calculated deleting the lowest score (Method 3), there would be only one *C*, four *B*'s, and two *A*'s. Note, too, that the one student who would receive a grade of *C* using Method 3 had unit grades consisting of just two *C*'s and three *B*'s. More important, no student would receive the same grade across all three methods. In fact, two students (4 and 5) could receive a grade of *A*, *B*, or *C*, depending on the tallying method employed!

The teacher responsible for assigning grades to the performance of these seven students has to answer a number of difficult questions. For example, which of these three methods is the fairest? Which method provides the most accurate summary of each student's achievement and level of performance? Do all seven students deserve the same grade, as the arithmetic average (Method 1) indicates, or are there defensible reasons to justify different grades for certain students? And if there are reasons to justify different grades, can these reasons be clearly specified? Can they be fairly and equitably applied to the performance of all students? Can these reasons be clearly communicated to students before instruction begins? Would it be fair to apply them if they were not?

The nature of the assessment information from which these scores are derived could make matters even more tangled. Might it make a difference, for example, if we knew the content of each unit assessment was cumulative? In other words, the assessment for Unit 2 contained material from Units 1 and 2, and the Unit 5 assessment included material from all five previous units. And if it did, would this make these grading decisions any easier for teachers, or would it further complicate summary calculations?

What should be evident in this example is that the use of computerized grading programs will not solve these complex grading problems. Although such programs can simplify numerical record keeping, the mathematical precision they offer doesn't make the grading process any more objective or any fairer. Calculating a summary score to the one hundred thousandth decimal point does not yield a more accurate depiction of students' achievement and level of performance. Each teacher still must decide what information goes into the calculation, what weight will be attached to each source of information, and what method will be used to tally and summarize that information.

Above all, we have to recognize that teachers' professional judgment will always be an essential part of the grading process. Teachers at all levels of education must make carefully reasoned decisions about the purpose of the grade, the components that will be included in determining the grade, how those components will be combined and summarized, and what format will be used in reporting those summaries. While computerized grading programs and electronic gradebooks are useful tools that help teachers record and mathematically tally numerical data, they do not relieve teachers of the professional responsibilities involved making these crucial decisions. In the end, teachers must still decide what grade offers the most accurate and fairest description of each student's achievement and level of performance over a particular period of time.

## Recommendation

Technology presents educators with innumerable options when it comes to communicating information about students' achievement and performance. Video report cards and digital portfolios offer authentic information to parents and others about what students know and are able to do. Computerized grading programs and electronic gradebooks greatly simplify record-keeping tasks by allowing teachers to gather increased amounts of evidence and then tally that evidence in highly efficient ways. These programs are particularly helpful when that evidence is numerical. For these reasons, we encourage educators at all levels to make thoughtful use of these various forms of technology.

At the same time, however, technology does not alleviate the need for sound and intelligent professional judgment in the grading process. While technology makes record keeping more efficient and numerical tallying easier, it doesn't alleviate teachers' professional responsibility to carefully weigh the various aspects of that evidence in determining the mark or grade that best summarizes students' achievement or performance. Computers can score certain kinds of assessments and do mathematical operations with great precision. They cannot, however, determine fair and appropriate grades.

The process of grading will always involve one group of human beings (teachers) making judgments about the achievement and performance of another group of human beings (students). Technology makes it easier to collect relevant evidence for making those judgments and permits results to be communicated in a variety of meaningful formats. Nevertheless, it does not lessen the obligation of educators to ensure that the marks or grades they assign are accurate, honest, and fair summaries of the quality of students' performance.

# Weighted Grades

A common practice in many high schools today is to assign greater weight or credit to the grades earned in courses considered exceptionally challenging than is assigned to regular or general courses (Mitchell, 1994). Honors courses and those designed to prepare students for Advanced Placement (AP) examinations, for example, might be given a weight of five credits while regular or general courses would have a weight of four credits. Other schools simply adjust grading scales so that a *B* in an honors or AP course is considered equivalent to an *A* in a regular or general course. Some schools make further adjustments by assigning less weight or credit to lower level courses or remedial courses.

The use of weighted grades is typically justified on the grounds of fairness. They are seen as a way to reward or compensate those students who enroll in more challenging courses. Many educators also believe that weighted grades are an enticement to bright students who might choose a less rigorous program of studies unless some form of special recompense or recognition is offered.

Before they choose to use weighted grades, however, educators should address two important questions: "What is their true purpose?" and "How will they be used?" In most schools today, weighted grades are used to differentiate students' performance for the purpose of selection. In determining who will be named on the honor roll, for instance, weighted grades allow students enrolled in challenging courses with lower grades to be eligible, while ensuring the exclusion of students with high grades in only remedial courses. Weighted grades are also a major factor in many high schools when it comes to naming the valedictorian. Apart from these selection and differentiation functions, however, weighted grades have little utility. We know of no evidence that shows they serve to motivate students to enroll in more challenging courses or dissuade students from enrolling in lower level or remedial courses (see Gilman & Swan, 1989).

## *Recommendation*

As we stressed earlier, students who attain a high level of achievement or performance deserve special recognition. Likewise, students should be encouraged to engage in challenging academic programs, and those who do well should be appropriately distinguished. Honor roll membership and other forms of academic recognition (letters, special commendations, etc.) serve this purpose well. But as we described in Chapter 7, educators need to be clear about the criteria used in conferring such "honors" designation. Specifically, they must decide if the high standards associated with "honors" mean challenging in the absolute sense of specific knowledge and skills or simply challenging for that particular student. If the former, then weighted grades allow more students in challenging courses to be recognized while making students with disabilities who receive *A*'s and *B*'s in lower level courses ineligible. If the latter, then weighted grades are irrelevant and unnecessary. In either case, however, it is an issue of differentiation and selection. It is not an academic issue.

The use of weighted grades in selecting a valedictorian is another matter altogether. Recall that in Chapter 3 we discussed the dilemmas caused by this process when selection is restricted to a single student. Our recommendation there was to name multiple valedictorians or to follow a process similar to that used in colleges and universities where graduates are distinguished as *magna cum laude* and *summa cum laude*. This provides special recognition for those students who have distinguished themselves academically while eliminating the detrimental effects that stem from the competition among students for that singular distinction.

Keep in mind, too, our discussion of how colleges and universities today look beyond class rank and GPA to the rigor of students' academic programs and the courses they have taken when making decisions about admission and scholarship awards (see Adelman, 1999). While weighted grades help college officials distinguish honors or AP courses in students' transcripts (Lockhart, 1990; Talley & Mohr, 1991), other means of identification can be used. For example, such courses can be specially marked, numbered differently, or highlighted in the transcript. Aside from this labeling function, weighted grades have little relevance.

In essence, the issue of weighted grades comes down to the basic purpose of grading and reporting. If the purpose is to communicate teachers' judgments about students' achievement and performance to parents, to the students themselves, or to others, then it is difficult to justify the use of weighted grades. On the other hand, if the purpose of grading is to select, identify, or group students for certain educational paths, programs, or honors, then weighted grades take on considerable significance. Remember, however, that no single grading method or reporting tool can serve both these purposes well. Our recommendation, therefore, is that educators first address the issue of purpose. Once decisions about purpose are made, questions about weighted grades will be much easier to address and resolve.

# Grade Inflation

Another issue that causes great debate among educators is grade inflation. Many argue that more students today receive high grades not because of excellence in achievement or performance but because of new grading schemes and teachers' concerns about students' self-esteem. According to these critics, teachers have relaxed their standards and, as a result, grades have become meaningless and have no validity (Beaver, 1997). To counter this problem, teachers are sometimes encouraged to "hold down" grades and restrict the number of high grades they assign (Agnew, 1993). Those opposed to such measures are labeled by critics as apathetic to the problem of grade inflation (Hills, 1991) and unwilling to take the steps necessary to address this problem (Gose, 1997; Zirkel, 1995).

Careful research on the issue of grade inflation shows, however, that the problem may be more imagined than real. At the college level, for example, studies show that although students' GPAs have generally risen over the past two decades, this increase is largely attributable to changes in the characteristics of entering students (Kwon & Kendig, 1997). Especially at selective colleges and universities, entering students today are older and more talented than those who entered a decade ago. An investigation at Brigham Young University, for instance, found that the average American College Testing (ACT) score of entering freshmen rose from the 70th percentile nationally in 1975 to the 90th percentile nationally in 1994. In essence, the lower third of the student body that existed 20 years before has disappeared (Olsen, 1997). Under such conditions, wouldn't an increase in students' GPAs be expected? When disparities in rising GPAs across colleges were investigated at Brigham Young University, researchers discovered that colleges that based grades on fixed performance standards were awarding higher grades than colleges that graded "on the curve." Again, should anyone be surprised by this result?

Bracey (1998) investigated the issue of grade inflation at the high school level using data from the 1997 edition of the U.S. Department of Education's *Condition of Education* report. This report compared students' high school GPAs with their scores on the Scholastic Aptitude Test (SAT). If grade inflation were occurring, then we would expect, over time, that the SAT scores of students with the top GPA would decline. In other words, if teachers are really assigning *A*'s to undeserving students, then the average SAT scores of *A* students should go down. On the other hand, if the assigned grades were justified, we would expect SAT scores to rise. The data that Bracey (1998) offered are shown in Table 8.2.

Notice that the scores in math rise for all but the lowest 5th, and they rise the most for the top two groups: the first 10th and second 10th. This suggests that the top 20% of students are accomplishing more during their high school careers. The verbal scores are steady, except for the lowest 5th, which also show a small decline.

Equally impressive are the differences between score groups. In 1995, those in the top 10% of their class showed a 65- to 75-point advantage over those in the second 10%. If teachers were indiscriminately awarding high grades, differences of this size would not be expected. The only place where there is not much difference is between the bottom groups: the fourth 5th and fifth 5th. This is precisely the opposite of what would be expected if teachers were giving more high grades than they should.

**Table 8.2** Scholastic Aptitude Test Scores for Students in Different Grade Point Average Groups

| GPA Standing | SAT Verbal | | SAT Math | |
|---|---|---|---|---|
| | 1977 | 1995 | 1977 | 1995 |
| Top 10th | 518 | 518 | 574 | 594 |
| Second 10th | 452 | 452 | 499 | 518 |
| Second 5th | 415 | 414 | 453 | 467 |
| Third 5th | 372 | 375 | 401 | 413 |
| Fourth 5th | 347 | 349 | 374 | 379 |
| Fifth 5th | 339 | 334 | 364 | 362 |

SOURCE: Bracey (1998).

Bracey points out that SAT scores are never a particularly good measure of educational trends because students who take the SAT are self-selected and the size and demographics of this group of students change over time. Still, these data offer no support for the idea that grade inflation is prevalent in high schools or that students' high grades are undeserved.

*Recommendation*

We believe the problem of grade inflation is not simply that more students are receiving high grades. Rather, the problem rests in the meaning of the grades assigned. When grades reflect teachers' judgments of students' achievement and performance in reference to clearly articulated learning goals or standards, the meaning of those grades is clear. When challenged on the grades they assign or accused of grade inflation, teachers only need point to the standards or goals used in determining the grades. So long as those standards are sufficiently rigorous and appropriate for that grade level or course, the assigned marks or grades can be easily defended. The best way to fight grade inflation, therefore, is not to assign fewer high grades but to push for clearer standards.

We would add, however, that developing more stringent guidelines for grading is not the same as raising learning standards (see Agnew, 1995). Many popular assumptions about how to address the question of standards (raising cut-scores, weighting grades, freeing teachers from external pressure, etc.) emphasize grades rather than standards (Basinger, 1997). In essence, they focus on the yardstick rather than on what it measures. Once learning goals and standards are clearly defined, however, the problem of grading inflation pretty much disappears.

### Grade Inflation Is Not the Real Issue

Grade inflation deeply concerns many university officials today and leads to many heated debates. Unfortunately, most of these debates focus on the wrong issues and, as a result, the solutions proposed are misguided. The problem with grade inflation isn't simply that more students are receiving high grades. Rather, it is that we're not sure what those grades mean.

The question that needs to be addressed in these debates is "What is the purpose of grading?" If, as some professors believe, the purpose of grading is to discriminate among students, then we must maximize the differences between students in terms of their performance. Since it's difficult to distinguish among students if many do well, we need to make sure the differences in their performance are as large as possible.

Of course, nothing maximizes those differences better than poor teaching. When students are taught poorly, only those who are able to teach themselves learn well and receive high marks. The majority of students who need the help and assistance of their professors learn very little and receive the low marks.

Maximizing differences among students is typically accompanied by "grading on the curve." This means that students are graded according to their relative standing among classmates. Grading on the curve makes it easy to adjust for grade differences between departments or classes by simply requiring that only a small percentage of students, say the top 20%, receive the highest grade.

But when students are graded on the curve, a high mark doesn't represent excellent performance, as some might think. It means only that the performance was somewhat better than that of others in the class, all of whom might have performed miserably.

Grading on the curve also makes learning highly competitive. Students must compete among themselves for the few scarce rewards (high grades) distributed by the professor. Under these conditions, students avoid helping each other because doing so is detrimental to their chances for success. Getting a high grade doesn't mean performing excellently. It means doing better than your classmates.

On the other hand, if the purpose of grading is to reflect how well students have learned, then we must follow different procedures. First, we must clarify what we want students to learn and be able to do. Second, we must identify clear criteria or standards by which their learning will be judged. That is, we must decide in advance what evidence best represents what students have learned.

Teaching then becomes an organized and purposeful effort to help all students meet those standards. The goal is to develop talent, not simply to identify and select it.

Grades that reflect well-defined learning standards have direct meaning. They describe what students have accomplished and the skills they've acquired. Grades based on learning standards also bring new significance to discussions of differences in grade distributions across departments and classes.

Students' grades in some professors' classes might be higher because the standards are less rigorous. A comparison of related learning criteria would address this issue. It also might be, however, that some professors are simply better than others at helping their students attain rigorous and challenging learning standards. Such evidence would be invaluable in efforts to improve instructional quality.

The problem is that defining clear learning standards and deciding what evidence best reflects those standards is hard work. It takes lots of time, clear thinking, and dedicated effort. Professors don't always agree on what standards are appropriate or what evidence should be used to verify students' attainment of those standards. But isn't this precisely the kind of debate that should be going on in colleges and universities?

Until we precisely identify what students are expected to learn, articulate the criteria by which their learning will be judged, and clearly communicate these criteria to students, grading will remain an arbitrary and highly subjective process that victimizes more students than it helps.

SOURCE: Adapted from an editorial by Guskey (1999c).

## Questionable Grading Practices

Some grading practices are clearly matters of opinion. Despite the heated arguments they sometimes provoke, no strong evidence either confirms their value or verifies their harm. An example is the relative importance of product, process, and progress grading criteria. For other practices, however, important evidence demonstrates their detrimental effects. As we indicated earlier, educators tend to use these practices simply because "it was done to them." Seldom have they thought seriously about such practices, examined their impact, or weighed other options.

Due to their potentially harmful effects, it's imperative that we consider these practices openly and honestly in light of current evidence. We also need to consider other, more positive alternatives. Three practices in particular that deserve special attention are (1) averaging scores to determine a grade, (2) the use of zeros, and (3) taking credit away from students or lowering their grade because of behavioral infractions.

## Averaging Scores to Determine a Grade

If a mark or grade is to provide an accurate description of what students have learned, then the practice of averaging falls far short. For example, students often are heard to say "I have to get a *B* on the final exam in order to pass this course." But does such a statement really make sense, or does it more accurately illustrate the inappropriateness of averaging? If a final examination or summative performance truly represents a comprehensive assessment of what students have learned, should a *B* level of performance translate to a *D* for the course grade? If the purpose of grading and reporting is to provide an accurate description of what students have learned, then averaging scores from past assessments with measures of current performance must be considered inappropriate.

Learning is a progressive and incremental process. Recognizing this, most teachers agree that students should have many opportunities to demonstrate their command of the subject. But should all those learning trials be considered in determining the grade? If at any time in the instructional sequence students demonstrate that they have learned the concepts well and mastered the intended learning goals, does that not make all previous information on their learning of those concepts and goals inadequate and invalid? Why then should such information be "averaged in" when determining students' grades?

Any single measure of learning surely can be unreliable. Consequently, most researchers recommend using several indicators in determining students' marks or grades—and most teachers concur (Natriello, 1987). Nevertheless, the key question is "What information provides the most accurate depiction of students' learning at this time?" In nearly all cases, the answer is "the most current information." If students demonstrate that past assessment information no longer accurately reflects their learning, that information must be discarded and replaced by the new information. Continuing to rely on past assessment data miscommunicates students' learning (Stiggins, 2001).

Another important factor to consider is the potentially detrimental effect of averaging on students' motivation. Suppose, for example, that a student does poorly on one or two major assessments administered early in the marking period. This is the case of Students 4 and 6 in Table 8.1, shown earlier in this chapter. Knowing that those scores will be "averaged in" as part of the final grade, what motivation do these students have to do well on other assessments? Even if they perform at the highest level from that point on, they have little chance of attaining a high grade. Why? Because of the practice of averaging.

We personally know of a student who, during the first marking period of his senior year in high school, experienced the death of a beloved family member. The trauma of that experience proved exceptionally difficult for this young man. As a result, he neglected his schoolwork completely and received failing grades in all of his courses. With help from teachers and family members, he recovered emotionally, rededicated himself, and with diligent effort, attained *A*'s in his courses during the other three marking periods over the school year. Because of the practice of averaging, however, his final course grades were *C*'s. Did those *C*'s accurately reflect what he had learned? Did they truly represent his achievement or level of performance? Was this fair? We think not!

In our work with teachers we frequently share the information in Table 8.1 and the student profiles that accompany the table. We then ask which of the three grading procedures (average, median, or average with the lowest score deleted) is "best" or "fairest." Never is there agreement. With great consistency, however, the majority of teachers rate "averaging" as the least fair. And even when forced to choose among the remaining options, nearly every teacher wants to add individual exceptions.

## Recommendation

Because any single measure or indicator of student learning can be flawed or unreliable, teachers at all levels must use multiple sources of information when assigning marks or grades to students' achievement or level of performance. But simply combining all those measures and calculating an average or even a weighted average is rarely appropriate or fair. Some educators argue that the median or middle score provides a more accurate summary (Wright, 1994), but as we showed in our discussion of Table 8.1, it can be problematic too. The mathematical precision of these approaches doesn't necessarily yield greater objectivity, validity, or fairness.

Instead, teachers must look for consistency in the evidence they've gathered. If that evidence is consistent across several indicators and a student's scores or marks are fairly uniform, then deciding what grade to assign is a relatively simple task. This would be the case, for example, for students whose scores on a class project, two summative examinations, and an oral report are all quite similar. Even these cases can get complicated, however, if that evidence is consistently near the cutoff between two grade categories. Note, for example, the case of Student 3 in Table 8.1.

If the evidence is not consistent, however, then teachers must look deeper and search for the reasons why (Brookhart, 1999). They also must face the difficult challenge of deciding what evidence or combination of evidence represents the truest and most appropriate summary of students' achievement and performance. In such cases, we recommend three general guidelines.

First, the most recent evidence should always be given priority or greater weight. Because grades are usually meant to represent students' current achievement status or level of performance, the most accurate evidence is generally the evidence collected most recently. Therefore, scores from assessments at the end of the marking period are typically more representative of what students have learned than those collected at the beginning.

Second, we would recommend giving priority or greater weight to the most comprehensive forms of evidence. If certain sources of evidence represent cumulative summaries of the knowledge and skills students have acquired, then these should hold the greatest weight in determining students' grades. Exceptions to this approach might be necessary, however, for students who suffer inordinate test or performance anxiety. Such students typically do remarkably well on assignments, quizzes, and class discussions but then "freeze" during larger assessments or performances. In such cases, teachers may have to consider sources of evidence other than major exams or assessments as more valid representations of these students' learning.

Our third recommendation would be to rank order the evidence gathered in terms of its importance to the course learning goals or standards. Those sources of evidence that relate to the most important or most crucial goals or standards for the course should then be given precedence. Teachers might, for example, attach greater importance to students' scores on a project that required the students to synthesize and apply what they learned than would be given to the scores students attained on assessments designed to tap basic knowledge and comprehension of course content.

---

**Guidelines for Considering Inconsistent Evidence on Students' Achievement and Performance**

1. Give priority to the most recent evidence.

2. Give priority to the most comprehensive evidence.

3. Give priority to evidence related to the most important learning goals or standards.

---

Of course, the best option is to offer multiple grades on different aspects of students' performance. Whenever diverse sources of evidence are combined into a single symbol, pertinent information is always lost. The use of multiple grades allows teachers to record separate marks or grades for different learning goals or standards. If the reporting form is appropriately structured, teachers might also record separate grades for product, process, and progress criteria. Moreover, multiple grades let teachers present a learner "profile" that communicates definite and useful information about students' achievement and performance. Such information is much more meaningful than that derived from a single grade in which multiple aspects of learning are combined.

Whatever strategy teachers choose, however, they must be sure to apply that strategy consistently across their students. Although exceptions due to unusual or extenuating circumstances are always permissible, fairness in grading dictates that teachers inform students about their grading policies and practices in advance and then faithfully and consistently apply those policies.

## The Use of Zeros

We always begin our work with educators on the topic of grading and reporting by asking them to consider its purpose. In other words, why do we do it? The answers they give typically fall into one of the following six categories outlined in Chapter 4:

1. To communicate the achievement status of students to parents and others

2. To provide information that students can use for self-evaluation

3. To select, identify, or group students for certain educational paths or programs

4. To provide incentives for students to learn

5. To evaluate the effectiveness of instructional programs

6. To provide evidence of students' lack of effort or inappropriate responsibility

After briefly discussing these purposes, we next ask everyone to rank them in order of their importance. That is, which purpose is most important and which is least? While there is seldom agreement about the most important purpose, nearly all agree that the least important purpose is #6: "To provide evidence of students' lack of effort or inappropriate responsibility."

We then turn to the topic of assigning zeros to students' work that is missed, neglected, or turned in late. On further reflection, most educators see that a zero is not an accurate reflection of students' learning (Raebeck, 1993). Instead, zeros are typically assigned to punish students for not displaying appropriate effort or responsibility (Canady & Hotchkiss, 1989; Stiggins & Duke, 1991). Obviously if the grade is to represent how well students have learned, then the practice of assigning zeros clearly misses the mark.

Finally we turn to the profound effect of zeros when combined with the practice of averaging. It's readily apparent that students who receive a single zero have little chance of success because such an extreme score so drastically skews the average. Note, for example, the scores of Students 6 and 7 in Table 8.1. That is why in scoring Olympic events like gymnastics, diving, or ice-skating, the highest and lowest scores are always eliminated. If they were not, one judge could control the entire competition simply by giving extreme scores.

Some teachers defend the practice of assigning zeros by arguing that they cannot give students credit for work that is incomplete or not turned in—and that's certainly true. But there are far better ways to motivate and encourage students to complete assignments than through the use of zeros, especially considering the overwhelmingly negative effects of assigning zeros.

One alternative approach is to assign an *I* or "Incomplete" grade. Remember our discussion in Chapter 3 of how some teachers use the *I* grade instead of assigning a failing grade to students' work. Students who receive an *I* grade are then required to do additional work to bring their performance up to an acceptable level. This same policy can be used in place of assigning zeros. Students whose work is incomplete or not turned in on time, for example, might be required to attend after-school study sessions or special Saturday school programs in order to complete their work. In other words, they are not "let off the hook" with a zero. Instead, students learn that they have certain responsibilities in school and that their actions have specific consequences.

### Recommendation

We believe that students should learn to accept responsibility and should be held accountable for their work. Nevertheless, we know of no evidence that shows assigning a zero helps teach students these lessons. Unless we are willing to admit that we use grades to show evidence of students' lack of effort or inappropriate responsibility, then alternatives to the practice of assigning zeros must be found.

The use of an *I* or "Incomplete" grade is an alternative to assigning zeros that is both educationally sound and potentially quite effective. Students who miss an assignment or neglect a project deadline receive a grade of *I* and then are required to attend after-school study sessions and/or special Saturday classes until their work is completed to a satisfactory level. As we described in Chapter 3, implementing such a policy may require additional funding and support. Still, the payoffs are likely to be great. Not only is it more beneficial to students than simply assigning a zero, it's also a lot fairer. In addition, it helps make the grade a more accurate reflection of what students have learned.

## Lowering Grades Because of Behavioral Infractions

Another typical grading practice with detrimental effects is to lower students' grades because of behavioral infractions. Some teachers deduct from students' grades for classroom disruptions and similar forms of misconduct. Other teachers consider class attendance in determining students' grades and often reduce the grades of students who miss a certain number of class sessions. Teachers also vary widely in how they handle offenses such as plagiarism, copying another student's work, or other forms of "cheating." For most teachers, however, such transgressions are weighed heavily when assigning students' grades.

The case of Student 7 in Table 8.1 is an excellent example. This particular student performed excellently in the first four units, but then was caught cheating on the assessment for Unit 5. For that infraction, the student received a score of zero for the unit, and most teachers would undoubtedly concur that this is "fair." Now, however, we come to the thornier issue of determining this particular student's course grade. Some teachers would look at the achievement history over the marking period, conclude that this incident was truly an exception, and give the student a high grade. Others would reason that the student probably attained high marks in earlier units through cheating as well but simply didn't get caught. Hence they would give the student a lower grade.

The important question we must address when considering infractions such as these is, again, "What is the purpose of grading?" If the purpose is to present teachers' summary judgments of students' achievement and performance, then to count these behavioral infractions in determining the grade clearly miscommunicates. Although we would never suggest that educators should ignore such infractions, it is clear that they are not part of the evidence that reflects what students have learned and what they are able to do.

### *Recommendation*

Behavioral infractions cannot be considered indicators of achievement or performance. Hence, they do not reflect product criteria. Including information about such infractions when determining students' grades, particularly lowering the grades of students who commit such infractions, yields an inaccurate representation of their learning.

The best strategy for considering behavioral infractions in grading is to offer multiple grades. If we report separate grades for product and process criteria, and include among the process criteria indicators of students' class behaviors or work habits, we can communicate this information to those for whom it has the greatest value: the students themselves and their parents. Although using multiple grades complicates both record keeping and grading procedures, the advantages in terms of better and more meaningful communication clearly outweigh those costs.

## Summary

What should be evident from this chapter is that our knowledge base on grading is quite extensive and offers us clear guidelines for better practice. Nevertheless, it does not show one method of grading or one set of grading policies to be best under all conditions or in all circumstances. Advances in technology, for example, have radically altered both grading and reporting practices. They have greatly simplified record-keeping tasks and enabled teachers to collect and summarize large amounts of information in precise and efficient ways. At the same time, the mathematical precision they offer does not necessarily lead to grades that are more accurate, honest, objective, or fair.

Grading remains a process of professional judgment that demands continuous reflection on its purpose. If grades are to represent information about the adequacy of students' achievement and performance, then the evidence used in determining grades must denote what students have learned and can do. Other factors related to students' work habits or behaviors, while important, should be reported separately. To include these factors as part of a single grade misrepresents students' learning attainments.

Grading requires careful planning, thoughtful judgment, a clear focus on purpose, excellent communication skills, and an overriding concern for students. Such qualities are necessary to ensure grading practices that provide high-quality information on student learning, regardless of the method employed.

# CHAPTER 9

# Model Reporting Forms

In this chapter, we turn our attention to model reporting forms developed by educators at various levels that are helping them meet the challenge of effective communication. Our work in this area began with the collection of over 100 elementary and secondary reporting forms gathered from communities throughout the United States and Canada where reporting is considered effective. Among these widely varied forms, however, we could find none that accomplished all of the reporting goals that teachers and parents say are important. Instead, we found in these communities that the report card is but one of several tools used to communicate with parents, students, and others. In other words, these communities have developed and implemented multifaceted reporting systems.

Still, at the center of every one of these reporting systems is a report card or reporting form of some type. In this chapter, we include examples of a variety of forms that efficiently convey students' achievement and level of performance, usually in relation to carefully articulated learning standards. In exploring and evaluating these various reporting forms we discovered that the format, organization, and graphic layout of the form are extremely important. These physical characteristics can enhance or detract from the intended message. For that reason, we also offer recommendations on ways to ensure that the "form" of the report does not get in the way of its "function."

## Developing a Model Reporting Form

As described above, we recently reviewed numerous report cards and reporting forms used at every grade level from preschool through Grade 12. This work, along with our informal surveys and interviews with parents, students, and teachers, have shown us that the reporting forms perceived most positively are those designed to fit a specific purpose and intended for a specific audience. In most cases, this means they are context specific. A form that works well in one setting with a particular audience may not work equally well in a different setting with a different audience.

In designing a reporting form, therefore, we believe two major issues must be given priority and considered at the very beginning of the development process. The first is what purpose we want the form to serve, and the second is what reporting format, method, or structure best serves that purpose. The reporting forms described in this chapter were developed with these issues foremost in mind. They come from highly diverse schools and school districts and illustrate how these critical issues can be addressed in positive and highly effective ways.

Because no single form can be considered best in all contexts, however, we chose not to include any reporting form in its entirety. Rather, we've included examples and segments of forms that are working well in specific contexts to illustrate the important points we want to make. We encourage educators to use these examples to design reporting forms that fulfill their own designated reporting purpose in a format that is well organized, easy to read, and understandable to the intended audience.

In most cases we also have not named the schools and school districts from which these examples are drawn. Because the educators who developed these forms are constantly engaged in the process of improvement, the forms shown here might not represent their most current version. Many of the forms have been adapted to illustrate particular points. Plus, we do not want any of our suggestions for improvement to be misinterpreted as criticisms. We applaud the efforts of these dedicated educators and hope that our ideas will be helpful to them and to others as they continue in their efforts to design and implement effective reporting systems.

## Information to Include in a Reporting Form

Once educators determine the primary purpose of their reporting form, they must then consider its structure. The reporting form's structure and the information it includes can vary widely from school to school and across grade levels. Differences range from the high school report card that lists a single letter grade for each course on a half page of paper to a lengthy, multipage elementary report that lists grade-level standards for each of six or seven subject areas and a complex series of marks related to students' learning progress.

In choosing what and how much information to include, educators must seek a balance between detail and practicality. A reporting form should present a comprehensive picture of students' academic strengths and weaknesses. At the same time, however, it should be compact, understandable, and not require inordinate time for teachers to prepare or for parents to interpret (Linn & Gronlund, 2000).

Although students, parents, and others sometimes express different wants with regard to the form and structure of reporting forms, they share many common preferences. These preferences relate to the type of information included on the form and the need for specific guidance in interpreting that information. Based on the results from our surveys and interviews with students and parents, along with our personal experiences as educators and parents, we offer the following recommendations.

## Separate Grades for Product and Process

Whenever possible in reporting, educators should separate information about students' achievement, performance, and academic products from information about their work habits, study skills, or other process skills. An example of how this might be done is presented in Figure 9.1. This form comes from an elementary school that serves students in kindergarten through Grade 5. Reporting forms such as this provide parents with information about different aspects of students' achievement and performance in each subject area, as well as independent information about students' engagement in learning processes.

Other forms accomplish this separation of product and process by including a special section on the report for "Social Development and Work Habits," as illustrated on the form in Figure 9.2. Teachers use this portion of the report to communicate information about students' consistency in demonstrating social skills such as "Demonstrates Self-Control" and work habits such as "Uses Time Profitably."

Multisection reporting forms give parents explicit information about students' academic performance in specific subject areas as well as important feedback about students' social development and work habits. This information allows parents to develop a clearer picture of their child as a learner. But perhaps more important, it helps parents better target improvement efforts when they are needed.

## Separate Grades for Product and Progress

To provide a clear picture of what students have accomplished, it is also best to separate information about students' achievement, performance, and academic products from information about how much learning progress they have made. As we described earlier, certain academically talented students might demonstrate a high level of achievement based on grade-level standards and yet make relatively little learning progress. Conversely, other students might make significant progress and still not reach a proficient level with regard to the standards. Such differences are important to parents in evaluating the performance of their children.

| MATHEMATICS GRADE: | 1st<br>B | 2nd | 3rd | 4th |
|---|---|---|---|---|
| Demonstrates understanding of concepts | 3 | | | |
| Demonstrates mathematical thinking | 3 | | | |
| Makes mental calculations and reasonable estimations | 4 | | | |
| Uses strategies to solve problems | 3 | | | |
| Collects, organizes & analyzes data | 2 | | | |
| Demonstrates a knowledge of basic facts | 3 | | | |
| Computes accurately | 3 | | | |
| Completes assignments on time | 4 | | | |

**Key to Subject Area Grades:**

**A** = Outstanding (90 – 100% Mastery of Subject Goals)
**B** = Very Good   (80 – 89% Mastery of Subject Goals)
**C** = Satisfactory (70 – 79% Mastery of Subject Goals)
**D** = Experiencing Difficulty (Below 70% Mastery of Subject Goals)

**Key to Skills Grades:**

**4** = Consistently or Independently
**3** = Usually
**2** = Sometimes
**1** = Seldom
**NE** = Not Evaluated

**Figure 9.1.** Elementary Reporting Form Illustrating a Grade for Achievement in the Subject Area With Separate Indicators for Process Skills

The high school reporting forms shown in Figures 9.3 and 9.4 provide examples of how this might be done. These forms offer a detailed account of students' progress in compiling a portfolio of work required for graduation. The educators who developed this form identified 10 academic standards di-

| SOCIAL DEVELOPMENT AND WORK HABITS | 1st | 2nd | 3rd | 4th |
|---|---|---|---|---|
| Works and plays cooperatively | | | | |
| Works well independently | | | | |
| Accepts responsibility for returning homework, books & school-related materials on time | | | | |
| Uses time profitably | | | | |
| Demonstrates self-control | | | | |
| Demonstrates neatness and organizational skills | | | | |
| Respects rights, opinions, and property of others | | | | |
| Follows rules and displays appropriate behavior | | | | |
| Follows oral directions | | | | |
| Follows written directions | | | | |
| Listens during instructional lessons | | | | |
| Seeks help when needed | | | | |
| Effectively solves social conflicts | | | | |

**Key to Skills Grades:**

**4** = Consistently or Independently

**3** = Usually

**2** = Sometimes

**1** = Seldom

**NE** = Not Evaluated

**Figure 9.2.** Elementary Reporting Form Illustrating Grades for Student Work Habits and Social Development

**Portfolio Standard 1: Careers**

**Students will prepare for careers of their own choosing.**

*While performing individual or group tasks, students will:*

1.01 Demonstrate awareness of a variety of career options.

1.02 Demonstrate awareness of the changing qualifications necessary for a variety of career options.

1.03 Maintain an accurate personal resume.

1.04 Demonstrate skills and knowledge necessary to accurately complete a variety of application forms for jobs, schools, colleges, and universities.

1.05 Demonstrate effective interviewing skills.

1.06 Demonstrate mastery of essential career skills, including CTBS & HCST.

**Figure 9.3.** Example of Portfolio Entries Related to the Career Standard

rectly related to skills needed in the workplace. Included are proficiencies such as career preparation, oral and written communication, and teamwork. The criteria for meeting each standard are clearly articulated for students, parents, and others, including employers.

As students advance through their four years in high school, they collect artifacts to demonstrate their mastery of each standard. The reporting form illustrates their progress on all 10 standards. Each marking period, the teacher records the number of artifacts assembled to date, the total number of artifacts required, and the percentage completion. In addition, every student has a "teacher advisor" who completes a brief narrative on the reporting form that describes both the level of achievement and amount of progress to date. Finally, students contribute to the form by writing recommendations and comments regarding their own work and progress.

The clarity and detail of this reporting form provides parents with specific information each marking period about where students stand on completing these important graduation requirements. Not only does it describe teachers' appraisals of the products and artifacts that students have compiled, it also gives parents and others a clear picture of how much progress students have made.

**PORTFOLIO ASSESSMENT REPORT**

Student: Drah Seirt                                                                 **Grade:** 11

**Advisor:** Ydaer Syawla

**Assessment Date:** November 20 (Report #1 of 4)

| Standard | I Careers | II Commu-nication | III Human Diversity | IV Human Relations | V Infor-mation | VI Math | VII Re-sources | VIII Systems | IX Tech-nology | X Think-ing |
|---|---|---|---|---|---|---|---|---|---|---|
| **Total Artifacts Presented** | 14 | 30 | 20 | 25 | 12 | 12 | 12 | 31 | 2 | 13 |
| **Total Artifacts Required** | 15 | 42 | 24 | 27 | 15 | 42 | 12 | 31 | 31 | 15 |
| **Percentage Completed** | 93 | 71 | 83 | 93 | 80 | 29 | 100 | 100 | 6 | 87 |

**Advisor's Recommendations and Comments:**

*Drah has been working hard this quarter and has made considerable progress since our last assessment. She has completed Core Portfolio requirements for Standards I, IV, VII, VIII, and X. Next she should concentrate on those standards below the 85% mark. In particular, Drah should try to focus on mathematics and technology during the next quarter. Drah's communication artifacts show excellent progress and she should soon complete this area of study. Good work, Drah!*

**Student's Recommendations and Comments:**

*I don't have too many items in mathematics or technology because I was in the Language Arts/Social Studies division this quarter. My goal is to complete either the mathematics or the technology standards before our next assessment. I worked really hard in my communications standards, and I'm not sure why I still don't have enough artifacts. I plan to do more of my work this time (I know I said that last time, but this time I really mean it!).*

**Figure 9.4.** Example of a Portfolio Assessment Report

Another important part of this same high school's reporting form is the "Work Ethic Checklist," an excerpt of which is shown in Figure 9.5. This checklist is an example of how secondary teachers might separately report process

**WORK ETHIC CHECKLIST**

Student: _____     Grade: _____

Advisor: _____

Reporting Period:   1   2   3   4

| Work Ethic Description | Evaluation | | |
|---|---|---|---|
| | Below Standard | Meets Standard | Exceeds Standard |
| 1. Dresses and grooms in a manner which satisfies the school dress code. | ☐ | ☐ | ☐ |
| 2. Comes to school on time each day, except for unavoidable personal emergencies & serious illness. | ☐ | ☐ | ☐ |
| 3. Accepts criticism and suggestions in a positive manner. | ☐ | ☐ | ☐ |
| 4. Is present and at work during all school hours. | ☐ | ☐ | ☐ |
| [Complete checklist includes 37 items] | | | |

Notes:

Comments:

**Figure 9.5.** Excerpt From a Work Ethics Checklist

skills. Again, these skills are directly related to the workplace and reflect the teachers' emphasis on employability skills for all students.

# Using Checklists and Rubrics to Evaluate Students' Performance

As we described in Chapter 6, an increasing number of elementary schools have developed standards-based reporting forms. The "Work Ethic Checklist" described in the previous section is an example of a similar development at the high school level. Standards-based reporting forms such as this give parents detailed information about teachers' judgments of students' performance in relation to clearly articulated learning goals or standards.

The "Elementary Progress Report" illustrated in Figure 9.6 is another example of a standards-based reporting form. This form is an extension of the reporting form shown in Figure 6.1 of Chapter 6. It is a four-page form used in kindergarten through Grade 5. The first three pages list the standards for each subject area, including reading, writing, communication, mathematics, science, social studies, technology, fitness, music, art, and social/learning skills. The last page includes a section for teacher comments and a record of goal-setting information.

What makes this form unique is the extensive documentation that accompanies it. Together with the reporting form parents receive a curriculum guidebook that describes what each standard means at each grade level, along with the associated skills. Also included is the rubric that defines students' level of progress in meeting each standard. An example of the mathematics criteria and accompanying rubrics for first grade and fifth grade are shown in Figures 9.7 and 9.8, respectively. The educators who developed this reporting form have done extensive work with parents and other community members to help them understand, interpret, and use the form effectively.

The strength of this type of reporting form lies in its consistency. Every elementary teacher in this particular school district uses the same form. Parents are not confused by a different form or reporting format at different grade levels. Rather, the form looks the same for each of six years. What changes are the grade-level standards and rubrics. Plus, parents gain a great deal of helpful information about what their child is learning each year from kindergarten through Grade 5.

We hasten to add, however, that educators who want to use reporting forms similar to the one illustrated in Figure 9.6 must commit themselves to educating parents about the content of the form and how it can be meaningfully interpreted. In this particular school district, the reporting form at each grade level is accompanied by approximately 20 pages of information. To some parents this may be overwhelming, especially those with limited literacy skills or those who speak a language other than English. With guidance, training, and good communication from teachers, however, we believe that many parents would welcome this form and the wealth of information it provides.

*text continues on page 159*

| Elementary Progress Report | | |
|---|---|---|
| Student: | | Grade: |
| Teacher: | School: | Year: |

This report is based on grade-level standards established for each subject area.
The ratings indicate your student's progress in relation to the year-end standard.

| **Evaluation Marks** | **Level Expectation Marks** | **Social Learning Skills & Effort Marks** |
|---|---|---|
| **4** = Exceptional | **++** = Advanced | **E** = Exceptional |
| **3** = Meets Standard | **+** = On Level | **S** = Satisfactory |
| **2** = Approaches Standard | **--** = Below Level | **U** = Unsatisfactory |
| **1** = Beginning Standard | | |
| **N** = Not Applicable | | |

| Mathematics | 1st | 2nd | 3rd | 4th |
|---|---|---|---|---|
| Uses mathematics to define and solve problems | | | | |
| Uses mathematical reasoning | | | | |
| Communicates knowledge and understanding in both everyday and mathematical language | | | | |
| Makes mathematical connections within mathematics, to other subject areas, and to real-life situations | | | | |
| Applies concepts and procedures of math in the following areas: | | | | |
|    Number Sense and Computation | | | | |
|    Measurement | | | | |
|    Geometric Sense | | | | |
|    Probability and Statistics | | | | |
|    Algebraic Sense | | | | |
| Work Habits | | | | |

| Social and Learning Skills | 1st | 2nd | 3rd | 4th |
|---|---|---|---|---|
| Respects others | | | | |
| Accepts responsibility | | | | |
| Follows directions | | | | |
| Cooperates with others | | | | |

**Figure 9.6.** Example of a Standards-Based Reporting Form

SOURCE: Adapted by Bellevue School District (Bellevue, WA) from a document created by Issaquah School (Issaquah, WA). Used by permission.

## FIRST GRADE
### Mathematics Criteria for Progress Report

| Problem Solving | Mathematical Reasoning | Number Sense and Computational Skills |
|---|---|---|
| This includes:<br>• Uses, creates and evaluates a variety of strategies to solve problems<br>• Formulates questions about problems, identifying necessary and unnecessary information<br>• Identifies the unknown in a problem<br>• Applies appropriate methods, operations and processes to construct a solution | This includes:<br>• Supports thinking using models, known facts, patterns and relationships<br>• Makes predictions, collects data, supports arguments and justifies results<br>• Reflects on and evaluates procedures | This includes:<br>• Identifies, represents and compares numbers up to 100<br>• Uses computational strategies to solve problems using addition and subtraction with numbers up to 20<br>• Writes numbers sentences for situations representing addition and subtraction |

**The Student . . .**

| | | | |
|---|---|---|---|
| 4<br>**Exceptional** | Consistently demonstrates an understanding of the concepts and processes of problem solving. | Consistently demonstrates an understanding of the concepts and processes of mathematical reasoning. | Consistently accurate in using number operations and demonstrating an understanding of number concepts and processes. |
| 3<br>**Meets Standard** | Usually demonstrates an understanding of the concepts and processes of problem solving. | Usually demonstrates an understanding of the concepts and processes of mathematical reasoning. | Usually accurate in using number operations and demonstrating an understanding of number concepts and processes. |
| 2<br>**Approaches Standard** | Sometimes demonstrates an understanding of the concepts and processes of problem solving. | Sometimes demonstrates an understanding of the concepts and processes of mathematical reasoning. | Sometimes accurate in using number operations and demonstrating an understanding of number concepts and processes. |
| 1<br>**Beginning Standard** | Seldom demonstrates an understanding of the concepts and processes of problem solving. | Seldom demonstrates understanding of the concepts and processes of mathematical reasoning. | Seldom accurate in using number operations and demonstrating an understanding of number concepts and processes. |

**Figure 9.7.** Example of First Grade Mathematics Criteria and Accompanying Rubrics

SOURCE: Adapted by Bellevue School District (Bellevue, WA) from a document created by Issaquah School (Issaquah, WA). Used by permission.

**FIFTH GRADE**
Mathematics Criteria for Progress Report

| Problem Solving | Mathematical Reasoning | Number and Sense Computational Skills |
|---|---|---|
| This includes:<br><br>• Uses, creates and evaluates a variety of strategies to solve problems<br>• Formulates questions about problems, identifying necessary and unnecessary information<br>• Identifies the unknown in a problem<br>• Applies appropriate methods, operations, and processes to construct a solution<br>• Organizes relevant information from multiple sources | This includes:<br><br>• Supports thinking using models, known facts, patterns and relationships<br>• Makes predictions, collects data, supports arguments and justifies results<br>• Tests conjectures and inferences and explains why they are true or false<br>• Checks for reasonableness of results | This includes:<br><br>• Identifies, represents and orders non-negative whole numbers<br>• Uses visual and physical models to describe the meaning of fractions, decimals, and percents<br>• Orders fractions with decimals and decimals with decimals<br>• Identifies equivalent fractions and simplifies fractions<br>• Describes prime and composite numbers, factors and multiples, and recognizes multiples of 2, 5, and 10<br>• Illustrates and compares equivalent fractions<br>• Adds, subtracts, multiplies and divides non-negative whole numbers<br>• Adds and subtracts decimals, fractions, and mixed numbers<br>• Uses mental arithmetic, paper and pencil, calculator, or computer as appropriate for a given situation |

**Figure 9.8.** Example of Fifth Grade Mathematics Criteria and Accompanying Rubrics

SOURCE: Adapted by Bellevue School District (Bellevue, WA) from a document created by Issaquah School (Issaquah, WA). Used by permission

The Student . . .

| | | | |
|---|---|---|---|
| **4**<br>**Exceptional** | Consistently demonstrates an understanding of the concepts and processes of problem solving. | Consistently demonstrates an understanding of the concepts and processes of mathematical reasoning. | Consistently accurate in using number operations and demonstrating an understanding of number concepts and processes. |
| **3**<br>**Meets**<br>**Standard** | Usually demonstrates an understanding of the concepts and processes of problem solving. | Usually demonstrates an understanding of the concepts and processes of mathematical reasoning. | Usually accurate in using number operations and demonstrating an understanding of number concepts and processes. |
| **2**<br>**Approaches**<br>**Standard** | Sometimes demonstrates an understanding of the concepts and processes of problem solving. | Sometimes demonstrates an understanding of the concepts and processes of mathematical reasoning. | Sometimes accurate in using number operations and demonstrating an understanding of number concepts and processes. |
| **1**<br>**Beginning**<br>**Standard** | Seldom demonstrates an understanding of the concepts and processes of problem solving. | Seldom demonstrates an understanding of the concepts and processes of mathematical reasoning. | Seldom accurate in using number operations and demonstrating an understanding of number concepts and processes. |

**Figure 9.8.** Continued

# Communicating Information on Self-Assessment and Goal Setting

In many schools and school districts, the standards developed for all students stress the importance of self-evaluation and goal setting. Hence these schools devote space on the reporting form for reflection and comments in these two areas, similar to that shown in Figure 9.9. This report is completed during a parent-teacher conference or student-led conference, and provides a focal point for conversations among students, parents, and teachers.

| Goal Setting Conference Summary | | |
|---|---|---|
| Student: | | Grade: |
| Teacher: | School: | Date: |
| **Step 1: Review Progress Report and All Evaluation Materials.** | | |
| | | |
| **Step 2: Parents' Goals:** | | |
| | | |
| **Step 3: Student's Goals:** | | |
| | | |
| **Step 4: Teacher's Goals:** | | |
| | | |
| **Step 5: Shared Discussion Items to Note:** | | |
| | | |
| **Student's Signature** | **Parent's Signature** | **Teacher's Signature** |

**Figure 9.9.** Example of a Goal Setting Conference Summary Report

Other schools accomplish the same purpose by attaching an extra page to the reporting form like the one illustrated in Figure 9.10. Students fill out this page during class with the help of their teacher. The student and teacher then discuss the outlined goals and complete an action plan together. Finally, the page is sent home to parents for their signatures and approval.

Forms like these have been used with very positive results at all grade levels. Teachers tell us that they find the goal-setting process particularly helpful at the start of the school year or when a new course of study is beginning. It provides a quick, informal assessment of each student's needs and encourages students to take increased responsibility for their learning. Both parents and students report that the self-evaluation and goal-setting information helps them reflect on progress and set high expectations.

# Special Comment Sections and Parent Reports to School

When the stated purpose of a school's reporting form is communicating information about students' learning to parents, it is vital that parents be able to read the form and understand the meaning of the information it contains. To obtain feedback from parents about their understanding of the report, some schools ask parents to add their own written comments on the reporting form. This not only guarantees that parents have received the form, it also encourages their input in the reporting process. Other shools consider it important for students to understand the reported information and, therefore, ask students to write their own comments in a section of the reporting form. In some cases, information is added about students' involvement in community service or extracurricular activities. The inclusion of such comments makes the reporting process much more encompassing and interactive. Figure 9.11 shows an example of a page that can be attached to any report card to record these special comments.

In an effort to encourage increased interaction and better two-way communication between teachers and parents, some schools include a section on the reporting form for parents to describe students' learning activities at home and the degree of parental involvement. We have seen this most often in the early elementary grades, kindergarten through Grade 2. Usually, it takes the form of a checklist that serves as a reminder to parents about the importance of reading to their child or providing extra support at home. An example of one such "Parent Report to School" is shown in Figure 9.12.

Still other schools have created a small section on the report form to record "Parent's Conference Attendance." This typically consists of a "yes" or "no"

*text continues on page 164*

---

## Self-Assessment and Goal Setting
*(To be completed by the student in consultation with the teacher.)*

**Accomplishments:**




**Goals for Next Reporting Period:**




**Action Plan:**




**Parental Support**
(Please discuss this evaluation with your child and respond below to his or her self-assessment and goal setting statements.  Then sign and return this page of the report to the teacher.)




Date: _____          Parent/Guardian Signature: _____

---

**Figure 9.10.** Example of a Self-Assessment and Goal Setting Conference Reporting Form

| SPECIAL COMMENTS SECTION | |
|---|---|
| **Teacher Comments:** | **Student Comments:** |
| **Community Involvement and Extracurricular Activities:** | **Parent Comments:** |

**Figure 9.11.** Example of a Report Attachment for Teacher, Parent, and Student Comments

| This is what I do at home: | 1st | 2nd | 3rd | 4th |
|---|---|---|---|---|

**PARENT REPORT TO SCHOOL**
Yarnick Elementary School

Student: | Grade:
Teacher: | School Year:

Please mark using the following key:

$N$ = Not yet          $S$ = Sometimes          $M$ = Most of the time

Marking Period

- I ask about my child's school day.
- I read to my child daily.
- I check my child's backpack for notes and schoolwork.
- I help my child with homework.
- I encourage my child to do his or her best in school
- I read school newsletters.
- I look over my child's graded papers and ask questions when needed.
- I value education and don't allow outside activities to take precedence over school work.
- I call the teacher whenever I have questions or concerns.

Please sign and return this report to your child's teacher.

_____          _____
Parent's Signature                               Date

**Figure 9.12.** Example of a Parent Report to School

check mark recorded by the dates of scheduled parent-teacher conferences during the school year. By keeping a record of conference attendance on the report card, parents are reminded of the importance of these events.

**Report of Special Services**

*A check mark (✔) under the marking period indicates that your child received that particular service. The name of each of your child's special services teachers is listed.*

| Special Services Received and Teacher's Name: | 1st | 2nd | 3rd | 4th |
|---|---|---|---|---|
| Title I Teacher for: <br> ❑ Reading  ❑ Math  ❑ Social Studies  ❑ Science | | | | |
| Reading Recovery Teacher | | | | |
| Speech and Language Teacher | | | | |
| Learning Center or Resource Room Teacher | | | | |
| Teacher for Gifted/Talented | | | | |
| Section 504 Coordinator | | | | |

**Figure 9.13.** Example of a Special Services Report

# Reports of Special Services

Some schools like to note on the reporting form the "special services" provided to each child. A sample checklist for such special services is shown in Figure 9.13. This information can be especially helpful to school personnel as children progress from one grade level to the next or move from one building or district to another.

# Reports on Physical Growth

Some elementary schools report information to parents about students' physical characteristics such as their height and weight, or their proficiency with particular motor skills. One checklist that we have seen, for example, reports on each child's progress in demonstrating balance and coordination, self-help skills, and skills in using writing tools. Parents often appreciate having this type of ongoing record of their child's growth and progress in these areas.

Once again, however, we stress that each school must examine and clearly articulate the purpose for reporting this kind of information. If information on students' physical development and mastery of specific motor skills is important in fulfilling the stated purpose of the reporting form, then it may be included. On the other hand, if such information does not fulfill the specified reporting purpose, then it should be ignored or eliminated. Reports to parents should be clear, concise, and free of nonessential information.

## Secondary Level Reporting Forms

Most secondary educators design reporting forms to include information about students' achievement and current level of performance. Many also offer information about the consistency of students' performance by listing current grades along with the grades earned in previous reporting periods. This allows both parents and students to note improvements or declines in performance. Others communicate information on students' progress toward specified graduation requirements, especially those involving service learning or community service. In addition, most secondary reporting forms include information about students' attendance and punctuality since these are believed to be crucial to students' academic success.

The staff of one high school we know uses a computer-generated reporting form to combine these varied pieces of information on student learning in an easy-to-read format. The report includes a short narrative description of the major learning goals for each class for that particular reporting period. These one- or two-sentence narratives are printed on each student's reporting form and are the same for all students in the class. Teachers then add one or two additional sentences commenting on each student's individual performance. This communicates to parents what was emphasized in the class as well as how their child performed.

Following these narrative descriptions, teachers record each student's grade to date. This information is then combined with the student's previous grade for the class, the number of credits earned toward graduation, and a record of school and class attendance. The final page of the reporting form contains information on students' goal setting and self-evaluation activities, along with space for parents' comments and signatures. This particular form even contains small photographs of each of the student's teachers. An adapted version of the form is shown in Figure 9.14.

Both parents and students consider the information on this reporting form extremely valuable. Nevertheless, providing this level of detail would be impossible without the necessary computer technology. The typical high

---

## GRIEDER HIGH SCHOOL REPORT CARD

| Student: **Eno Trams** | Grade: **10** | Year |
|---|---|---|

| Course: **English 10**     Teacher: **A. Miller** | Mark to Date: | A |
|---|---|---|
| Narrative: *In English 10 this term, students worked in groups to write and produce an original play. The class continues to learn to compare and contrast tragedy and comedy through various reading and writing assignments. Eno completed all assignments related to play production. He continues to excel in this class by completing all work, contributing actively, and progressing nicely in developing his writing skills.* | Previous Mark: | A |
| | Final Mark: | -- |
| | Credits Earned: | -- |
| | Absences: | 2 |
| | Times Tardy: | 0 |

| Course: **Biology 10**     Teacher: **F. Crick** | Mark to Date: | B |
|---|---|---|
| Narrative: *The class is currently studying the respiratory system and recently completed a unit on the digestive system. Students are expected to recognize and label organs and describe the functions of each system. Eno has two assignments missing (one diagram and one short essay). Completing work on time and making sure all assignments are complete will improve his grade. Eno is a capable student who demonstrates good knowledge of the subject when he completes required work.* | Previous Mark: | A |
| | Final Mark: | -- |
| | Credits Earned: | -- |
| | Absences: | 2 |
| | Times Tardy: | 1 |

| Course: **Social Studies 10**     Teacher: **S. Gould** | Mark to Date: | A |
|---|---|---|
| Narrative: *In Social Studies this term, the class has been preparing to take the statewide social studies exam which assesses students' knowledge of history, economics, and government. Students have completed essays, multiple choice quizzes, and short research studies in each area. Eno's daily work and tests show that he is well prepared to take the state exam. His knowledge of government and economics is exceptional. He works well in groups, completes all assignments, and actively participates in class discussions. Great job, Eno!* | Previous Mark: | A |
| | Final Mark: | -- |
| | Credits Earned: | -- |
| | Absences: | 2 |
| | Times Tardy: | 0 |

| Course: **Spanish II**     Teacher: **S. Gonzales** | Mark to Date: | A |
|---|---|---|
| Narrative: *Our Spanish class has been studying advanced concepts in grammar and syntax. We have continued to build vocabulary for use in meaningful oral and written expression. We also have researched and discussed several cultural traits of various Spanish speaking countries. Eno's performance on class tests has shown significant improvement and he contributes much more frequently in class. He is developing a much better facility and appreciation for the language.* | Previous Mark: | B |
| | Final Mark: | -- |
| | Credits Earned: | -- |
| | Absences: | 2 |
| | Times Tardy: | 0 |

**Figure 9.14.** Adapted Version of a Secondary Reporting Form

school teacher who sees 120 to 150 students each day would never be able to offer such extensive information if it had to be recorded by hand. The technology available to these teachers, however, allows them to enter and manage a highly detailed database in an efficient and highly effective manner.

As we have emphasized with all reporting forms, secondary educators must first decide the primary purpose they want their reporting device to serve and what information best fits that purpose. Evaluating the technology available might then open up a broad array of reporting options. With careful thought and planning, secondary educators can design reporting forms that are informative, helpful, and yet manageable.

## Combining Methods of Reporting

The most effective reporting forms are those that use a combination of methods to provide clear and concise information to parents, students, and others. With deliberate planning and technological support, it is possible to design reporting forms that include all of the following components:

- Checklists that show students' progress toward subject area standards
- Narratives to clarify student strengths or areas of concern in each subject
- Ratings of the student's work habits or social development
- Records of attendance and special services
- Sections for students to complete on self-assessment and goal setting
- Reports of progress on portfolio or service learning requirements
- Space for parents' comments, questions, and signatures

If design efforts begin by establishing the purpose of the reporting form, then decisions about what information to include are much easier to make. Teachers and school administrators usually find that including parents and sometimes students in these discussions also helps in the decision-making process. When teachers, administrators, parents, and other stakeholders work together to design the reporting form, the product is usually something that all find useful and informative.

## Format, Organization, and Graphic Layout

In addition to a statement of purpose, most reporting forms include on the first page an explanation of the marks or codes used in the form. This usually takes the form of a legend or "key to marks," with accompanying definitions. If the purpose of the reporting form is to communicate students' progress toward articulated learning goals, then those who receive the form should be able to understand the information it contains and easily interpret what it communicates in terms of students' performance.

If the purpose of the reporting form is clearly stated and the marks or grades are precisely explained, then the organization and graphic layout of the form can vary widely and still communicate effectively. In our review of reporting forms used at different grade levels, we found a multitude of different organizational styles, formats, and graphic layouts. Some schools use a very modest, simple, one-page, black-and-white reporting form. Others use graphic representations and two or three colors of ink to emphasize different aspects of the report. Still others have developed glossy, multipage, detailed reports that include photographs of the student, teachers, and even the school building.

The graphic design and layout of the reporting form can enhance or detract from its intended message. If not carefully considered, they can also serve to distort or mislead. One kindergarten reporting form that we reviewed, for example, listed the letters of the alphabet in very large, bold type. Teachers would circle those letters that students recognized visually and phonetically. Because this section of the report visually stood out from all other sections, it gave the appearance that the teachers placed great emphasis on letter recognition.

When we questioned the building principal about this, she told us that the kindergarten teachers did not stress this skill over other literacy skills. They had not noticed, however, that the layout of the report made this skill more prominent than any other skill. After reviewing the form and realizing the many inconsistencies between the form layout and message they wanted to communicate, staff members completely redesigned the form. Educators must always keep in mind that the format and graphical layout of a reporting form contribute greatly to the message communicated by the form.

Many schools and school districts use experienced graphic designers to gain advice and direction regarding format and layout options when developing their reporting form. Font sizes and print style, graphic and photo options, paper quality, report length, and color all must be considered in designing the form. A person knowledgeable in graphic design also can help ensure that design details enhance rather than detract from the report's intended message.

## Encouraging Input in the Design Process

One way to secure acceptance of a new reporting form is to encourage broad-based involvement during the design process. In one school district that we know, for example, the committee working to design a new reporting form included teachers, administrators, parents, local business people, board members, and students. After developing a draft version of a new reporting form, committee members organized parent focus groups at each grade level to gain additional feedback on their work. These groups were asked to comment on the report's stated purpose, the marking system, the vocabulary used, the organization, and the design. Based on this feedback, the committee made several excellent changes to enhance the form's effectiveness. This process also established a great deal of community support for the new reporting form before it was implemented. The committee continues to meet annually to make minor revisions in the form and other elements of the school's reporting system. The community is well pleased with these efforts and sees them as part of the school's commitment to better communication between the school and home.

## Consistency in Reporting Forms

Another vital consideration in designing reporting forms is consistency. Once the form is drafted, all documents should be carefully inspected to ensure consistency in several areas. First, reviewers should look for consistency in terminology and vocabulary. Although educators regard certain terms as interchangeable, their mixed use can be quite confusing to parents and others (Guskey, 1999b). For example, are we reporting on "standards," "learning goals," or "learner expectations?" Also, are the standards explained in terms of "criteria," "indicators," "benchmarks," or "rubrics?" While any of these terms is appropriate, consistency and clarity in the terminology used to communicate with parents is essential. Involving parents in the development of reporting forms can help ensure that the terms and vocabulary chosen are clear and understandable.

Next, reviewers should look for consistency in the format and organization of reporting forms used at different grade levels. In many schools and school districts, reporting forms differ drastically from one grade level to the next. In one school district that we know, for example, the teachers at each grade level in each school designed their own reporting form. The district has six elementary schools, each serving students in kindergarten through Grade 5. Hence at the elementary level alone there were 36 different reporting forms used in this district. The typical parent encountered six different reporting forms during their child's elementary school years! And the parents of students who transfer from one school to another at the same grade level within the district would have to interpret a totally different report. This resulted in confusion for parents, students, and teachers alike.

If the purpose of the reporting form is to communicate clearly, then it is best to have consistency in the format and organization of forms across grade levels and from building to building within the district. The best way to accomplish this is to include staff members and parents from different buildings in the district on development committees. In addition, the input of teachers at different levels (i.e., elementary, middle, and secondary) can be valuable as well. Such broad-based involvement further ensures good communication across grade levels and buildings throughout the district.

Consistency is also vital in conveying the importance of each subject area. Some of the elementary reporting forms we reviewed, for example, go into great detail in listing standards or expectations for reading, writing, and mathematics. On the same report, however, students' achievement in science, social studies, art, music, and physical education is described by only two or three broadly defined indicators such as "Understands subject area concepts" or "Participates well in class." Whether intended or not, this communicates that science, social studies, and other subjects are not as important as reading, writing, and math. In elementary schools where literacy and mathematics are intentionally emphasized, this may be quite appropriate. On the other hand, if these other subjects are considered comparably important, then greater consistency in reporting among the subjects should be sought when designing the reporting form.

# Frequency of Reports

A final consideration in developing reporting forms is the number and frequency of reporting periods. As we indicated earlier, teachers and parents often disagree on how frequently reporting forms should be distributed. Most teachers prefer only three or four reporting periods per year. They stress that they want to get to know students, understand their learning styles, and accurately determine students' individual strengths and weaknesses before having to report to parents. In addition, preparing reports requires a significant time commitment from teachers; time that must be taken away from preparing lessons and planning quality instructional activities.

Most parents, on the other hand, would like to receive reports on their child's performance in school at least six or eight times per year. Parents emphasize that the sooner they know about learning problems or weaknesses, the sooner they can take steps to help their child. In our interviews and discussions with parents, they continually stressed their desire for frequent and consistent communication from teachers.

The solution to this dilemma rests in the development of a multifaceted reporting system. Few parents will be satisfied if the only information they receive on their child's achievement and performance in school comes in a reporting form sent home just three or four times per year. However, if that reporting form is but one element in a multifaceted reporting system that offers parents regular and meaning information in a variety of formats, then parents are much more likely to feel their needs and concerns are being met.

## Summary

The most important issue that needs to be addressed in any effort to design a new reporting form or revise an existing one is to clarify its purpose. Specifically, developers need to ask, What is this reporting form intended to accomplish? For whom is the information intended? and What are they expected to do with the information? Including a statement of purpose on the first page of the reporting form is always a good idea. This helps all stakeholders clarify the intent of the form and how the information is to be used.

Because the most effective reporting forms are designed to fit a specific purpose and intended for a specific audience, it is impossible to identify one exemplary model form. Instead, forms must be adapted to fit particular contexts. Nevertheless, development efforts guided by a clear understanding of the knowledge base and involving a broad base of stakeholders can yield reporting forms that are practical, useful, and an enhancement to teaching and learning processes.

CHAPTER **10**

# Guidelines for Developing Effective Reporting Systems

Throughout this book we have emphasized that as the goals of schooling become more complex, the need for better quality and more detailed communication about student learning grows increasingly important. We've also argued that no single reporting device can adequately serve these ever expanding communication needs. That's why reform efforts that focus on report cards alone so often fail. Either they attempt to accomplish too much with a single reporting device, or they ignore important principles of effective communication.

What we need instead are comprehensive, multifaceted reporting systems that communicate multiple types of information to multiple audiences in multiple formats. At the base of such systems is a redesigned report card that serves as a model for effective communication. But these systems also include a wide variety of other communication tools, each with a specific purpose and designed for a particular audience. Reporting systems such as these are built on the premise that successful reporting is more a challenge in effective communication than simply a process of documenting student achievement.

In this chapter, we turn our attention to the steps involved in building comprehensive reporting systems. We outline a set of guidelines for educators to follow to ensure that their reporting systems focus on the qualities of effective communication. We then describe some of the various reporting tools that might be included in such systems. Finally, we show how adhering to the principles of honesty and fairness helps ensure that grading and reporting systems are true enhancements to teaching and learning processes.

## The Importance of Purpose

The most critical issue to be addressed in selecting the tools included in a reporting system is what purpose or purposes we want to serve. In other words, why are we conveying this information, and what do we hope to accomplish? To determine the purpose or purposes, three aspects of communication must be considered, as shown in the box below. Once our purposes are clarified we can then select the tool or tools that best serve those purposes.

---

**Critical Aspects in Determining Communication Purposes**

1. What information or message do we want to communicate?

2. Who is the primary audience for that message?

3. How would we like that information or message to be used?

---

A major error committed by many educators in selecting reporting tools or creating reporting systems is that they choose their reporting tools first without giving careful attention to the purpose. Many schools and school districts, for example, charge headlong into the development of a standards-based report card without first addressing core questions about why they are doing it. Others incorporate student portfolios or implement student-led conferences simply because "they seem to be a good idea" and "other schools are doing it."

Such efforts typically encounter unexpected resistance and rarely bring the foretold positive results. Parents and teachers often perceive them as new-fangled fads that require extra work and present no real advantage over more traditional reporting methods. As a result, many of these efforts end up being short-lived experiments that are abandoned after a few troubled years of implementation.

Efforts that begin by clarifying their purpose, on the other hand, make intentions explicit from the start. This not only helps mobilize everyone involved in the reporting process, it also keeps efforts on track. Furthermore, being clear about the purpose prevents distraction by peripheral issues that waste crucial time and divert energy (Guskey, 2000). In essence, the famous adage that guides architecture also applies to reporting student learning: *Form follows function.* In other words, purpose must always come first. Once the purpose or function is decided, questions regarding form become more relevant and much easier to address.

This is not to imply, however, that there is or ever should be a single purpose in reporting student learning. Most schools and school districts recognize multiple reporting purposes. That is why they require comprehensive reporting systems that include multiple reporting tools, each with a specific and clearly articulated purpose.

# The Challenge of Communication

Most teachers and school administrators want to do a better job of communicating student learning, especially to parents. They recognize that such communication is essential to involving parents in students' learning efforts and to gaining parents' support for school programs. At the same time, many have no idea how to go about building a positive and effective communication system and, consequently, are fearful of trying (Epstein, 1995).

Teachers and school administrators are also aware of the formidable barriers to parent involvement. These include both parents working, single parents with heavy responsibilities, transportation difficulties, child-care needs, cultural and language barriers, and some parents just too stressed or too depressed to care (Kirschenbaum, 1999). Still, strong evidence indicates that parents at all socioeconomic levels and of all educational backgrounds are willing to help their children succeed in school. Many are dependent, however, on guidance from the school, and especially their child's teacher, as to how best to offer that support (Chrispeels, Fernandez, & Preston, 1991).

Surveys of parents consistently show that most would like more information about their child's progress in school. They want to receive that information more regularly and in a form they understand and can use. As we described earlier, parents generally perceive the report card as the primary and sometimes only source of such information. Therefore, the majority of parents indicate they want to receive report cards more often than the typical three or four times per year (Wemette, 1994). A reporting system that includes multiple reporting tools distributed at different times throughout the school year can address this parental concern. If thoughtfully designed, such multi-tool systems offer students, parents, and others precisely the kind of information they want and deserve.

# Tools for a Comprehensive Reporting System

The list of reporting tools that can be included in a school or school district's reporting system is extensive. In fact, advances in communication technology make the number and variety of options available to educators virtually unlimited. The reporting systems most highly regarded by parents typically include a mix of traditional and more modern reporting tools. Some of the tools most commonly used are listed in the accompanying box and described in detail on the following pages.

---

**Tools That Might Be Included in a
Comprehensive Reporting System**

1. Report Cards
2. Notes Attached to Report Cards
3. Standardized Assessment Reports
4. Phone Calls to Parents
5. Weekly/Monthly Progress Reports
6. School Open-Houses
7. Newsletters to Parents
8. Personal Letters to Parents
9. Evaluated Projects or Assignments
10. Portfolios or Exhibits of Students' Work
11. Homework Assignments
12. Homework Hotlines
13. School Web Pages
14. Parent-Teacher Conferences
15. Student-Teacher Conferences
16. Student-Led Conferences

---

## Report Cards

Report cards form the foundation of nearly every reporting system. For that reason, much of our discussion in previous chapters focused on report cards and other similar reporting forms. If the primary purpose of the report card is to communicate information to parents about teachers' judgments of students' achievement and performance, then parents should be closely involved in developing the report card. Their perspectives and input should be thoroughly considered and their pertinent concerns addressed. To serve as an effective communication tool, parents must understand the information on the report card and know what it means (Wiggins, 1994). They also must be able to interpret that information correctly and use it appropriately to guide any improvement efforts that might be required.

On the other hand, if the primary purpose of the report card is to communicate information to students for self-evaluation, then it is students who must be able to understand and accurately interpret the information included. This, in turn, means that students should be involved in the development of the report card so that their perspectives and concerns can be taken into account.

Whatever purpose is chosen, however, we recommend that purpose be clearly stated on the report card itself. It can be printed in a small box on the top of the report card or on the first page. This should be done on traditional, paper report cards, on digital report cards, or announced at the beginning of a video report card. Clearly stating the purpose helps everyone know what the report card represents, the intended audience, and how the included information might be used.

> *Great job in math, Chris!*
> *Next time, let's try to*
> *bring up those marks*
> *in social studies*

**Figure 10.1.** Example of a Report Card Note From the Principal

## Notes Attached to Report Cards

The manner in which a principal interacts with students and the things that students subsequently tell their parents about the school greatly affect parents' perceptions of the school and their relationships with educators. One way that many principals have found to strengthen their relationships with students and parents is to attach short, personal notes to each student's report card. In some cases, the notes are intended for the parents. More often, however, they are addressed to the students themselves. The purpose of these notes is usually twofold. First, they express the principal's interest in each student's learning progress. Second, they allow principals to recognize students' accomplishments and to offer encouragement for improvement (see Figure 10.1).

In our interviews with parents and students, we were surprised to find how much they value and appreciate these small notes. Many indicated that it's the first thing they read on the report card and that these notes are always saved. Teachers told us that they, too, read the notes and deeply appreciate the principal's personal interest in their students. Although preparing such notes requires time and commitment on the part of principals, they are an effective communication tool that reinforces positive home-school relations (Giba, 1999).

## Standardized Assessment Reports

Many schools and school districts administer commercially prepared, standardized tests and assessments to gain another perspective on students' achievement and performance. These assessments are typically given just once a year, and because they must be sent off to be scored, results generally are not available to teachers, students, or their parents until several months later.

Students' scores on standardized assessments are usually compared to score distributions obtained from a "national sample" of students who are of similar age or at the same grade level. Comparative results are then reported in percentiles, stanines, normal curve equivalents, or some other standardized score. Test manufacturers prepare score summaries for each student along with brief descriptions of what the scores mean. These summaries are recorded in students' permanent school files and also sent home to parents who interpret the scores as depicting how their child ranks among age mates or classmates across the entire nation.

Of all reporting tools, standardized assessment reports are probably the most frequently misinterpreted. The statistical procedures used to generate students' scores (e.g., item response theory models) confuse school counselors and bewilder most parents. Even seemingly simple conveyances such as "grade equivalents" are almost always misunderstood (Hills, 1983). Complicating matters further is the fact that most standardized assessments are not well aligned with the curriculum being taught and hence tend to be an inadequate measure of how well students have learned (Barton, 1999). For these reasons, standardized assessment reports typically require detailed explanation from school personnel and extensive parent training.

## Phone Calls to Parents

Phone calls are one of the easiest and most efficient means of communication between educators and parents. Of all reporting tools, however, phone calls are probably the most underused and misused. In our surveys with parents, for example, over 70% indicated that they "feared" phone calls from school. When we investigated this unexpected response in follow-up interviews, parents clarified what they meant. They told us they feared phone calls from school because they receive a call for only one of two reasons. The first reason is that their child had done something wrong and was in trouble. And the second reason is that their child was sick or hurt. Is it any wonder that parents fear phone calls from school if these are the only reasons educators call them?

To change this perspective, many teachers have started making regular phone calls to parents and, in the process, have discovered countless benefits. Most begin by checking school records to determine with whom their students are living and make a special note when surnames differ. Next, they notify parents during an open-house meeting or in a special note sent home of their intention to call once a month or every other month. Most tell their students as well. Typically teachers emphasize to parents that they have no set agenda for the call. Rather, they simply want to hear parents' concerns and answer any questions the parents might have. Finally, the teachers set aside a time each week to make the calls (Gustafson, 1998).

Teachers report that some weeks they complete the calling in 10 to 15 minutes, with the majority of calls resulting in messages left on answering machines. Other weeks, however, every call is answered by a parent eager to talk. Most teachers begin the conversation with an open-ended statement such as "Hi, this is Ms. Hartman, ____'s teacher at Walsh. I'm making my regular

## One Teacher's Experience With Phone Calls

A middle school's faculty with which we worked decided to initiate a "Phone Home Program" in which every teacher agreed to call the parents or guardians of three students each week. During the calls teachers informed parents of classroom events, reported on students' recent learning progress, and inquired about questions or concerns that parents might have. One first-year teacher misinterpreted the plan, however, and began the school year by making three phone calls *each night*.

When the principal observed this beginning teacher's class during the third week of school, he was delighted to find she had no classroom management problems, no student behavior problems, and 100% completion rates on homework assignments. When asked how she was able to curtail problems that typically plague first-year teachers, she replied simply, "I've talked to all my kids' parents, and they're helping me."

This teacher went on to relate the following conversation she had with Jason, a student who had been a challenge to his former teachers.

Jason came into class frowning one morning and indignantly asked his teacher, "You called my mom last night, didn't you?"

"Yes, Jason, I did," replied the teacher.

"Why'd you do that? I haven't done anything wrong."

"No you haven't, Jason, and that's just what I told your mother. In fact, I told her that you've been doing very well and that I thought this was going to be a really great year for you."

"You really told her that, huh?"

"Yes, I did."

(Pause)

"You know, she won't let me watch television now until I finish my homework."

"We talked about that, too."

(Pause)

"Are you going to be talking with my mom again?"

"I'm sure I will, Jason. I told your mother that I plan to call each month. And I'm certain I'll have some good things to tell her about how you're doing."

(Pause)

"This year's sure going to be different, isn't it?"

"Yes, Jason, I think it will . . . "

phone call and wanted to know if you have any questions, or if there is anything you would like to talk about." Teachers find that parents generally take it from there.

Regular phone calls to parents help teachers keep up to date on their students' lives. Without them, for example, the teacher might not know that one quiet girl often had late assignments because she was competing in gymnastics, that a boy's father was taking over custody, that several fourth-grade girls were picking on one another at recess, or that a beloved grandfather had died. Regular calls also give parents the opportunity to check on the information their children bring home from school (Gustafson, 1998).

---

### One Principal's Experience With Phone Calls

An elementary school principal we know uses her cell phone to communicate to parents what she calls "The Good News." She carries her phone with her as she walks through the hallways, visits the cafeteria, supervises the playground, and observes teachers' classes. When she sees a student performing well in class, assisting a classmate, or helping to improve the school, she immediately calls that student's parent or guardian on her phone and announces, "Hello, this is Ms. Johnson, the principal at Judd Elementary School. I just saw Tonya . . . " After explaining what she observed and complimenting the child, she hands the phone to the child so that he or she can talk briefly with the parent or guardian. Everyone leaves with a big smile.

When asked about calls to parents concerning student problems, Ms. Johnson explains, "Those I save for after school. Often, I have to think more carefully about what I'm going to say and what strategies I'm going to recommend. When I see a child doing something wonderful, however, I want to let the parents know about that right away. And I never have to weigh my words. Plus, I think it means more to the child."

The principal's phone calls have completely altered the culture of this school. Parent involvement and participation in school events is at an all-time high, and their regard for Ms. Johnson and the school staff is exceptionally positive. It's a small thing, but it has made a big difference.

---

Phone calls can also be used to inform parents of special events and to invite their participation. This might include classroom celebrations, choir performances, science fairs, or open-house meetings. Receiving a call not only reminds parents of the event but tells them it's important enough that someone took the time to contact them. And once they've promised to be there, parents are likely to keep their promise (Kirschenbaum, 1999).

Nearly all teachers tell us the first phone call is the most difficult. Time and again we've heard stories of parents answering the phone and, upon learning the call is from their child's teacher, ask, "What did he do now?" Automatically, they assume something must be wrong. After learning the nature of the call, parents often express a sense of relief and usually end the call by adding "I'm really glad you called." Making regular phone calls to parents takes time and dedication on the part of teachers. Most teachers tell us, however, that the benefits far outweigh the costs.

## Weekly/Monthly Progress Reports

Another reporting tool that many school staffs use to inform parents about what's going on in school and how they can become involved is weekly or monthly progress reports. In some cases, these are short checklists or mini report cards that give parents a brief summary of students' learning progress between report cards. Others are designed simply to inform parents about the curriculum and teachers' expectations.

An example of one such report is illustrated in Figure 10.2. This form is completed by each teacher and distributed to students to take home to their parents at the beginning of each month. It lets parents know what will be the curriculum focus in each class during the coming month, as well as the planned learning goals. Equally important, it offers parents specific suggestions about how they might help at home. Most teachers find that completing a form such as this for each class takes relatively little time and effort. Still, it is deeply appreciated by parents and frequently leads to improvements in student learning.

## School Open-Houses

A school open-house is a brief meeting, usually held in the evening, where parents are invited to the school to visit their child's classrooms and meet with the teachers. In most cases the open-house is parents' first encounter with their child's teachers and the teachers' first opportunity to interact with parents.

Because open-house meetings tend to be brief and rarely involve detailed discussions about individual students, most teachers regard them casually and spend little time preparing for them. Parents, on the other hand, attach great importance to open-house meetings. A recent *Phi Delta Kappan* poll showed, for example, that nearly 90% of parents consider school open-house meetings to be the most effective communication device for gathering information about the school and their child's teachers (Langdon, 1999).

To make the most of school open-houses, teachers should keep in mind our discussion in Chapter 1 regarding what parents most want to know about their child's teachers. Recall, parents want to know (1) that their child's teachers are competent, and (2) that those teachers care about their child as an individual. Teachers who focus on communicating these two things to parents at open-house meetings create a positive impression among parents and do much to ensure parents' cooperation and assistance throughout the school year.

---

## Morton Middle School

Parent Information & Involvement Form

*Teacher* _____ *Class* _____

---

During the next month, the major topics we will be studying are:

---

Our goal in studying these topics is for students to be able to:

---

Parents can help at home by:

---

**Figure 10.2.** Example of a Monthly Class Report

How teachers communicate these two things to parents, of course, is vitally important. In our informal interviews and discussions with parents, we learned, for example, that few are impressed by a teacher's long list of degrees or training experiences. Instead, they want to know what the teacher has planned for the class, what learning goals have been set, and how the teacher intends to help students reach those goals. Parents also appreciate hearing about special projects, classroom procedures, and tips on how they can help at home. Perhaps most important, parents want to know that the teacher is personable, approachable, and willing to make special efforts to help students learn. Teachers who convey this in their presentations to parents not only open pathways to better communication, they also facilitate a better working partnership between school and home.

## Newsletters to Parents

When it comes to fostering communication between school and home, the majority of both teachers and parents say that conventional forms of communication are more effective than newer ones, such as Internet Web sites and hotlines (Landgon, 1999). Among the more conventional forms, both teachers and parents consider newsletters to be one of the most effective.

Newsletters provide parents and others with everyday details about the school. They can describe upcoming events, thank parents by name for their assistance, announce student award winners in each class, and provide ideas for specific learning activities that parents can do with their children. Some newsletters contain profiles of new teachers or staff members, and many have a special column by the principal (Kirschenbaum, 1999). Most schools distribute newsletters once each month, and parents typically assist in their preparation.

In addition to regular newsletters, many schools distribute an attractive calendar and handbook to parents at the beginning of each school year. The calendar notes school events, indicates when interim reports and report cards will be distributed, encourages parents' involvement, and offers detailed suggestions on how parents can support their child's education at home (Kirschenbaum, 1999). The handbook offers information about the school and staff members, describes school policies, and indicates where and how parents can find more details.

## Personal Letters to Parents

Personal letters to parents allow teachers to model honest communication by notifying parents when their child has done exceptionally well or by informing parents as soon as academic or behavioral problems arise. Letters that report good news should congratulate the child and emphasize the quality and effort displayed in the student's work. Letters that identify problems should make suggestions to parents as to how the problem might be addressed and stress the teacher's willingness to work with parents toward a solution. This approach keeps parents informed and demonstrates the importance of sharing children's successes as well as their difficulties with parents (Kreider & Lopez, 1999).

## Evaluated Projects or Assignments

Evaluated projects and assignments represent a highly effective means for teachers to communicate learning goals and expectations to parents. But the form of this evaluation information makes a difference. Projects or assignments that come home with only a single mark or grade at the top of the page provide neither students nor their parents with much useful information. Although it may communicate the teacher's overall appraisals of students' achievement or performance, it offers no guidance for improvement.

Parents seeking to become more involved in their child's learning need direction from educators, and particularly their child's teacher, as to how they can help. Evaluated assignments or assessments that include specific comments from the teacher, along with clear suggestions for improvement, offer parents that needed direction. Projects or papers accompanied by explicit scoring rubrics similarly provide parents with a clear description of what the teacher expects and the criteria by which students' work is evaluated. With this information parents can make sure their efforts at home are well aligned with what the teacher expects at school.

## Portfolios or Exhibits of Students' Work

Another efficient and highly effective way of sharing information about students' achievement and performance with parents is to collect evaluated samples of students' work in a portfolio. Portfolios are simply collections of evidence on student learning that serve three major purposes: (1) to display students' work around a theme, (2) to illustrate the process of learning, and (3) to show growth or progress (Davies, 2000). Some portfolios are specific to a class or subject area, whereas others combine students' work across several subjects (Robinson, 1998). Teachers at all levels report that parents are enthusiastic about the use of portfolios as a reporting tool and often indicate that they learn more from the portfolio than they do from the report card (Balm, 1995).

Most schools use portfolios in conjunction with report cards to clarify the marks or grades on the report card. In some schools, however, portfolios serve to inform parents about students' learning on a more regular and ongoing basis. One school that we know, for example, uses "Friday Folders" to keep parents abreast of their children's performance. A collection of evaluated papers, assignments, and assessments, along with notes from teachers and notices of school events, are placed in the folder and sent home each Friday. Parents sign the folder each week and record any comments or questions they might have. Students then return the folder to their teacher when they come to school the following Monday.

Exhibits of students' work represent yet another good way to communicate information about students' achievement. The athletic and fine arts departments in schools have long scheduled sporting events, concerts, and plays for parents and interested community members to attend. These events communicate important and meaningful information to those who watch or listen about "what students can do." Exhibits designed expressly for the purposes of communicating how well students perform in academic tasks can do the same (Brookhart, 1999).

To make the best use of portfolios and exhibits of students' work, however, teachers must be able to articulate the qualities of good work and help students learn to recognize these qualities in their own work. Teachers also must teach their students how to select the examples to exhibit and how to articulate the reasons for their selections. These are important assessment-related skills that help students become more thoughtful judges of their own work and lead to higher levels of student performance.

## Homework Assignments

Most teachers see homework as a way to offer students additional practice on what they learned in class and to extend students' involvement in learning activities. Many consider homework an opportunity for students to review academic skills and to explore topics of special interest through individual reports and independent projects. But homework is also an excellent way for teachers to communicate with parents. It provides a means for teachers to let parents know what is being emphasized in class, what is expected of students, and how students' work will be evaluated (Cooper, 1989).

Students' engagement in homework is closely related to measures of achievement and academic performance at the high school level, although this relationship has more to do with the quality of homework in which students engage than simply the quantity. At the elementary level, however, the relationship between homework and performance in school is much more modest. In the elementary grades, homework serves best to inform parents about what students are doing in school and to involve parents in students' learning tasks (Cooper, 1994).

Homework assignments at the elementary level, therefore, should be specifically designed so that parents and students can work together. For example, an assignment might involve questions that students are to ask their parents or guardian, issues that students and parents are to explore together, or a procedure for students to complete and then have their parent check. Experiences such as these give parents the opportunity to become involved in their children's schoolwork, to encourage good work habits, and to emphasize the importance of learning.

## Homework Hotlines

To facilitate completion of homework assignments, many schools develop "homework hotlines." The simplest hotlines permit students and their parents to telephone the school, follow a series of simple instructions, and then hear a recorded message from the teacher describing the homework assignment for that day. Some teachers simply describe the assignment and the due date in their message. Others specify the goal of the assignment, offer suggestions for completion, and outline the criteria by which the assignment will be evaluated. These messages allow students to check on assignments and clarify those of which they are unsure. They also permit students who are absent from school to get a head start on their makeup work.

In other schools, homework hotlines are actually staffed by teachers or teaching assistants who offer direct assistance to students on their homework assignments. Students who get stuck on some aspect of an assignment can call the hotline and get immediate help. They need not wait until their next class to ask a question or to get the assistance they need. Although setting up homework hotlines requires additional expense and effort on the part of educators, the service offers a variety of benefits to both students and their parents.

## School Web Pages

As schools become increasingly sophisticated in their use of technology, more are establishing their own Internet Web pages. Some school Web pages simply offer information about the school, administrators, and faculty; school policies; and the time and dates of special events. Others include information about various programs of study and about each course or class within the program. In addition to a general description of the classes, many include information about the learning standards or goals, the grading criteria or scoring rubrics for particular class projects, and a schedule of assignments. In some cases, descriptions are regularly updated to provide information about daily homework assignments and special class events.

Another important advantage of school Web pages is that they offer the opportunity for two-way communication. Most Web pages are combined with e-mail systems that list the e-mail address of each school administrator, teacher, and staff member. Parents who have questions or concerns can correspond with their child's teacher directly and need not worry about interrupting the teacher's busy schedule. Teachers, in turn, can respond to parents' questions and concerns at a time convenient to them. Furthermore, e-mail allows teachers time to think about their response, include pertinent information, offer suggestions or recommendations, and then keep a record of the communication. Although most schools report that few parents correspond with teachers or staff members via e-mail, those who do find it a very useful form of communication.

## Parent-Teacher Conferences

Parent-teacher conferences hold special promise as a reporting tool because the communication is interactive and can be highly individualized. Teachers can select different pieces for information or even different themes to discuss for different students (Brookhart, 1999). Conferences also offer teachers the opportunity to discuss a wide range of school-related but nonacademic aspects of learning, such as attendance and tardy rates, class participation, attentiveness, social interactions, and class behavior (Nelson, 2000). But like other forms of reporting, teachers rarely receive pre-service training or professional development on how to prepare for these face-to-face encounters with parents (Little & Allan, 1989).

Poorly planned parent-teacher conferences can be a frustrating experience for parents and teachers alike. In our interviews with parents, for example, many expressed occasional disappointment with parent-teacher conferences. Some said that the time allotted for the conference was too short to get a clear picture of how their child was doing. Others related stories of having to stand in long lines to have only a few minutes with the teacher. Teachers expressed different but equally serious frustrations. Several described spending hours preparing for conferences and then having only a few parents show up. The parents who did show up often were not the ones with whom the teacher really hoped to speak. Still other teachers told of the difficulties they encountered in dealing with angry and disgruntled parents.

When parent-teacher conferences are well planned, however, they can be key to developing a positive working relationship between parents and teachers. To aid in that process, we offer a series of procedural recommendations for planning and conducting effective parent-teacher conferences in Table 10.1. These recommendations are based on information gleaned from our interviews with parents and teachers. They are divided in the table among things to do before the conference, during the conference, and then after the conference (see also Bernick, Rutherford, & Elliott, 1991).

Table 10.1  Recommendations for Effective Parent-Teacher Conferences

| Before the conference... | During the conference... | After the conference... |
|---|---|---|
| • Encourage parents to review student work at home, note concerns or questions, and bring those to the conference. | • Provide child care, refreshments, and transportation, if needed. | • Provide parents with a telephone number and schedule of specific times so they may call you with concerns. |
| • Schedule times that are convenient for both working and nonworking parents. | • Show multiple samples of student work and discuss specific suggestions for improvement. | • Follow up on any questions or concerns raised during the conference. |
| • Notify parents well ahead of scheduled conference times. | • Actively listen and avoid the use of educational jargon. | • Plan a time to meet again, if necessary. |
| • Provide staff development for new teachers on the purpose for conferences, preparation, and scheduling. | • Communicate expectations and describe how parents can help. | • Encourage parents to discuss the conference with their child. |
| • Consider alternative locations, such as churches or community centers for parents' convenience. | • Develop a system for ongoing communication with each parent that recognizes parents as partners. | • Ask parents for a written evaluation of the conference and encourage them to make suggestions. |
| • Print conference schedules and materials in multiple languages, if necessary. | • Provide resources or materials that parents might use at home to strengthen students' skills. | • Debrief with colleagues to look for ways to improve future conferences. |

Parent-teacher conferences also appear to be most efficient and effective when they focus on four major issues:

1. What is the student able to do?

2. What areas require further attention or skill development?

3. What help or support does the student need to be successful?

4. How is the student doing in relation to established learning standards for students in a similar age range or grade level? (Davies, 1996).

With careful planning and organization, parent-teacher conferences can be both informative and productive. They are an effective way to build positive, collaborative relationships between parents and teachers and should be part of every school's comprehensive reporting system.

## Student-Teacher Conferences

Another highly effective but often neglected conference form is the student-teacher conference. Like parent-teacher conferences, student-teacher conferences require careful planning and organization. In particular, if the conferences are held during class time, teachers must ensure that students not involved in the conference are engaged in meaningful learning activities. Student-teacher conferences also have their own dynamics and require different approaches to communication about academic work. Nevertheless, they provide for both students and teachers a form of one-to-one, interpersonal communication that cannot be achieved through other communication formats.

Student-teacher conferences should focus on discussions of the qualities of good work and students' current work in relation to those qualities. Work samples can be reviewed with specific suggestions for improvement. Teachers should express their positive expectations for students' learning and behavior along with their willingness to help students in efforts to improve. And most important, teachers should actively listen to students to determine how they might be most helpful.

Some teachers conduct student-teacher conferences just twice per year, while others schedule conferences with students at the beginning of each marking period. This regular schedule of conferences allows them to review students' immediate past work while setting improvement goals for forthcoming marking periods or instructional units.

## Student-Led Conferences

A third highly effective conference form is student-led conferences. In the typical parent-teacher conference and student-teacher conference, teachers lead the discussion regarding students' learning progress. In contrast, in a student-led conference the students are responsible for leading the discussion and reporting on their learning to parents. The teacher serves primarily as facilitator and observer.

Most teachers organize student-led conferences so that several conferences (typically four) are conducted simultaneously in the classroom, with family groups seated far enough apart to allow privacy. The teacher then circulates among family groups, stopping long enough to make pertinent comments and answer questions. Students direct the conversation during the conference, focusing both on the work samples they have in their conference portfolio and on their performance in relation to expected learning goals or standards.

The real power in this conference format is that students take responsibility for reporting what they have learned. To prepare for this responsibility, students must be given regular opportunities to evaluate and reflect on the quality of their work. They also must be given guidance on how to thoughtfully organize their work in a portfolio and how to explain their work to others. In other words, students must be actively involved in all aspects of the reporting process.

Despite these additional preparation responsibilities, teachers at all levels generally favor the use of student-led conferences. Most indicate that the necessary preparation does not require an inordinate amount of instructional time. Plus, preparation tasks blend well with regular classroom routines as a way to promote student accountability. In addition, many teachers consider student-led conferences an extremely efficient way to meet and talk with the parents of their students.

Student-led conferences also are an effective means of promoting parent involvement. Schools that have implemented student-led conferences consistently report dramatic increases in parent attendance at conferences (Little & Allan, 1989).

Through our surveys and interviews with parents we learned that they too regard student-led conferences very highly. One parent of an elementary student said, "I didn't know my son could speak so well about his work. He usually tells me he 'learned nothing today.' He really does know what he's doing!" Parents of high school students similarly expressed appreciation for all of the preparation and reflection that went into the portfolio of the student's work. Many told us that they especially liked having their son or daughter present to talk about concerns and to ask questions during the conference.

There are many ways to organize student-led conferences, and teachers vary in their format preferences. Important factors to consider when designing a specific format include the age and number of students involved, the flexibility of any previously established school district schedule for conference times, the amount of time available for student preparation, the comfort level of all participants with the concept of student-led conferences, and the specific goals for reporting student learning. It is also important to again consider purpose and context in choosing a format (Little & Allan, 1989).

Student-led conferences represent a highly effective way to communicate directly and authentically with parents. When students direct the reporting process, information is communicated in a form everyone can understand and use. As learning becomes increasingly complex from kindergarten throughout high school, the portfolio becomes a detailed reporting tool that demonstrates students' growth and progress over time. Reviewing the portfolio during the conference becomes a learning experience for everyone involved. As such, student-led conferences are an especially important part of the comprehensive reporting system.

# Guidelines for Better Practice

We now turn to a few brief guidelines for better practice. As we've stressed from the beginning, most teachers try hard to be fair in their grading and reporting policies and practices. They inform students of the components that will be used in grading and how those components will be weighed or combined. Nevertheless, grading practices vary considerably from teacher to teacher, especially in the perceived meaning of grades and in the factors considered in determining grades (Brookhart, 1994). Furthermore, few teachers have thought seriously about how they grade or considered the potential impact of their grading policies and practices on students.

To develop and implement better grading policies and practices, we need to become more thoughtful about what we do. We need to make better use of the significant knowledge base on grading and reporting that has been accumulated over the past century. We also must become more conscientious about the application of that knowledge. The following guidelines are offered to help educators at all levels in that process.

## Begin With a Clear Statement of Purpose

Many of the dilemmas faced with regard to grading and reporting can be resolved if we are clearer about our purpose. Grading and reporting today are an integral part of teaching and learning. But as we have shown, not all educators agree on the purpose of grading or on the intended outcomes. As a result, grading and reporting policies and practices tend to be fragmented, ambiguous, and generally confusing to students, to parents, and to many teachers.

The first step in this clarification process is distinguishing the formative and summative purposes of grading and reporting. As we described in Chapter 4, most of a teacher's grading and reporting tasks are actually *formative* in nature; that is, they are designed to offer students prescriptive feedback on their performance. Only occasionally must teachers synthesize that information in order to assign a cumulative, *summative* grade to students' achievement and performance (Bloom et al., 1971). By keeping this distinction in mind and by using more thoughtful ways to combine the various sources of information in order to determine summative grades, teachers can emphasize their role as advocates for students while still fulfilling their evaluation responsibilities.

The second step is for educators to recognize that no single reporting tool can serve all reporting purposes well. Improvements in grading and reporting will be best accomplished therefore through the development of comprehensive reporting systems. Reporting systems include multiple reporting tools, each designed to fit a specific, well-defined purpose. They communicate multiple types of information to multiple audiences in multiple formats. Such comprehensive reporting systems serve educators' diverse communication needs far better than can any single reporting device.

## Provide Accurate and Understandable Descriptions of Student Learning

At all levels of education teachers must be able to identify what they want their students to learn, what evidence they will use to verify that learning, and what criteria will be used to judge that evidence. These decisions form the basis for grading and reporting.

Educators also must decide if they want to report on aspects of students' learning apart from evidence on achievement or academic performance. For example, is it important to consider information about students' work habits, effort, or other process criteria? Should information about the amount of improvement or progress criteria be included as well? If information on these types of learning criteria is considered significant in the reporting process, it should be reported separately from evidence on achievement or performance. As we emphasized in earlier chapters, it is far better to offer multiple marks or grades on different aspects of students' learning than it is to combine all aspects into a single symbol with fine gradations.

Once such decisions are made, educators must consider how best to communicate this information. If the primary audience for the information is parents or students, we must ensure that information is free of jargon and complex technical language. It should be explicit and precise, and relate to clearly defined learning goals. Most important, it should communicate students' strengths and what they have achieved, identify any shortcomings or areas of weakness, and recommend practical suggestions for making improvements.

Finally, we must always remember that reporting involves two-way communication. Not only must the information be understood by the audience for whom it is intended, procedures must be in place for questions or concerns to be expressed and addressed. Effective grading and reporting is far more a challenge in effective communication than simply a process of documenting student achievement.

## Use Grading and Reporting to Enhance Teaching and Learning

Educators today are becoming increasingly skilled in measurement and assessment techniques. Many use a variety of authentic assessment formats and score students' performance with carefully constructed rubrics. At the same time, however, their efforts to communicate the results of those assessments to parents and other interested persons are undeveloped and rarely adequate. Few teachers today have thoroughly considered the consequences of their grading policies and practices or explored possible alternative procedures. As a result, they persist in the use of unsound grading practices that can have profoundly negative effects on students' attitudes, confidence, achievement, self-concept, motivation, and future education (Stiggins et al., 1989). The indiscriminate use of averaging to obtain a course grade, assigning zeros, and lowering students' grades due to behavioral infractions are just a few examples. How teachers grade is a serious matter and one that needs serious attention.

The changes required to eliminate these harmful effects are relatively small and seldom require a significant amount of extra work. However, it does mean developing grading and reporting systems that provide more chances for success, more guidance, more detailed feedback, more corrective instruction, and more positive encouragement. In essence, it means ensuring that grades provide an accurate and understandable description of students' achievement, performance, and progress in learning. Grades are harmful only if they misinform or mislead, or are based on factors that have nothing to do with learning.

Parents consistently tell us that they want to know more about how their children are doing in school. Most are willing to become more involved in their children's education but are highly dependent on the school, and especially their child's teacher, for guidance as to how to do so. Information that lets them know what is expected of their children, how their children are performing in relation to those expectations, and how they can assist in the process is particularly helpful. Information supported by teachers' records, observations, and samples of students' work is even better. Information that students develop, reflect upon, and then report to their parents and others is better still. Such practices adhere to important principles of honesty and fairness and help ensure that grading and reporting systems are true enhancements to teaching and learning processes.

## Conclusion

By its very nature, grading is a subjective process. It involves one group of human beings (teachers) making judgments about the performance of another group of human beings (students). But as we have stressed throughout this book, being subjective doesn't mean that grades lack credibility or are indefensible. Rather, it simply implies that grading is and will always be an exercise in professional judgment. Grades provide parents, students, and other interested persons with the means to interpret the professional judgments that teachers have made.

If those professional judgments are to remain meaningful and accurate, teachers must continuously reflect on their purpose in grading. They must constantly review what information they want to communicate, who is the primary audience for that information, and what result they hope to accomplish. If grades are to present information to parents about the adequacy of students' achievement and performance, then the evidence used in determining grades must relate directly to what students have learned and can do. Other factors related to students' work habits, behaviors, or learning progress, while important, must be reported separately. To include these factors as part of a single grade misrepresents students' learning attainments.

Above all else, grading and reporting require careful planning, thoughtful judgment, and a clear focus on purpose. They also require a profound sense of fairness, excellent communication skills, and an overriding concern for students. Such qualities are necessary to ensure grading practices that provide high-quality information on student learning, regardless of the method employed. They also ensure that grading and reporting will be a positive and beneficial aspect of students' learning experiences.

# Resource A

# MESA UNIFIED SCHOOL DISTRICT #4
## REPORT CARD

**Student Name**

**Student Number**

| Grade | Home Room | Counselor Phone No. | Parent Phone No. |
|---|---|---|---|

### Grade Legend

A = Superior (4.0)
B = Above Average (3.0)
C = Average (2.0)
D = Below Average (1.0)
D- = Min. Progress (0.5)
F = Failure (0.0)
INC = Incomplete (0.0)
W/D = Withdrawn (0.0)
AUD = Audit (0.0)
P/F = Pass/Fail (0.0)

### Graduation Requirements

COMPETENCY REQUIREMENTS ACHIEVED

☐ READING   ☐ MATH   ☐ WRITING

| SUBJECT | *CREDITS REQUIRED | EARNED |
|---|---|---|
| ENGLISH | 4 | |
| MATH | 2 | |
| SCIENCE | 2 | |
| SOCIAL STUDIES | 3 | |
| FINE / PRAC. ART | 1 | |
| PHYS. ED. | 1 | |
| ELECTIVES | 8 | |
| TOTAL | 21 | |

* Credits earned on a semester basis. This is an unofficial credit report. See your counselor for official totals.

**Please Contact Teacher**

1. Excellent Student
2. Good Attitude / Behavior in Class
3. Good Participation in Class
4. Shows Extra Effort
5. Assignments Complete and Accurate
6. Showing Improvement
7. Student Tries But Experiences Difficulty
8. Low Test Scores Negatively Affect Grade
9. Needs to Bring Materials to Class
10. Needs to Turn in Homework / Make-up Work or Tests
11. Needs to Improve Classroom Behavior
12. Absences / Tardies Affect Work
13. Needs to Follow Correct Techniques / Procedure
14. Needs to Demonstrate More Effort / Time on Task

| Period | Course Number | Course Title | Teacher | 1st Qtr Gd | 2nd Qtr Gd | Final Exam Gd | Sem Gd | 1 | 2 | 3 | 4 | 5 | 6 | 7 | 8 | 9 | 10 | 11 | 12 | 13 | 14 | 15 |
|---|---|---|---|---|---|---|---|---|---|---|---|---|---|---|---|---|---|---|---|---|---|---|
| | | | | | | | | | | | | | | | | | | | | | | |

**Grade Point Averages**

Qtr:
Sem:
Cum:

TO:

Congratulations are in order where success is evident.
Encouragement or teacher contact is appropriate where problems now exist.

Rev. 12-2-93

196

# DISTRITO ESCOLAR UNIFICADO DE MESA #4
## REPORTE DE CALIFICACIONES

**Requisitos Para Graduacion**

REQUISITOS DE COMPETENCIA LOGRADOS

☐ LECTURA ☐ MATEMATICAS ☐ ESCRITURA

| ASIGNATURA | *CREDITOS | |
|---|---|---|
| | OBLIGATORIOS | ACUMULADOS |
| INGLES | 4 | |
| MATEMATICAS | 2 | |
| CIENCIA | 2 | |
| CIENCIAS SOCIALES | 3 | |
| ARTES FINAS/PRAC. | 1 | |
| EDUCACION FISICA | 1 | |
| ELECTIVAS | 8 | |
| TOTAL | 21 | |

* Los créditos se acumulan cada semestre.
Este no es un reporte oficial de créditos.
Consulta con tu consejero/a para los totales oficiales.

### LEYENDA DE CALIFICACIONES

A = Sobresaliente (4.0)
B = Más del Promedio (3.0)
C = Promedio (2.0)
D = Menos del Promedio (1.0)
D- = Progreso Mínimo (0.5)
F = Deficiencia (0.0)
INC = Incompleto (0.0)
W/D = Se Salió (0.0)
AUD = Audit (0.0)
P/F = Aprobar Reprobar (0.0)

**Favor de Comunicarse con la Maestra/o.**

| | |
|---|---|
| 1 | Estudiante Sobresaliente |
| 2 | Actitud/Comportamiento Bueno en la Clase |
| 3 | Buena Participación en la Clase |
| 4 | Muestra Esfuerzo Extra |
| 5 | Las Asignaturas Son Completas y Correctas |
| 6 | Muestra Progreso |
| 7 | Estudiante se Esfuerza Pero Experimenta Dificultad |
| 8 | Las Puntuaciones Bajas en Exámenes Afectan las Calificaciones Negativamente |
| 9 | Necesita Traer los Útiles a Clase |
| 10 | Necesita Entregar Tarea/Trabajo Atrasado o Exámenes |
| 11 | Necesita Mejorar el Comportamiento en el Salón de Clase |
| 12 | Faltas/Tardanzas Afectan su Trabajo |
| 13 | Necesita Seguir las Técnicas/Procedimientos Correctos |
| 14 | Necesita Demostrar más Esfuerzo/Tiempo en Trabajos |

**Nombre del Estudiante** | **Num del Estudiante**

**Grado** | **Salón Principal** | **Teléfono de Consejero/a** | **Teléfono de Padres**

| Periodo | Num. Del Curso | Titulo del Curso | Maestra/o | Calificacion del Primer Trimestre | Calificacion del Segundo Trimestre | Calificacion del Examen Final | Calificacion Semestral |
|---|---|---|---|---|---|---|---|
| | | | | | | | |
| | | | | | | | |
| | | | | | | | |

Cuando el éxito sea evidente, las felicitaciones podrian ser extendidas. El estimulo y la
comunicación con el maestro/a es apropiada donde existen problemas actuales.

DIRIGIDO A:

**Promedios de Calificaciones**

Trimestre:
Semestre:
Cumulativo:

Rev. 12-2-93

English and Spanish Versions of a High School Reporting Form

SOURCE: Report card of Mesa Public Schools (Mesa, AZ). Used by permission.

# References

Abedi, J. (1999, Spring). CRESST report points to test accommodations for English language learning students. *The CRESST Line: Newsletter of the National Center for Research on Evaluation, Standards, and Student Testing,* 6-7.

Abedi, J., Lord, C., & Hofstetter, C. (1998). *Impact of selected background variables on students' NAEP math performance.* Los Angeles: University of California, Center for the Study of Evaluation/National Center for Research on Evaluation, Standards, and Student Testing.

Abou-Sayf, F. K. (1996). An investigation of different grading practices: Reliability, validity, and related psychometric considerations. *Journal of Applied Research in the Community College, 4*(1), 39-47.

Adelman, C. (1999). *Answers in the tool box: Academic intensity, attendance patterns, and bachelor's degree attainment.* Washington, DC: Office of Educational Research and Improvement, U.S. Department of Education.

Afflerbach, P., & Sammons, R. B. (1991). *Report cards in literacy evaluation: Teachers' training, practices, and values.* Paper presented at the annual meeting of the National Reading Conference, Palm Springs, CA.

Agnew, E. (1993). *Department grade quotas: The silent saboteur.* Paper presented at the annual meeting of the Conference on College Composition and Communication, San Diego, CA.

Agnew, E. (1995). Rigorous grading does not raise standards: It only lower grades. *Assessing Writing, 2*(1), 91-103.

Airasian, P. W. (1994). Grading pupil performance. In *Classroom assessment* (2nd ed., chap. 9, pp. 281-330). New York: McGraw-Hill.

Allison, E., & Friedman, S. J. (1995). Reforming report cards. *Executive Educator, 17*(1), 38-39.

American Federation of Teachers, National Council for Measurement in Education, & National Education Association. (1990). *Standards for teacher competence in educational assessment of students.* Washington, DC: Author.

Andrade, H. G. (2000). Using rubrics to promote thinking and learning. *Educational Leadership, 57*(5), 13-18.

Arter, J. A., & Spandel, V. (1992). Using portfolios of student work in instruction and assessment (ITEMS module). *Educational Measurement: Issues and Practice, 12*(1), 36-44.

August, D., & Hakuta, K. (Eds.). (1997). *Improving schooling for language-minority children: A research agenda.* Washington, DC: National Academy Press.

Austin, S., & McCann, R. (1992). *"Here's another arbitrary grade for your collection": A statewide study of grading policies.* Paper presented at the annual meeting of the American Educational Research Association, San Francisco.

Azwell, T., & Schmar, E. (Eds.). (1995). *Report card on report cards: Alternatives to consider.* Portsmouth, NH: Heineman.

Bailey, J., & McTighe, J. (1996). Reporting achievement at the secondary level: What and how. In T. R. Guskey (Ed.), *Communicating student learning. 1996 Yearbook of the Association for Supervision and Curriculum Development* (pp. 119-140). Alexandria, VA: Association for Supervision and Curriculum Development.

Baker, E. L., Linn, R. L., & Herman, J. L. (1996, Summer). CRESST: A continuing mission to improve educational assessment. *Evaluation Comment,* pp. 1, 4-23. Los Angeles: UCLA Center for the Study of Evaluation/National Center for Research on Evaluation, Standards, and Student Testing.

Balm, S. S. M. (1995). Using portfolio assessment in a kindergarten classroom. *Teaching and Change, 2*(2), 141-151.

Barnes, L. L. B., Bull, K. S., Perry, K., & Campbell, N. J. (1998). *Discipline-related differences in teaching and grading philosophies among undergraduate teaching faculty.* Paper presented at the annual meeting of the American Educational Research Association, San Diego, CA.

Barnes, S. (1985). A study of classroom pupil evaluation: The missing link in teacher education. *Journal of Teacher Education, 36*(4), 46-49.

Barton, P. (1999). *Too much testing of the wrong kind; too little of the right kind in K-12 education.* Princeton, NJ: Educational Testing Service.

Basinger, D. (1997). Fighting grade inflation: A misguided effort? *College Teaching, 45*(3), 88-91.

Beaver, W. (1997). Declining college standards: It's not the courses, it's the grades. *College Board Review, 181,* 2-7.

Bennett, R. E., Gottesman, R. L., Rock, D. A., & Cerullo, F. (1993). Influence of behavior perceptions and gender on teachers' judgments of students' academic skill. *Journal of Educational Psychology, 85*(2), 347-356.

Berg, M. H., & Smith, J. P. (1996). Using videotapes to improve teaching. *Music Educators' Journal, 82*(4), 31-37.

Bernetich, E. (1998, February 6). *Personal communication to Thomas R. Guskey from Edward Bernetich, Principal of Beachwood Middle School, Beachwood, OH.*

Bernick, R., Rutherford, B., & Elliott, J. (1991). *School and family conferences in the middle grades.* Washington, DC: Office of Educational Research and Improvement (OERI), U.S. Department of Education.

Bishop, J. H. (1992). Why U.S. students need incentives to learn. *Educational Leadership, 49*(6), 15-18.

Block, J. H., Efthim, H. E., & Burns, R. B. (1989). *Building effective mastery learning schools.* New York: Longman.

Bloom, B. S. (1968). Learning for mastery. *Evaluation Comment, 1*(2), 1-12.

Bloom, B. S. (1971). Mastery learning. In J. H. Block (Ed.), *Mastery learning: Theory and practice.* New York: Holt, Rinehart & Winston.

Bloom, B. S. (1976). *Human characteristics and school learning.* New York: McGraw-Hill.

Bloom, B. S. (1981). *All our children learning: A primer for parents, teachers and other educators.* New York: McGraw-Hill.

Bloom, B. S., Hastings, J. T., & Madaus, G. F. (1971). *Handbook on formative and summative evaluation of student learning.* New York: McGraw-Hill.

Bloom, B. S., Madaus, G. F., & Hastings, J. T. (1981). *Evaluation to improve learning.* New York: McGraw-Hill.

Boothroyd, R. A., & McMorris, R. F. (1992). *What do teachers know about testing and how did they find out?* Paper presented at the annual meeting of the National Council on Measurement in Education, San Francisco, CA.

Bracey, G. W. (1994). Grade inflation? *Phi Delta Kappan, 76*(4), 328-329.

Bracey, G. W. (1998). More about grade inflation or lack of it. *Phi Delta Kappan, 79*(8), 629-630.

Bracey, G. W. (1999). Getting that sheepskin. *Phi Delta Kappan, 81*(2), 169-170.

Brewer, W. R., & Kallick, B. (1996). Technology's promise for reporting student learning. In T. R. Guskey (Ed.), *Communicating student learning. 1996 Yearbook of the Association for Supervision and Curriculum Development* (pp. 178-187). Alexandria, VA: Association for Supervision and Curriculum Development.

British Columbia Ministry of Education. (1994). *Policy for reporting student progress in British Columbia: Kindergarten to Grade 12.* Victoria, BC: Author.

Brookhart, S. M. (1991). Grading practices and validity. *Educational Measurement: Issues and Practice, 10*(1), 35-36.

Brookhart, S. M. (1993). Teachers' grading practices: Meaning and values. *Journal of Educational Measurement, 30*(2), 123-142.

Brookhart, S. M. (1994). Teachers' grading: Practice and theory. *Applied Measurement in Education, 7*(4), 279-301.

Brookhart, S. M. (1999). Teaching about communicating assessment results and grading. *Educational Measurement: Issues and Practice, 18*(1), 5-13.

Brown, D. W. (1972). Look, mom, here's my video report card! *Audiovisual Instruction, 17*(10), 20-22.

Bursuck, W. D., Munk, D. D., & Olson, M. M. (1999). The fairness of report card grading adaptations: What do students with and without disabilities think? *Remedial and Special Education, 20*(2), 84-92, 105.

Bursuck, W. D., Polloway, E. A., Plante, L., Epstein, M. H., Jayanthi, M., & McConeghy, J. (1996). Report card grading and adaptations: A national survey of classroom practices. *Exceptional Children, 62*(3), 301-318.

Calhoun, M. L., & Beattie, J. (1984). Assigning grades in the high school mainstream: Perceptions of teachers and students. *Diagnostique, 9*(4), 218-225.

Cameron, J., & Pierce, W. D. (1994). Reinforcement, reward, and intrinsic motivation: A meta-analysis. *Review of Educational Research, 64*(3), 363-423.

Cameron, J., & Pierce, W. D. (1996). The debate about rewards and intrinsic motivation: Protests and accusations do not alter the results. *Review of Educational Research, 66*(1), 39-51.

Canady, R. L., & Hotchkiss, P. R. (1989). It's a good score! Just a bad grade. *Phi Delta Kappan, 71*(1), 68-71.

Cangelosi, J. S. (1990). Grading and reporting student achievement. In *Designing tests for evaluating student achievement* (chap. 9, pp. 196-213). New York: Longman.

Carnevale, A. P., & Desrochers, D. M. (1999). *School satisfaction: A statistical profile of cities and suburbs.* Princeton, NJ: Educational Testing Service.

Cattermole, J., & Robinson, N. (1985). Effective home/school communication—From the parents' perspective. *Phi Delta Kappan, 67*(1), 48-50.

Chang, L. (1993). *Using confirmatory factor analysis of multitrait-multimethod data to assess the psychometrical equivalence of 4-point and 6-point Likert-type scales.* Paper presented at the annual meeting of the National Council on Measurement in Education, Atlanta, GA.

Chang, L. (1994). A psychometric evaluation of 4-point and 6-point Likert-type scales in relation to reliability and validity. *Applied Psychological Measurement, 18*(3), 205-215.

Chapman, H. B., & Ashbaugh, E. J. (1925, October 7). Report cards in American cities. *Educational Research Bulletin, 4,* 289-310.

Chastain, K. (1990). Characteristics of graded and ungraded compositions. *Modern Language Journal, 74*(1), 10-14.

Chrispeels, J., Fernandez, B., & Preston, J. (1991). *Home and school partners in student success: A handbook for principals and staff.* San Diego, CA: San Diego City Schools Community Relations and Integration Services Division.

Cizek, G. J., Fitzgerald, S. M., & Rachor, R. E. (1996). Teachers' assessment practices: Preparation, isolation, and the kitchen sink. *Educational Assessment, 3*(2), 159-179.

Cohen, S. B. (1983). Assigning report card grades to the mainstreamed child. *Teaching Exceptional Children, 15*(2), 86-89.

Cooper, H. (1989). Synthesis of research on homework. *Educational Leadership, 47*(3), 85-91.

Cooper, H. (1994). *The battle over homework: An administrator's guide to setting sound and effective policies.* Thousand Oaks, CA: Corwin.

Corey, S. M. (1930). Use of the normal curve as a basis for assigning grades in small classes. *School and Society, 31,* 514-516.

Cross, L. H., & Frary, R. B. (1996). *Hodgepodge grading: Endorsed by students and teachers alike.* Paper presented at the annual meeting of the National Council on Measurement in Education, New York.

Cuban, L. (1990). Reforming again, again, and again. *Educational Researcher, 19*(1), 3-13.

Davies, A. (1996). *Student-centered assessment & evaluation.* Merville, British Columbia: Classroom Connections International.

Davies, A. (2000). Seeing the results for yourself: A portfolio primer. *Classroom Leadership, 3*(5), 4-5.

Davis, J. D. W. (1930). Effect of the 6-22-44-22-6 normal curve system on failures and grade values. *Journal of Educational Psychology, 22,* 636-640.

Dettmer, P. (1994). IEPs for gifted secondary students. *Journal of Secondary Gifted Education, 5*(1), 52-59.

Donohoe, K., & Zigmond, N. (1990). Academic grades of ninth-grade urban learning-disabled students and low-achieving peers. *Exceptionality, 1*(1), 17-27.

Durm, M. W. (1993). An *A* is not an *A* is not an *A:* A history of grading. *The Educational Forum, 57*(3), 294-297.

Dwyer, C. A. (1996). Cut scores and testing: Statistics, judgment, truth, and error. *Psychological Assessment, 8*(4), 360-362.

Eames, K., & Loewenthal, K. (1990). Effects of handwriting and examiner's expertise on assessment of essays. *Journal of Social Psychology, 130*(6), 831-833.

Eastwood, K. W. (1996). Reporting student progress: One district's attempt with student literacy. In T. R. Guskey (Ed.), *Communicating student learning. 1996 Yearbook of the Association for Supervision and Curriculum Development* (pp. 65-78). Alexandria, VA: Association for Supervision and Curriculum Development.

Ebel, R. L. (1979). *Essentials of educational measurement* (3rd ed.). Englewood Cliffs, NJ: Prentice Hall.

Edwards, N., & Richey, H. G. (1947). *The school in the American social order.* Cambridge, MA: Houghton Mifflin.

Engel, P. (1991). Tracking progress toward the school readiness goal. *Educational Leadership, 48*(5), 39-42.

Epstein, J. L. (1995). School/family/community partnerships: Caring for the children we share. *Phi Delta Kappan, 76*(9), 701-712.

Esty, W. W., & Teppo, A. R. (1992). Grade assignment based on progressive improvement. *Mathematics Teacher, 85*(8), 616-618.

Farley, B. L. (1995). "A" is for average: The grading crisis in today's colleges. In *Issues of education at community colleges: Essays by Fellows in the Mid-Career Fellowship Program at Princeton University.* Princeton, NJ: ERIC Document Service No. ED 384384.

Feldman, A., Kropf, A., & Alibrand, M. (1996). *Making grades: How high school science teachers determine report card grades.* Paper presented at the annual meeting of the American Educational Research Association, New York.

Feldmesser, R. A. (1971). *The positive functions of grades.* Paper presented at the annual meeting of the American Educational Research Association, New York.

Ferrara, S. (1995). *Ways in which teachers communicate learning targets, criteria, and standards for performance to their students.* Paper presented at the annual meeting of the American Educational Research Association, San Francisco.

Frary, R. B., Cross, L. H., & Weber, L. J. (1993). Testing and grading practices and opinions of secondary teachers of academic subjects: Implications for instruction in measurement. *Educational Measurement: Issues and Practice, 12*(3), 23-30.

Frase, L. E., & Streshly, W. (1994). Lack of accuracy, feedback, and commitment in teacher evaluation. *Journal of Personnel Evaluation in Education, 8*(1), 47-57.

Friedman, S. J., & Frisbie, D. A. (1995). The influence of report cards on the validity of grades reported to parents. *Educational and Psychological Measurement, 55*(1), 5-26.

Friedman, S. J., & Manley, M. (1992). Improving high school grading practices: Experts vs. practitioners. *NASSP Bulletin, 76*(544), 100-104.

Friedman, S. J., Valde, G. A., & Obermeyer, B. J. (1998). Computerized report card comment menues: Teacher use and teacher/parent perceptions. *Michigan Principal, 74*(3), 11-14, 21.

Frisbie, D. A., & Waltman, K. K. (1992). Developing a personal grading plan. *Educational Measurement: Issues and Practices, 11*(3), 35-42.

Galen, H. (1994). Developmentally appropriate practice: Myths and facts. *Principal, 73*(5), 20-22.

Garcia, G. E. (1991). Factors influencing the English reading test performance of Spanish-speaking Hispanic children. *Reading Research Quarterly, 26*(4), 371-392.

Gatta, L. A. (1973). An analysis of the pass/fail grading system as compared to the conventional grading system in high school chemistry. *Journal of Research in Science Teaching, 10*(1), 3-12.

Gersten, R., Vaughn, S., & Brengelman, S. U. (1996). Grading and academic feedback for special education students and students with learning difficulties. In T. R. Guskey (Ed.), *Communicating student learning: 1996 Yearbook of the Association for Supervision and Curriculum Development* (pp. 47-57). Alexandria, VA: Association for Supervision and Curriculum Development.

Giba, M. A. (1999). Forging partnerships between parents and teachers. *Principal, 78*(3), 33-35.

Gilman, D. A., & Swan, E. (1989). Solving GPA and class rank problems. *NASSP Bulletin, 73*(515), 91-97.

Gitomer, D. H., & Pearlman, M. A. (1999). Are teacher licensing tests too easy? Are standards too low? *ETS Developments, 45*(1), 4-5.

Goldstein, K. M., & Tilker, H. A. (1971). Attitudes toward *A-B-C-D-F* and *Honors-Pass-Fail* grading systems. *Journal of Educational Research, 5*(3), 99-100.

Good, W. (1937). Should grades be abolished? *Education Digest, 2*(4), 7-9.

Gose, B. (1997, March 21). Duke rejects controversial plan to revise calculation of grade point averages. *Chronicle of Higher Education,* p. A53.

Gray, K. (1993). Why we will lose: Taylorism in America's high schools. *Phi Delta Kappan, 74*(5), 370-374.

Greenwood, T. W. (1995). Let's turn on the VCR and watch your report card. *Principal, 74*(4), 48-49.

Gribbin, A. (1992). Making exceptions when grading and the perils it poses. *Journalism Educator, 46*(4), 73-76.

Gronlund, N. E. (2000). *How to write and use instructional objectives* (6th ed.). Upper Saddle River, NJ: Merrill.

Gulliksen, A. R. (1993). Matching measurement instruction to classroom-based evaluation: Perceived discrepancies, needs, and challenges. In S. L. Wise (Ed.), *Teacher training in measurement and assessment skills.* Lincoln, NE: Buros Institute of Mental Measurements.

Gulliksen, A. R., & Hopkins, K. D. (1987). Perspectives on educational measurement instruction for preservice teachers. *Educational Measurement: Issues and Practice, 6*(3), 12-16.

Guskey, T. R. (1987). Rethinking mastery learning reconsidered. *Review of Educational Research, 57*(2), 225-229.

Guskey, T. R. (1989). Feedback, correctives, and enrichment. In L. W. Anderson (Ed.), *The effective teacher: Study guide and readings* (pp. 353-363). New York: Random House.

Guskey, T. R. (1993). Should letter grades be abandoned? *ASCD Update, 35*(7), p. 7.

Guskey, T. R. (1994). Making the grade: What benefits students. *Educational Leadership, 52*(2), 14-20.

Guskey, T. R. (Ed.). (1996a). *Communicating student learning: 1996 Yearbook of the Association for Supervision and Curriculum Development.* Alexandria, VA: Association for Supervision and Curriculum Development.

Guskey, T. R. (1996b). Reporting on student learning: Lessons from the past—Prescriptions for the future. In T. R. Guskey (Ed.), *Communicating student learning: 1996 Yearbook of the Association for Supervision and Curriculum Development* (pp. 13-24). Alexandria, VA: Association for Supervision and Curriculum Development.

Guskey, T. R. (1997). *Implementing mastery learning* (2nd ed.). Belmont, CA: Wadsworth.

Guskey, T. R. (1999a). Apply time with wisdom. *Journal of Staff Development, 20*(2), 10-15.

Guskey, T. R. (1999b). Making standards work. *School Administrator, 56*(9), 44.

Guskey, T. R., (1999c, April 1). Inflation not the issue; focus on grades' purpose. *Lexington Herald-Leader,* p. A19.

Guskey, T. R. (2000). *Evaluating professional development.* Thousand Oaks, CA: Corwin.

Guskey, T. R., & Huberman, M. (Eds.). (1995). *Professional development in education: New paradigms and practices.* New York: Teachers College Press.

Guskey, T. R., & Piggott, T. D. (1988). Research on group-based mastery learning programs: A meta-analysis. *Journal of Educational Research, 81*(4), 197-216.

Gustafson, C. (1998). Phone home. *Educational Leadership, 56*(2), 31-32.

Gutek, G. L. (1986). *Education in the United States: An historical perspective.* Englewood Cliffs, NJ: Prentice Hall.

Haertel, E. H., & Wiley, D. E. (1993). Representations of ability structures: Implications for testing. In N. Frederiksen, R. J. Mislevey, & I. I. Bejar (Eds.), *Test theory for a new generation of tests* (pp. 359-384). Hillsdale, NJ: Lawrence Erlbaum.

Haladyna, T. M. (1999). *A complete guide to student grading.* Boston: Allyn & Bacon.

Hall, K. (1990). *Determining the success of narrative report cards.* Princeton, NJ: ERIC Document Service No. ED 334013.

Hargis, C. H. (1990). *Grades and grading practices.* Springfield, IL: Charles C Thomas.

Heck, A. O. (1938). Contributions of research to classification, promotion, marking and certification. Reported in *The science movement in education (Part II), Twenty-Seventh Yearbook of the National Society for the Study of Education.* Chicago: University of Chicago Press.

Henderson, A., & Berla, A. (1995). *A new generation of evidence: Family involvement is critical to students' achievement.* Columbia, MD: National Committee for Citizens in Education.

Hendrikson, J., & Gable, R. A. (1997). Collaborative assessment of students with diverse needs: Equitable, accountable, and effective grading. *Preventing School Failure, 41*(4), 159-163.

Hill, G. E. (1935). The report card in present practice. *Education Methods, 15*(3), 115-131.

Hills, J. R. (1983). Interpreting grade-equivalent scores. *Educational Measurement: Issues and Practice, 2*(1), 15, 21.

Hills, J. R. (1991). Apathy concerning grading and testing. *Phi Delta Kappan, 72*(7), 540-545.

Hoover-Dempsey, K. V., & Sandler, H. M. (1997). Why do parents become involved in their children's education? *Review of Educational Research, 67*(1), 3-42.

Huber, J. (1997). Gradebook programs: Which ones make the grade? *Technology Connection, 4*(1), 21-23.

Johnsen, S. (1995). How did you do? The myths and facts about grades. *Gifted Child Today Magazine, 18*(2), 10,12-13.

Johnson, D. W., & Johnson, R. T. (1989). *Cooperation and competition: Theory and research.* Endina, MN: Interaction.

Johnson, D. W., Skon, L., & Johnson, R. T. (1980). Effects of cooperative, competitive, and individualistic conditions on children's problem-solving performance. *American Educational Research Journal, 17*(1), 83-93.

Johnson, R. H. (1918). Educational research and statistics: The coefficient marking system. *School and Society, 7*(181), 714-716.

Johnson, R. T., Johnson, D. W., & Tauer, M. (1979). The effects of cooperative, competitive, and individualistic goal structures on students' attitudes and achievement. *Journal of Psychology, 102,* 191-198.

Juarez, T. (1994). Mastery grading to serve student learning in the middle grades. *Middle School Journal, 26*(1), 37-41.

Kirschenbaum, H. (1999). Night and day: Succeeding with parents at School 43. *Principal, 78*(3), 20-23.

Kirschenbaum, H., Simon, S. B., & Napier, R. W. (1971). *Wad-ja-get? The grading game in American education.* New York: Hart.

Kohn, A. (1993). *Punishment by rewards: The trouble with gold stars, incentive plans, A's, praise, and other bribes.* Boston: Houghton Mifflin.

Kohn, A. (1994). Grading: The issue is not how but why. *Educational Leadership, 52*(2), 38-41.

Kovas, M. A. (1993). Make your grading motivating: Keys to performance based evaluation. *Quill and Scroll, 68*(1), 10-11.

Kreider, H. M., & Lopez, M. E. (1999). Promising practices for family involvement. *Principal, 78*(3), 16-19.

Krumboltz, J. D., & Yeh, C. J. (1996). Competitive grading sabotages good teaching. *Phi Delta Kappan, 78*(4), 324-326.

Kuehner, J. C. (1998, January 31). Bad news for bad grades: Beachwood school puts teeth in D's and F's by requiring extra classes or summer school. *Plain Dealer,* pp. 1A, 7A.

Kulik, C. C., Kulik, J. A., & Bangert-Drowns, R. L. (1990a). Effectiveness of mastery learning programs: A meta-analysis. *Review of Educational Research, 60*(2), 265-299.

Kulik, J. A., Kulik, C. C., & Bangert-Drowns, R. L. (1990b). Is there better evidence on mastery learning? A response to Slavin. *Review of Educational Research, 60*(2), 303-307.

Kwon, I. G., & Kendig, N. L. (1997). Grade inflation from a career counselor's perspective. *Journal of Employment Counseling, 34*(2), 50-54.

LaCelle-Peterson, M., & Rivera, C. (1994). Is it real for all kids? A framework for equitable assessment policies for English language learners. *Harvard Educational Review, 64*(1), 55-75.

Lake, K., & Kafka, K. (1996). Reporting methods in grades K-8. In T. R. Guskey (Ed.), *Communicating student learning. 1996 Yearbook of the Association for Supervision and Curriculum Development* (pp. 90-118). Alexandria, VA: Association for Supervision and Curriculum Development.

Langdon, C. A. (1999). The fifth Phi Delta Kappa poll of teachers' attitudes toward the public schools. *Phi Delta Kappan, 80*(8), 611-618.

Libit, H. (1999). Report card redux. *The School Administrator, 56*(10), 6-10.

Linn, R. L. (1983). Testing and instruction: Links and distinctions. *Journal of Educational Measurement, 20*(2), 179-189.

Linn, R. L., & Gronlund, N. E. (2000). Grading and reporting. In *Measurement and assessment in teaching* (8th ed., chap. 15, pp. 377-404). Upper Saddle River, NJ: Prentice Hall.

Little, A.W., & Allan, J. (1989). Student-led parent-teacher conferences. *Elementary School Guidance and Counseling, 23*(3), 210-218.

Lockhart, E. (1990). Heavy grades? A study on weighted grades. *Journal of College Admission, 126,* 9-16.

Marzano, R. J. (1999). Building curriculum and assessment around standards. *High School Magazine, 6*(5), 14-19.

McMillan, J. H., Workman, D., & Myran, S. (1999). *Elementary teachers' classroom assessment and grading practices.* Paper presented at the annual meeting of the American Educational Research Association, Montreal.

Mehring, T. A. (1995). Report card options for students with disabilities in general education. In T. Azwell & E. Schmar (Eds.), *Report card on report cards: Alternatives to consider* (pp. 11-21). Portsmouth, NH: Heineman.

Middleton, W. (1933). Some general trends in grading procedure. *Education, 54*(1), 5-10.

Million, J. (1999). Restaurants, report cards, and reality. *NAESP Communicator, 22*(8), 5,7.

Mitchell, B. M. (1994). Weighted grades. *Gifted Child Today, 17*(4), 28-29.

Munk, D. D., & Bursuck, W. D. (1998a). Can grades be helpful and fair? *Educational Leadership, 55*(4), 44-47.

Munk, D. D., & Bursuck, W. D. (1998b). Report card grading adaptations for students with disabilities: Types and acceptability. *Intervention in School and Clinic, 33*(3) 306-308.

Natriello, G. (1987). The impact of evaluation processes on students. *Educational Psychologist, 22*(2), 155-175.

Natriello, G., Riehl, C. J., & Pallas, A. M. (1994). *Between the rock of standards and the hard place of accommodation: Evaluation practices of teachers in high schools serving disadvantaged students.* Baltimore, MD: Center for Research on Effective Schooling for Disadvantaged Students, Johns Hopkins University.

Nava, F. J. G., & Loyd, B. H. (1992). *An investigation of achievement and nonachievement criteria in elementary and secondary school grading.*

Paper presented at the annual meeting of the American Educational Research Association, San Francisco.

Nelson, K. (2000). Measuring the intangibles. *Classroom Leadership, 3*(5), 1, 8.

Nitko, A. J., & Niemierko, B. (1993). *Qualitative letter grade standards for teacher-made summative classroom assessments.* Paper presented at the annual meeting of the American Educational Research Association, Atlanta, GA.

O'Connor, K. (1999). *How to grade for learning.* Arlington Heights, IL: Skylight.

O'Donnell, A., & Woolfolk, A. E. (1991, August). *Elementary and secondary teachers' beliefs about testing and grading.* Paper presented at the annual meeting of the American Psychological Association, San Francisco.

Olsen, D. R. (1997). *Grade inflation: Reality or myth? Student preparation level vs. grades at Brigham Young University, 1975-1994.* Paper presented at the Annual Forum of the Association for Institutional Research, Orlando, FL.

Olson, L. (1995, June 14). Cards on the table. *Education Week,* pp. 23-28.

Ornstein, A. C. (1994). Grading practices and policies: And overview and some suggestions. *NASSP Bulletin, 78*(559), 55-64.

Page, E. B. (1958). Teacher comments and student performance: A seventy-four classroom experiment in school motivation. *Journal of Educational Psychology, 49*(2), 173-181.

Page, E. B., & Petersen, N. S. (1995). The computer moves into essay grading: Updating the ancient test. *Phi Delta Kappan, 76*(7), 561-565.

Pardini, P. (1997). Report card reform. *School Administrator, 54*(11), 19-20, 22-25.

Payne, D. A. (1974). *The assessment of learning.* Lexington, MA: Heath.

Peckron, K. B. (1996). Beyond the A: Communicating the learning progress of gifted students. In T. R. Guskey (Ed.), *Communicating student learning: 1996 Yearbook of the Association for Supervision and Curriculum Development* (pp. 58-64). Alexandria, VA: Association for Supervision and Curriculum Development.

Phillips, S. E. (1998). Standards and grading for disabled students: Part I. *National Council on Measurement in Education Newsletter, 6*(3), 2.

Phillips, S. E. (1999). Response to Friedman regarding the Oklahoma grading case. *National Council on Measurement in Education Newsletter, 7*(2), 2, 4.

Polloway, E. A., Bursuck, W. D., Jayanthi, M., Epstein, M. H., & Nelson, J. S. (1996). Treatment acceptability: Determining appropriate interventions within inclusive classrooms. *Intervention in School and Clinic, 31*(2), 133-144.

Polloway, E. A., Epstein, M. H., Bursuck, W. D., Roderique, T. W., McConeghy, J. L., & Jayanthi, M. (1994). Classroom grading: A national survey of policies. *Remedial and Special Education, 15*(2), 162-170.

Raebeck, B. (1993). *Exploding myths, exploring truths: Humane, productive grading and grouping in the quality middle school.* Paper presented at the annual conference and exhibit of the National Middle School Association, Portland, OR.

Reedy, R. (1995). Formative and summative assessment: A possible alternative to the grading-reporting dilemma. *NASSP Bulletin, 79*(573), 47-51.

Retish, P., Horvath, M., Hitchings, W., & Schmalle, B. (1991). *Students with mild disabilities in the secondary school.* New York: Longman.

Rich, D. (1998). What parents want from teachers. *Educational Leadership, 55*(3), 37-39.

Robins, L. S., Fantone, J. C., Oh, M. S., Alexander, G. L., Shlafer, M., & Davis, W. K. (1995). The effect of pass/fail grading and weekly quizzes on first-year students' performances and satisfaction. *Academic Medicine, 70*(4), 327-329.

Robinson, D. (1998). Student portfolios in mathematics. *Mathematics Teacher, 91*(4), 318-325.

Roderick, M., & Camburn, E. (1999). Risk and recovery from course failure in the early years of high school. *American Educational Research Journal, 36*(2), 303-343.

Rugg, H. O. (1918). Teachers' marks and the reconstruction of the marking system. *Elementary School Journal, 18*(9), 701-719.

Schafer, W. D., & Lissitz, R. W. (1987). Measurement training for school personnel: Recommendations and reality. *Journal of Teacher Education, 38*(3), 57-63.

Schulz, H. W. (1999). *Reporting student progress, grades, and the role of parent-teacher conferences.* Paper presented at the annual meeting of the American Educational Research Association, Montreal, Canada.

Scott, E. L. (1995). "Mokita," the truth that everybody knows, but nobody talks about: Bias in grading. *Teaching English in the Two-Year College, 22*(3), 211-216.

Selby, D., & Murphy, S. (1992). Graded or degraded: Perceptions of letter-grading for mainstreamed learning-disabled students. *British Columbia Journal of Special Education, 16*(1), 92-104.

Shuster, C., Lemma, P., Lynch, T., & Nadeau, K. (1996). *A study of kindergarten and first grade report cards: What are young children expected to learn?* Paper presented at the annual meeting of the American Educational Research Association, New York.

Smith, D. (1999, July 2). *Personal communication to Thomas R. Guskey from David Smith, Principal of West Springfield High School, Springfield, VA.*

Spear, M. (1997). The influence of contrast effects upon teachers' marks. *Educational Research, 39*(2), 229-233.

Sprouse, J. L., & Webb, J. E. (1994). *The pygmalion effect and its influence on the grading and gender assignment of spelling and essay assessments.* Master's thesis, University of Virginia.

Stallings, W. M., & Smock, H. R. (1971). The pass/fail grading option at a state university: A five semester evaluation. *Journal of Educational Measurement, 8*(3), 153-160.

Starch, D., & Elliott, E. C. (1912). Reliability of the grading of high school work in English. *School Review, 20,* 442-457.

Starch, D., & Elliott, E. C. (1913). Reliability of the grading of high school work in mathematics. *School Review, 21,* 254-259.

Stewart, L. G., & White, M. A. (1976). Teacher comments, letter grades and student performance. *Journal of Educational Psychology, 68*(4), 488-500.

Stiggins, R. J. (1991). Assessment literacy. *Phi Delta Kappan, 72*(7), 534-539.

Stiggins, R. J. (1993). Teacher training in assessment: Overcoming the neglect. In S. L. Wise (Ed.), *Teacher training in measurement and assessment skills* (pp. 27-40). Lincoln, NE: Buros Institute of Mental Measurements.

Stiggins, R. J. (1999). Evaluating classroom assessment training in teacher education programs. *Educational Measurement: Issues and Practice, 18*(1), 23-27.

Stiggins, R. J. (2001). Report cards. In *Student-involved classroom assessment* (3rd ed., chap. 13, pp. 409-465). Upper Saddle River, NJ: Merrill/Prentice-Hall.

Stiggins, R. J., & Duke, D. L. (1991). *District grading policies and their potential impact on at-risk students.* Paper presented at the annual meeting of the American Educational Research Association, Chicago.

Stiggins, R. J., Frisbie, D. A., & Griswold, P. A. (1989). Inside high school grading practices: Building a research agenda. *Educational Measurement: Issues and Practice, 8*(2), 5-14.

Sweedler-Brown, C. O. (1992). The effect of training on the appearance bias of holistic essay graders. *Journal of Research and Development in Education, 26*(1), 24-29.

Talley, N. R., & Mohr, J. I. (1991). Weighted averages, computer screening, and college admission in public colleges and universities. *Journal of College Admission, 132,* 9-11.

Thomas, B. J. (1987). Comparison of rural kindergarten report card grades. *Journal of American Indian Education, 26*(2), 7-17.

Thompson, P. J., Lord, J. E., Powell, J., Devine, M., & Coleman, E. A. (1991) Grading versus pass/fail evaluation for clinical courses. *Nursing and Health Care, 12*(4), 480-482.

Tomlinson, T. (1992). *Hard work and high expectations: Motivating students to learn.* Washington, DC: Office of Educational Research and Improvement, U.S. Department of Education.

Truog, A. L., & Friedman, S. J. (1996). *Evaluating high school teachers' written grading policies from a measurement perspective.* Paper presented at the annual meeting of the National Council on Measurement in Education, New York.

Turmbull, E., & Farr, B. (Eds.). (2000). *Grading and reporting student progress in an age of standards.* Norwood, MA: Christopher-Gordon.

Tyler, R. W. (1949). *Basic principles of curriculum and instruction.* Chicago: University of Chicago Press.

U.S. Department of Education. (1997). *Nineteenth annual report to Congress on the implementation of the Individuals with Disabilities Education Act.* Washington, DC: Government Printing Office.

Valdes, K. A., Williamson, C. L., & Wagner, M. M. (1990). *The national transition study of special education students* (Vol. 1). Menlo Park, CA: SRI International.

Vaughn, S., Schumm, J. S., Klingner, J., & Saumell, L. (1995). Students views of instructional practices: Implications for inclusion. *Learning Disability Quarterly, 18*(3), 236-348.

Vaughn, S., Schumm, J. S., Niarhos, F. J., & Gordon, J. (1993). Students' perceptions of two hypothetical teachers' instructional adaptations for low achievers. *Elementary School Journal, 94*(1), 87-102.

Vockell, E. L., & Fiore, D. J. (1993). Electronic gradebooks: What current programs can do for teachers. *Clearing House, 66*(3), 141-145.

Waltman, K. K., & Frisbie, D. A. (1994). Parents understanding of their children's report card grades. *Applied Measurement in Education, 7*(3), 223-240.

Watts, K. H. (1996). Bridges freeze before roads. In T. R. Guskey (Ed.), *Communicating student learning: 1996 Yearbook of the Association for Supervision and Curriculum Development* (pp. 6-12). Alexandria, VA: Association for Supervision and Curriculum Development.

Weller, L. D. (1983). The grading nemesis: An historical overview and current look at pass/fail grading. *Journal of Research and Development in Education, 17*(1), 39-45.

Wemette, J. F. (1994). *Personal communication to Thomas R. Guskey relating the results of a parent survey on grading conducted by the North St. Paul, Maplewood, Oakdale School District 662, Maplewood, MN.*

Whittington, D. (1999). Making room for values and fairness: Teaching reliability and validity in the classroom context. *Educational Measurement: Issues and Practice, 18*(1), 14-22, 27.

Wiggins, G. (1994). Toward better report cards. *Educational Leadership, 52*(2), 28-35.

Wiggins, G. (1996). Honesty and fairness: Toward better grading and reporting. In T. R. Guskey (Ed.), *Communicating student learning: 1996 Yearbook of the Association for Supervision and Curriculum Development* (pp. 141-176). Alexandria, VA: Association for Supervision and Curriculum Development.

Wiggins, G. (1997). Tips on reforming student report cards. *School Administrator, 54*(11), 20.

Wiggins, G., & McTighe, J. (1998). *Understanding by design.* Alexandria, VA: Association for Supervision and Curriculum Development.

Wiles, C. A. (1992). Investigating gender bias in the evaluations of middle school teachers of mathematics. *School Science and Mathematics, 92*(6), 295-298.

Willis, S. (1993). Are letter grades obsolete? *ASCD Update, 35*(7), pp. 1, 4, & 8.

Wood, L. A. (1994). An unintended impact of one grading practice. *Urban Education, 29*(2), 188-201.

Wresch, W. (1993). The imminence of grading essays by computer—25 years later. *Computers and Composition, 10*(2), 45-58.

Wright, R. G. (1994). Success for all: The median is the key. *Phi Delta Kappan, 75*(9), 723-725.

Zigmond, N., & Thornton, H. (1985). Follow-up of postsecondary age learning disabled graduates and dropouts. *Learning Disabilities Research, 1*(1), 50-55.

Zirkel, P. A. (1995, March 8). Grade inflation: A problem and a proposal. *Education Week,* p. 28.

# Name Index

Abedi, J., 123
Abou-Sayf, F. K., 70
Adelman, C., 40, 135
Afflerbach, P., 34, 107
Agnew, E., 136, 137
Airasian, P. W., 46
Alexander, G. L., 95
Alibrand, M., 19, 130
Allan, J., 187, 190
Allison, E., 1, 53, 107
American Federation of Teachers, National
    Council for Measurement in Education,
    & National Education Association, 11
Andrade, H. G., 57, 84
Arter, J. A., 57
Ashbaugh, E. J., 27
August, D., 122
Austin, S., 34, 52
Azwell, T., 6

Bailey, J., 28, 42
Baker, E. L., 46, 47
Balm, S. S. M., 184
Bangert-Drowns, R. L., 101
Barnes, L. L. B., 16, 31
Barnes, S., 34
Barton, P., 178
Basinger, D., 137
Beattie, J., 113
Beaver, W., 136
Bennett, R. E., 33
Berg, M. H., 129
Berla, A., 22
Bernetich, E., 35, 77
Bernick, R., 187
Bishop, J. H., 31, 37
Block, J. H., 102
Bloom, B. S., 27, 31, 32, 37, 38, 49, 97, 98, 100,
    191
Bookhart, S. M.
Boothroyd, R. A., 34
Bracey, G. W., 27, 39, 136, 137
Brengelman, S. U., 41, 113, 117, 120

Brewer, W. R., 129
British Columbia Ministry of Education, 107
Brookhart, S. M., 1, 12, 13, 28, 33, 41, 56, 58,
    62, 141, 185, 187, 191
Brown, D. W., 129
Bull, K. S., 16
Burns, R. B., 102
Bursuck, W. D., 16, 111, 112, 117, 118, 119,
    120, 121

Calhoun, M. L., 113
Camburn, E., 36
Cameron, J., 6, 34, 51
Campbell, N. J., 16
Canady, R. L., 130, 143
Cangelosi, J. S., 40
Carnevale, A. P., 10
Cattermole, J., 22
Cerullo, F., 33
Chang, L., 71
Chapman, H. B., 27
Chastain, K., 34, 51
Chrispeels, J., 175
Cizek, G. J., 1, 12, 56
Cohen, S. B., 120
Coleman, E. A., 95
Cooper, H., 59, 185
Corey, S. M., 27
Cross, L. H., 28, 41, 62
Cuban, L., 29

Davies, A., 184, 189
Davis, J. D. W., 27
Davis, W. K., 95
Desrochers, D. M., 10
Dettmer, P., 125
Devine, M., 95
Donohoe, K., 111
Duke, D. L., 143
Durm, M. W., 94
Dwyer, C. A., 71, 72

213

Eames, K., 34
Eastwood, K. W., 129
Ebel, R. L., 34, 51
Edwards, N., 25
Efthim, H. E., 102
Elliott, E. C., 26
Elliott, J., 187
Engel, P., 38
Epstein, J. L., 175
Epstein, M. H., 16, 117, 119
Esty, W. W., 41

Fantone, J. C., 95
Farley, B. L., 71
Farr, B., 6
Feldman, A., 19, 130
Feldmesser, R. A., 34, 50
Fernandez, B., 175
Ferrara, S., 13
Fiore, D. J., 130
Fitzgerald, S. M., 1, 12, 56
Frary, R. B., 28, 41, 62
Frase, L. E., 31
Friedman, S. J., 1, 41, 42, 53, 59, 60, 105, 106, 107
Frisbie, D. A., 16, 30, 41, 42, 50, 67, 105, 193

Gable, R. A., 110
Galen, H., 21
Garcia, G. E., 122
Gatta, L. A., 95
Gersten, R., 41, 113, 117, 120
Giba, M. A., 177
Gilman, D. A., 134
Gitomer, D. H., 81
Goldstein, K. M., 95
Good, W., 27
Gordon, J., 111
Gose, B., 136
Gottesman, R. L., 33
Gray, K., 36, 37
Greenwood, T. W., 129
Gribbin, A., 114
Griswold, P. A., 41, 193
Gronlund, N. E., 46, 47, 85, 148
Gulliksen, A. R., 13
Guskey, T. R., 6, 20, 24, 29, 31, 32, 45, 50, 84, 99, 101, 102, 138, 139, 170, 174
Gustafson, C., 178, 180
Gutek, G. L., 25

Haertel, E. H., 47
Hakuta, K., 122
Haladyna, T. M., 6, 24, 36, 38, 94, 95, 101, 114
Hall, K., 106
Hargis, C. H., 6, 20, 71, 112
Hastings, J. T., 27, 31, 32, 37, 38, 49, 97, 100, 191
Heck, A. O., 27
Henderson, A., 22
Hendrikson, J., 110
Herman, J. L., 46, 47
Hill, G. E., 27
Hills, J. R., 33, 136, 178
Hitchings, W., 114
Hofstetter, C., 123
Hoover-Dempsey, K. V., 22
Hopkins, K. D., 13
Horvath, M., 114
Hotchkiss, P. R., 130, 143
Huber, J., 130
Huberman, M., 29

Jayanthi, M., 16, 117, 119
Johnsen, S., 126
Johnson, D. W., 36
Johnson, R. H., 27
Johnson, R. T., 36
Johnson, S.
Juarez, T., 96

Kafka, K., 27
Kallick, B., 129
Kendig, N. L., 136
Kirschenbaum, H., 25, 96, 175, 180, 183
Klingner, J., 119
Kohn, A., 6
Kovas, M. A., 40
Kreider, H. M., 22, 184
Kropf, A., 19, 130
Krumboltz, J. D., 36
Kuehner, J. C., 35
Kulik, C. C., 101
Kulik, J. A., 101
Kwon, I. G., 136

LaCelle-Peterson, M., 122
Lake, K., 27
Langdon, C. A., 181, 183
Lemma, P., 93

Libit, H., 68, 77
Linn, R. L., 46, 47, 50, 148
Lissitz, R. W., 34
Little, A. W., 187, 190
Lockhart, E., 135
Loewenthal, K., 34
Lopez, M. E., 22, 184
Lord, C., 123
Lord, J. E., 95
Loyd, B. H., 41
Lynch, T., 93

Madaus, G. F., 27, 31, 32, 37, 38, 49, 97, 100, 191
Manley, M., 41
Marzano, R. J., 85
McCann, R., 34, 52
McConeghy, J. L., 16, 117
McMillan, J. H., 1, 12, 56
McMorris, R. F., 34
McTighe, J., 28, 42, 84, 85
Mehring, T. A., 111
Middleton, W., 24, 27
Million, J., 21, 22
Mitchell, B. M., 134
Mohr, J. I., 135
Munk, D. D., 111, 112, 117, 118, 119, 120, 121
Murphy, S., 35, 111
Myran, S., 1, 12, 56

Nadeau, K., 93
Napier, R. W., 25, 96
Natriello, G., 41, 140
Nava, F. J. G., 41
Nelson, J. S., 119
Nelson, K., 187
Niarhos, F. J., 111
Niemierko, B., 81
Nitko, A. J., 81

Obermeyer, B. J., 105, 106
O'Connor, K., 6, 9
O'Donnell, A., 33
Oh, M. S., 95
Olsen, D. R., 136
Olson, L., 44
Olson, M. M., 111, 119, 120
Ornstein, A. C., 32, 42

Page, E. B., 28, 29, 129
Pallas, A. M., 41
Pardini, P., 1, 53
Payne, D. A., 68
Pearlman, M. A., 81
Peckron, K. B., 125, 126
Perry, K., 16
Petersen, N. S., 129
Phillips, S. E., 110, 115, 116
Pierce, W. D., 6, 34, 51
Piggott, T. D., 50, 101
Plante, L., 117
Polloway, E. A., 16, 117, 119
Powell, J., 95
Preston, J., 175

Rachor, R. E., 1, 12, 56
Raebeck, B., 143
Reedy, R., 53
Retish, P., 114
Rich, D., 22
Richey, H. G., 25
Riehl, C. J., 41
Rivera, C., 122
Robins, L. S., 95
Robinson, D., 184
Robinson, N., 22
Rock, D. A., 33
Roderick, M., 36
Roderique, T. W., 16, 117
Rugg, H. O., 27
Rutherford, B., 187

Sammons, R. B., 1-7, 34
Sandler, H. M., 22
Saumell, L., 119
Schafer, W. D., 34
Schmalle, B., 114
Schmar, E., 6
Schulz, H. W., 71
Schumm, J. S., 111, 119
Scott, E. L., 33
Selby, D., 35, 111
Shlafer, M., 95
Shuster, C., 93
Simon, S. B., 25, 96
Skon, L., 36
Smith, D., 39
Smith, J. K., 79
Smith, J. P., 129

Smock, H. R., 95
Spandel, V., 57
Spear, M., 34
Sprouse, J. L., 34
Stallings, W. M., 95
Starch, D., 26
Stewart, L. G., 29
Stiggins, R. J., 10, 13, 17, 41, 42, 46, 68, 140, 143, 193
Streshly, W., 31
Swan, E., 134
Sweedler-Brown, C. O., 33

Talley, N. R., 135
Tauer, M., 36
Teppo, A. R., 41
Thomas, B. J., 33
Thompson, P. J., 95
Thornton, H., 111
Tilker, H. A., 95
Tomlinson, T., 42
Truog, A.L., 41, 59, 60, 105
Turmbull, E., 6
Tyler, R. W., 85

U. S. Department of Education, 109

Valde, G. A., 105, 106
Valdes, K. A., 111

Vaughn, S., 41, 111, 113, 117, 119, 120
Vockell, E. L., 130

Wagner, M. M., 111
Waltman, K. K., 16, 30, 42, 50, 67
Watts, K. H., 22
Webb, J. E., 34
Weber, L. J., 41
Weller, L. D., 94
Wemette, J. F., 53, 175
White, M. A., 29
Whittington, D., 12
Wiggins, G., 6, 41, 42, 84, 85, 107, 111, 176
Wiles, C. A., 34
Wiley, D. E., 47
Williamson, C. L., 111
Willis, S., 74
Wood, L. A., 27, 38
Woolfolk, A. E., 33
Workman, D., 1, 12, 56
Wresch, W., 129
Wright, R. G., 130, 141

Yeh, C. J., 36

Zigmond, N., 111
Zirkel, P. A., 136

CORWIN
PRESS

**The Corwin Press logo**—a raven striding across an open book—represents the happy union of courage and learning. We are a professional-level publisher of books and journals for K–12 educators, and we are committed to creating and providing resources that embody these qualities. Corwin's motto is "Success for All Learners."